121

MW00563211

To ~~████████ ████ ████████████~~

Hope this will
increase your knowledge
Merry Christmas.

~ Tom

SINGAPORE

SINGAPORE
SMART CITY **SMART STATE**

KENT E. CALDER

Brookings Institution Press
Washington, D.C.

The Brookings Institution is a private nonprofit organization devoted to research, education,
and publication on important issues of domestic and foreign policy. Its principal purpose
is to bring the highest quality independent research and analysis to bear on current and
emerging policy problems. Interpretations or conclusions in Brookings publications should
be understood to be solely those of the authors.

Library of Congress Cataloging-in-Publication data
Names: Calder, Kent E., author.
Title: Singapore : smart city, smart state / Kent E. Calder.
Description: Washington, D.C. : Brookings Institution Press, [2016] | Includes
    bibliographical references and index.
Identifiers: LCCN 2016029970 (print) | LCCN 2016037654 (ebook) | ISBN
    9780815729471 (paperback : alkaline paper) | ISBN 9780815729488 (ebook)
Subjects: LCSH: Singapore—Politics and government—1990– | Singapore—Social policy.
    | Singapore—Economic policy. | Urban policy—Singapore. | City and town life—
    Singapore. | Community life—Singapore. | City-states—Case studies. | Globalization—
    Case studies. | BISAC: BUSINESS & ECONOMICS / International / Economics. |
    POLITICAL SCIENCE / Globalization. | BUSINESS & ECONOMICS / Development
    / Economic Development.
Classification: LCC DS610.7 .C35 2016 (print) | LCC DS610.7 (ebook) | DDC
    959.5705—dc23
LC record available at https://lccn.loc.gov/2016029970

9 8 7 6 5 4 3 2 1

Typeset in Adobe Garamond and Myriad Pro
Composition by Cynthia Stock

To my students across the years,
who have so often become my teachers,
as the years roll by. . . .

Contents

Acronyms and Abbreviations

ALS	Area Licensing Scheme
CAAS	Civil Aviation Authority of Singapore
COE	Certificate of Entitlement
COP	Conference of the Parties
CPF	Central Provident Fund
CREATE	Campus for Research Excellence and Technological Enterprise
EAGLES	Edusave Awards for Achievement and Good Leadership and Service
EDB	Economic Development Board
EIP	Ethnic Integration Policy
EMA	Energy Market Authority
ERP	Electronic Road Pricing
FDPA	Five Power Defense Arrangements
FSA	Financial Services Agency (Japan)
GIS	Genome Institute of Singapore
GLC	Government-linked company
GST	Goods and services tax
HDB	Housing and Development Board
ICT	Information and communications technology
IES	International Enterprise Singapore
INSEAD	Institut Européen d'Administration des Affaires
IoT	Internet of Things
JTC	Jurong Town Corporation
LTA	Land Transport Authority
MAS	Monetary Authority of Singapore

NHB	National Heritage Board
NRF	National Research Foundation
NTUC	National Trades Union Congress
NUS	National University of Singapore
PA	People's Association
PAP	People's Action Party
PPS	Principal private secretaries
PSC	Public Service Commission
PTC	Public Transport Council
PUB	Public Utilities Board
RSIS	Rajaratnam School of International Studies
SCE	Singapore Cooperation Enterprise
SCP	Singapore Cooperation Program
SEZ	Special economic zone
SIMEX	Singapore International Monetary Exchange
SIT	Singapore Improvement Trust
STB	Singapore Tourism Board
SWF	Sovereign wealth fund
URA	Urban Redevelopment Authority
VAT	Value added tax
VQS	Vehicle Quota System
WSQ	Workforce Qualification System

Preface

One size never fits all—neither in tailoring nor in the real world. An increasingly global world, however, has an inevitable thirst for paradigms—concrete cases that can yield insight into the origins of the wealth, stability, and well-being of nations. Few are timeless, and virtually all such paradigms are profoundly related to their times.

The early twenty-first century, it is increasingly clear, is the era of the Digital Revolution. The deepening power of computing and telecommunications, coupled with their deepening integration, is radically reconfiguring economics, politics, and administration around the globe. In this radically new and volatile environment, international business and political centers must urgently study both best practice and emerging challenges from one another.

I went to Singapore first as a boy of eight, on vacation with my family from Burma, where my father was helping to establish a School of Business Administration at the University of Rangoon. I still remember the vivid orange of the flame trees along the road from Changi Airport, as we first arrived, while Singapore still slept under colonial rule. That natural beauty has continued to impress me over the twenty-odd trips I have made back to the Lion City over the intervening half century and more.

Apart from the continuity of the flame trees, however, Singapore for me has over the years been a fascinating whirlpool of continual change. In this book, my first effort at conceptualizing developments in Singapore since *The Eastasia Edge*, published in 1982, I have focused particularly on the city-state's adaptability. I have been curious as to how and why that once somnolent Southeast Asian nation has morphed into a paradigm of pragmatic, technologically sensitive policy adaptation of relevance to both developing and advanced industrial nations throughout the world.

A diverse and remarkable group, to whom I owe a profound debt of gratitude, has accompanied me on various stages of this intellectual journey. First, of course, are a loyal and unfailingly helpful group of Singaporean students, who have consistently been among the most able students with whom I have worked, at all of the three schools where I have taught. Khoo Boon Hui, a member of one of my first public policy seminars at Harvard, who later served with distinction as Singapore commissioner of police and president of Interpol, offered generous advice and correction on this manuscript, for which I am grateful. Serene Hung, my very last Princeton student, and the very first Reischauer Policy Research Fellow at SAIS, before leaving for the Harvard Government Department began the research that culminated in this book. Eric Teo, Alpana Roy, Kaijiun Wong, and Jason Ho, among others, are additional brilliant Singaporean students who have become my teachers and contributed to the work presented here.

Other Singaporean friends, many of them acquaintances from my tenure as the Rajaratnam Professor of Strategic Studies at RSIS, Nanyang University, also contributed greatly to my understanding. Prominent among them have been Dean Joseph Liow and his colleagues and staff at RSIS, including Ambassador Ong Keng Yong and Barry Desker, as well as Dean Kishore Mahbubani and his colleagues at NUS. I also owe special debts to numerous members of Singapore's outstanding foreign service, beginning with Ambassadors Chan Heng Chee and Ashok Mirpuri, as well as Bilahari Kausikan and Albert Chua, together with senior members of the Economic Development Board and other agencies, including Keat Chuan.

This is, of course, an academic volume, and scholars have been important in supporting my research efforts, providing advice, and deepening my insights regarding Singapore and its global role. I am grateful especially to the Johns Hopkins School of Advanced International Studies (SAIS), and to the Reischauer Center for East Asian Studies within it, under whose auspices this book is published. Vali Nasr, Peter Lewis, John Harrington, Karl Jackson, Bill Weiss, Deborah Brautigam, David Lampton, Anthony Rowley, and Lynn White have all deepened my understanding. Zongyuan Liu, Sophie Yang, Yun Han, Ivy Cao, Aileen McLaren, Alexander Evans, Olivia Schieber, Alicia Henry, Michale Kotler, Joshua Nair, Gyung-hee Kim, Nanum Jeon, Ivy Back, and Jaemin Choi have all provided important research assistance.

After completing twelve books, I have come to appreciate the importance of the end game—the conversion of a complex set of ideas into a concise and persuasive publication. This process can at times be unutterably frustrating, but moves with remarkable efficiency and good cheer, in my experience, at Brookings Press. I am especially grateful for end-game support to Bill Finan, Janet Walker, Vicky Macintyre, and, of course to my family. Without their gentle needling, combined with insightful commentary, this book would never have been completed.

I have thus received backing and support from a diverse range of valued sources. No doubt there is much sound advice that did not get through. For that, and for the final product, I as the author take full responsibility and ask the reader's indulgent understanding.

Washington, D.C.
September 2016

SINGAPORE

Introduction
SINGAPORE AND A WORLD OF CHANGE

Ju an si wei, jie she yi jian
[Watch for danger in times of peace. Be thrifty in times of plenty.]

—CHANCELLOR WEI ZHENG (580–643)

Rarely in the course of human affairs has the pace of socioeconomic and political change been so rapid as since the mid-1990s. The cold war has ended, the former Soviet bloc has become a more integrated part of the global economy, and the Internet revolution has transformed societies of both the industrialized and developing worlds. Meanwhile, massive urbanization has created a complex new plethora of cities, large and small. Today over 54 percent of the world's people live in cities—nearly double the ratio half a century ago. And by 2050 that ratio is expected to rise to two-thirds of the earth's entire population.[1]

Sweeping and accelerating global change has intensified the search for new institutional mechanisms and policy tools capable of dealing with such change. The traditional Western welfare state, relying on expensive universal entitlements to shield citizens from poverty, ill health, unemployment, and the vicissitudes of social transformation, has been found wanting. In country after country, beginning in Western Europe and then Japan and the United States, the welfare state has generated huge fiscal deficits, while arguably reducing impulses to save and to economize.[2]

At the international level, classical forms of organization, beginning with traditional empires like those of France, Britain, and the Soviet Union, have proved wanting as well. For their part, nation-states continue to struggle with the blistering pace of change in controlling multinational firms, as transnational relations among corporations, religious institutions, unions, and other types of nongovernmental organizations (NGOs) grow more active.[3] Even the utility and effectiveness of formal alliances between nations have come into question, especially in the developing world, as the skepticism manifested by emerging giants like India and China makes clear.[4] Even the United Nations has not shown itself to be as effective as hoped.

If traditional nation-states—even the most efficient of them—have difficulty delivering the lightning-quick reactions and extraordinary levels of foresight needed to handle such changes, who can? What alternative modes of governance and what policy paradigms are viable in the new, global world now emerging? And who formulates and implements paradigms most effectively? With what consequences?

Why Singapore?

One of the greatest challenges for today's rapidly changing world—one central to the concerns of this book—is the problem of governance. It lies in finding governmental structures that can cope effectively with the increasingly complex problems now faced by local, national, multinational, and supranational entities everywhere. This problem is especially perplexing for huge, rapidly developing societies like China, India, and Indonesia that aspire to the affluence and freedoms of the advanced Western nations but cannot afford or cannot countenance the costs and contentiousness of their welfare states.[5]

Speculation has begun on what form of governance might suit the 21st century's global circumstances. In both the West and beyond, there is a growing consensus that any future structures cannot or should not be modeled on the conventional welfare state. Some see a key role, at the international level, for "virtual states" of minimal geographic or political-military scale that nevertheless serve as important connectors and that disseminate ideas.[6] Others would favor governing structures that lighten the fiscal burden of government, while stressing individual rights in preference to universal social mandates.[7]

Meeting the challenges of governance naturally involves responses at multiple levels of social interaction, with significant changes in organizational design quite plausible in the future. Problems of global environment, and related matters of transportation and energy efficiency, have classically been addressed at the national and international levels, but progress in solving such problems has been slow. Cities, as political analyst Benjamin Barber and others have suggested, might be more effective than nations in tackling issues of this nature, since they tend to be more focused on everyday concerns and typically deal with less challenging interest-group configurations.[8] Indeed, the C-40 global group of mayors has already begun to address such pressing, albeit mundane, global environmental challenges with some success, while the Conference of the Parties (COP) series of national dialogues have made frustratingly meager concrete progress.

In a world of conspicuous institutional failure, one entity that still offers some important lessons for the practice of governance is Singapore. It stands strategically at the cusp of two levels of governance—each with distinctive capabilities in the volatile, increasingly global world now emerging. It is a nation-state—one of 193 members of the United Nations. This standing gives it the legitimacy, autonomy, and resources to act authoritatively and flexibly on the global scene. Singapore is also, however, a single, cohesive urban community—a diminutive unit, from a global perspective, of less than 6 million people inhabiting a physical space less than four times the size of Washington, D.C. Although Singapore is tiny from a national perspective, it is obviously much more substantial from a municipal standpoint. It joins the more than 1,000 cities worldwide having a population in excess of 500,000, which together house over one-third of the world's people and whose number is expected to rise to near 1,400 by the year 2030.[9]

Singapore thus has two dimensions: as a *city,* and as a *state.* Both are a source of strength on the international scene and allow Singapore to enjoy the best of both the national and municipal worlds. On one hand, its diminutive city-state character facilitates the pragmatic, flexible, nonideological domestic politics typical of cities that Barber describes. On the other hand, its national standing provides the legitimacy and resources required to play credibly on the international scene in areas of its clear competence.

Singapore's dual character is also a compelling reason for its importance as a global paradigm. In its capacity as a "smart city," Singapore is a veritable laboratory for global solutions—especially those bringing informatics to bear. It has devised methods, capitalizing on the enormous potential of digital technology, to meet the pressing challenges of urban transition, in their multifaceted energy, environmental, sanitary, and transport-related dimensions. At the national level, the efforts of Singapore's "smart state" to provide enabling, economical alternatives to traditional Western entitlement programs in the health and welfare areas as societies grow older—once again with a technological twist—deserve broader consideration as well.

Singapore as Number One?

More than 35 years ago, Harvard scholar Ezra Vogel examined the organizational capabilities of an emerging industrial nation in *Japan as Number One*.[10] For the manufacturing world of which he wrote, the organizational features that he stressed were plausible strengths on the global stage, even if Japan in the long run could not easily sustain them. Despite Japan's faults, its distinctive organizational forms did provide lessons, as Vogel suggested, for an America whose own industrial base was steadily crumbling at the time.

We live in a very different and more cosmopolitan world today. Manufacturing is less salient, and services are more central to the livelihood of advanced industrial nations. Societies are more interdependent economically, and increasingly capable of learning from one another through the power of advanced telecommunications, including the Internet. For the more fluid, more global, and less manufacturing-oriented world now emerging, clearly a paradigm transcending the Japanese successes of an earlier age is now needed.

Policy borrowing from state-of-the-art practice around the world is becoming ever more possible and important. And as the world approaches the mid-21st century, performance in the services is central to success. These realities are leading global affairs toward a fresh and paradoxical paradigm, in which the small and vulnerable inform the great: potentially Singapore as Number One. Singapore is simply smart and adaptive—as both a nation and as an urban community—in a volatile global world. The tiny city-state is vulnerable, of course, but that very fragility breeds responsiveness as well.

In recent years, as the world has grown more integrated and global, a proliferation of surveys has ranked the nations of the world on performance indicators: economic achievement, international competitiveness, market orientation, regulatory transparency, avoidance of corruption, and so on. To a remarkable degree, these surveys have placed Singapore at or near the top of the list. And they have done so for sustained periods of time.

The World Bank, for example, has for 10 years in succession (2006 through 2015) considered Singapore the easiest country on earth in which to do business.[11] The World Economic Forum's *Global Competitiveness Report* has for 5 years in succession (2011 through 2015) ranked Singapore as second only to Switzerland in overall competitiveness among 148 nations. In both 2014 and 2015 Singapore was first in networked readiness, which measures information and communications technology (ICT) factors. And it was likewise ranked first in meeting the basic requirements for competitiveness.[12] Singapore also traditionally ranks high in transparency of government policymaking (number 1 in 2015); public trust in politicians (also number 1); absence of corruption (number 3); and quality of intellectual protection (number 4).[13]

Singapore does not, of course, rank at the top in everything, in part owing to its distinctive, often controversial, yet efficiency-driven approach to public policy. There are important nuances in its global standing, although it tends to rank remarkably high overall. A sector-by-sector review provides a useful introduction to this unusual city-state, beginning with the most striking element of Singapore's global profile: its economy, which consistently receives high marks as a global center.

As just mentioned, Singapore is broadly ranked as the easiest place in the world to do business; the average start-up time for a new company, for example, is less than 2.5 days.[14] It is also said to provide strong protection for intellectual property, through a high-quality judicial system, and ranks as having the most open economy worldwide for international trade and investment.[15] Singapore has a strong long-term anticorruption record, even though there has recently been a disturbing, albeit mild, erosion of international perceptions of Singapore in this area.[16] By the numbers, located as it is in the heart of the world's most populous and rapidly growing region, Singapore seems well suited to become a global hub.

Not surprisingly, Singapore hosts a large concentration of high-tech firms as a consequence of its hospitable business environment and strong intellectual-property protection. IBM, for example, has established its Asia-Pacific Cloud Computing Data Center and Smart Cities Research Program in Singapore, while Dell Computer, Semantec, and Infineon Technologies have placed their Asia-Pacific regional headquarters there. Singapore also attracts a broad range of other multinationals, including Procter and Gamble, which moved its global headquarters for beauty and baby-care products to Singapore in 2012, and General Motors, which moved its international operations headquarters from Shanghai to Singapore in the second quarter of 2014.[17] In 2015 McKinsey, the global consulting firm, launched a Digital Campus in Singapore, to execute digital initiatives at scale, while in April 2016 Visa opened a similar facility for innovation in commerce and payments.[18] In all, over 7,000 multinational firms operate in the tiny city-state, employing more than 110,000 expatriates.[19] Relative to net international

Figure 1-1. *Singapore's Rising Affluence in Comparative Perspective, 1970–2014*

GDP per capita (current US$)

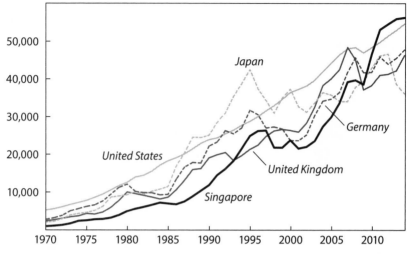

Source: World Bank, *World Development Indicators* (1970–2014) (http://data.worldbank.org/indicator/NY.GDP.PCAP.CD).

investment position as a share of GDP, Singapore ranked as the top country in the world in 2012.[20]

Turning from business evaluations to more abstract performance indicators, Singapore's production of goods and services provides some of the most notable evidence of its economic success. As a tiny city-state of less than 6 million people, its nominal GDP may not equal the world's largest but ranks surprisingly high given its diminutive scale—35th highest nominal GDP of 185 countries figuring in the World Bank's evaluation.[21] Its per capita ranking is of course higher: 9th out of 248 countries.[22] And as indicated in figure 1-1, that per capita standing has risen inexorably in recent years, outstripping that of Britain, Germany, Japan, and even the United States.

The relative pace of Singapore's ascent was particularly striking after the World Trade Center and Pentagon attacks of September 2001, paralleling the rapid rise of nearby China and India in international affairs. In the short run of 2014–16, the city-state was, to be sure, adversely affected by the slowing of Chinese growth, together with a related collapse of global energy prices and a strengthening of the U.S. dollar. Nominal GDP growth fell to 2 percent in 2015, while per capita GDP fell 6 percent to US$53,004.[23] Yet the long-term logic of rising economic fortunes in a heavily populated surrounding region will continue to provide Singapore with a powerful tail wind toward the future.

Singapore is clearly also amassing financial assets and reducing liabilities: its foreign exchange and gold reserves rank 11th highest of 84 nations, while its external debt places it 16th highest among 102 countries.[24] And it is investing those assets well: its national investment company, Temasek Holdings, which pays taxes like other firms in Singapore, is at the forefront in the efficiency of its operations out of 52 such institutions ranked internationally in 2016.[25] Singapore's financial firepower and the shrewdness with which its funds are deployed are clearly leveraging the tiny city-state's global influence.

Among the most distinctive and, in the view of business people and conservative politicians, most felicitous aspects of Singapore's economic environment is its relatively low tax rate.[26] Personal income tax rates start at zero and are capped at 20 percent for residents, while nonresidents are taxed at a uniform level of 15 percent.[27] The corporate income tax rate is only 17 percent, and there are incentives such as the Start-Up Tax Exemption scheme that reduce effective tax rates still further. Singapore's goods and services tax (GST) or value added tax (VAT) is also relatively low—just 7 percent. Furthermore, there is no dividend tax, no estate duty, and no capital gains tax.

Singapore is a wealthy nation, but it enjoys high performance in many basic social as well as economic indicators. Its unemployment rate was only 1.7 percent in 2014—less than a 3rd of American levels, and the 4th lowest in the world.[28] The technical quality of its health care system has recently been ranked as the 3rd best in the world.[29] And the World Health Organization (WHO) considers Singapore's health care system the finest in Asia, ahead even of Japan, which ranked 10th globally.[30] The WHO also indicates that Singapore has the 2nd lowest rate of infant mortality in the world, partly because of outstanding hospitals and clinics.[31] The International Institute for Management Development rates Singapore's health infrastructure, including those high-quality hospitals and clinics, as being the 4th best of 55 nations rated.[32]

Singapore also has a consistently high-quality educational system, from preschool through university. At the secondary level, this is demonstrated by the performance of its students on international math and science exams, where it has recently ranked among the top three in the world.[33] At the postsecondary level, Singapore sends many of its best and brightest to the finest universities in the West. Even so, the National University of Singapore

(NUS) was the highest-ranked Asian institution in the *Times Higher Education World University Rankings* for 2015–16—the first time that the continent reached that prominent spot in the rankings' 12-year history.

This strong global position owes much to Singapore's professional and technical schools.[34] Both the NUS Business School and that of Nanyang Technological University have recently been ranked among the top 32 business schools worldwide, while in 2015 the Nanyang Executive MBA program was rated 10th best in the world by the *Financial Times*.[35] According to another well-regarded indicator, Nanyang ranked 2nd globally in 2016 among universities less than 50 years old.[36]

Singapore's geography, transportation, infocommunications, and institutional infrastructure all help to facilitate the movement of people, goods, and ideas, thus enhancing economic-growth potential. Although far removed from major world economic centers in Europe and North America, Singapore is equipped with first-rate telecommunications that link it intimately to the "global village." In 2014 Singapore had the fifth highest Internet penetration in the Asia-Pacific region.[37] Singapore is also considered Asia's most "network-ready" country in terms of political and regulatory preparation for efficient connectivity.[38] Both its government and its private sector are capitalizing on the policy and the commercial implications of being so "wired up": it ranks second of 12 countries surveyed for "accessible electronic government" and first in Southeast Asia as a venue for online shopping.[39]

Singapore also has an outstanding transportation infrastructure, which likewise helps to connect it securely to major world centers. Changi Airport, together with Incheon in Korea, has been consistently ranked as the best airport internationally. It boasts excellent airline connections, efficient facilities and services, and the world's finest duty-free shopping. Changi also has a spotless safety and efficiency record; with over 450 awards, it is the world's most consistently applauded airport.[40] Singapore has likewise been named the best seaport in Asia and ranks second among the top seaports on earth in terms of tonnage.[41]

Although Singapore provides open access to carriers from throughout the world, it has also nurtured its own aviation sector. In terms of both service and efficiency, Singapore Air Lines is consistently rated one of aviation's finest carriers. It has developed an extensive long-haul network of direct flights to Singapore from Europe, the United States, the Middle East, Japan, and Australia, covering more than 60 cities in over 30 countries.[42] Singapore also leverages its strategic location to provide important refueling and repair facilities to the U.S. military, for which it is an important informal ally. Through both commercial and geopolitical initiatives, Singapore thus turns the "tyranny of distance"—close to 10,000 miles separating it from the core political-economic centers of the world—from a disadvantage into a strength.

Given its first-rate transport and communications infrastructure—not to mention its exotic location astride the equator in the heart of Southeast Asia—Singapore is a natural tourist destination. It has leveraged this as a duty-free port by becoming an attractive place to shop, although the high cost of land and labor is increasingly complicating this equation.

Broadening its attractiveness to tourists still further, Singapore recently went so far as to inaugurate the world's first nighttime Formula One race and to build two casinos.[43] The first Formula One Grand Prix race was run in 2008; Resorts World Sentosa (RWS) opened in February 2010, followed by the Marina Bay Sands Casino two months later. With its spicier new image, Singapore experienced a sharp rise of nearly 50 percent in its inflow of foreign tourists from the end of 2009 to the end of 2012, although growth deceleration in East Asia blunted tourism somewhat during 2013–16. On the World Economic Forum's Travel and Tourism Competitiveness Index, Singapore in 2015 ranked 11th of 141 countries as an attractive tourist destination.[44]

For a variety of reasons, Singapore has also emerged as one of the most livable cities on earth—for most of its permanent residents, as well as for tourists. Gallup recently ranked it the most favored immigration destination, attracting such Asian celebrities as Jet Li, Vicki Zhao, and Gong Li.[45] It has also increasingly pulled in new, long-term expatriate dwellers from the Middle East, Europe, and even North America. Among its new residents are one of the cofounders of Facebook, Eduardo Saverin; Jim Rogers, the well-known and well-regarded stock market analyst; and New Zealand–born investor Richard Chandler; as well as property tycoons Raj Kumar and Kishin RK.[46] With their rapid increase in recent years, foreigners now number more than 2 million and make up nearly 40 percent of Singapore inhabitants.[47]

Many of Singapore's foreigners, of course, are neither celebrities nor entrepreneurs. Around 80 percent are low-skilled workers from surrounding developing nations, striving for a better life than they left behind at home. Concentrated in the construction, domestic services, manufacturing, and marine industries, most such guest workers live in crowded dormitories or servants' quarters, with little access to friends or family. Many, especially natives of neighboring Indonesia and Malaysia, as well as Bangladesh and India, are Muslim. The number of manual guest workers grew over 70 percent between 2000 and 2010, surpassing 1 million, although rates of increase have tapered off since 2012.[48] Not surprisingly, the stability and future prospects of the immigrant community, including guest workers, are becoming an issue of first-order political, security, and humanitarian concern.

Why Singapore is so livable—for the bulk of its citizens and wealthy expatriates, at least—is a complex, subjective matter, although enlightened transport, land-use, housing, and environmental policies no doubt contribute, as explained at length in chapter 5. One additional element clearly is personal safety, placing Singapore at the top of this category in Asia and eighth globally in 2016.[49] There have been absolutely no instances of mass shootings, serial killings, terrorist bombing attacks, or major civil unrest, despite substantial turbulence in the surrounding region. A related strength is the absence of corruption.

Air and water quality are also distinctively high, even if that reality is less well recognized. Although Singapore is heavily populated, ranking second among 215 countries and territories in population density,[50] recent surveys indicate its residents are highly satisfied in this regard. Gallup, for one, finds 95 percent of Singaporeans pleased with their water quality (number 5 globally) and 91 percent with their air quality (number 6 globally).[51] And Singapore's air quality has also consistently been rated the best in Asia—in striking contrast to much more polluted Asian economic powerhouses such as Shanghai and Hong Kong.

Thanks to a distinctive combination of economic opportunity, social amenities, labor-influx controls, and effective training programs, Singapore has in addition succeeded in nurturing and motivating an unusually high-quality and highly motivated labor force. According to recent surveys, that workforce is among the top 10 most motivated in Asia, and 17th most motivated worldwide.[52] Singapore also has some of the most skilled labor in Asia. Much of this workforce comes from surrounding countries, under labor regulations that are among the most business oriented, albeit simultaneously restrictive in human terms, of any in Asia.[53]

Shadows?

Most of its longer-term inhabitants, especially expatriates, consider Singapore a convenient, efficient, and pleasant place to live. Yet residing there does have its challenges. The city is crowded and without a readily accessible hinterland to provide some escape from town. Moreover, owning a car to get around is extremely expensive, and there are only limited sports and recreation facilities nearby. Reflecting perhaps in part the difficulties of family life, the birth rate in Singapore is extremely low, with a 2014 fertility-level estimate of 1.25 that ranked 196th among 200 countries and regions around the world.[54]

Singapore has what is broadly regarded as one of the most efficient bureaucracies on earth, and arguably the best and least corrupt in Asia.[55] The World Economic Forum has found a higher trust of politicians there and less burden from government regulation than in any other country worldwide.[56] According to Transparency International, Singapore is also among the least corrupt nations on earth.[57] And the rule of law clearly prevails there to a much greater degree than in any of the surrounding countries.

Singapore does have regular democratic elections and a nominally competitive party system. Yet the city-state's distinctive policy approach, it must be noted, does impose more severe constraints on civil liberties and political rights than are typical in most Western industrial democracies. Singapore comes in at only "partly free" in the Freedom House democracy rankings, for example, a standing that has improved just slightly over the past 15 years.[58] Its 2015 Freedom House ranking for freedom of the press was only 148th in the world—along with Afghanistan, Kyrgyzstan, and Qatar.[59] Amnesty International, Human Rights Watch, and other observers have periodically criticized its treatment of guest workers.[60] Such workers have become a substantial share of the total population in recent years, with the share of foreign workers in the labor force—80 percent of whom are blue-collar—rising from 3.2 to 34.7 percent between 1970 and 2010.[61] Most guest workers come without their families, under tight social restrictions, and typically without the benefit of basic social services.[62] Not surprisingly, there has been occasional unrest among such employees in Singapore, precipitated by grievances over pay and other working conditions. And the influx of guest workers, which has helped push Singapore's population from 4 million in 2000 to over 5.5 million today, has stirred concerns about security and overcrowding among middle-class Singaporeans as well.[63]

Given its pleasant overall environment, Singapore is also quite an expensive place to live, ranking as the most expensive global city out of 133 worldwide in 2015.[64] While food and clothing appear to be quite reasonably priced, owing in part to Singapore's character as a free trade economy, housing is expensive, reflecting both its stimulative government policies and desirability as a destination for both tourists and long-term inhabitants.

As a result of its market-oriented ethos, attractiveness for wealth-oriented entrepreneurs, and high housing costs, Singapore is becoming an increasingly unequal society. The share of the very wealthiest Singaporeans in gross

Figure 1-2. *Share of Top 1 Percent in Gross Domestic Income, 1981–2011*

Percent

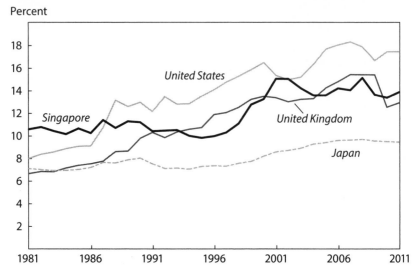

Source: *Chartbook of Economic Inequality* (www.chartbookofeconomicinequality.com/).

domestic income has been expanding steadily for at least the past 20 years (figure 1-2). Meanwhile, rising real estate prices and home rentals may be compounding inequality of assets, although data are inadequate on that point. Singapore's middle class, its living standards eroding in relative terms, has understandably begun to feel pressured and frustrated.

Comparative analysis confirms this long-term pattern, especially when factoring in the Singapore government's market-oriented policies, which may intensify it. Singapore's Gini coefficient of inequality after taxes, for example, appears to have been steadily rising, and rising faster since 2000, than in either Japan or the United Kingdom. Singapore's broad index of inequality does appear to still be lower than that of the United States, however (figure 1-3). Since the Lehman shock of 2008, its level of inequality may also have moderated compared with that of the United States, although evidence remains incomplete on this point and statistics are somewhat contradictory.[65]

International Leaders' Reactions

From the standpoint of international economic analysts and the global business community, Singapore's overall performance has been overwhelmingly positive. It has also received high marks from a broad range of statesmen,

Figure 1-3. *Singapore's Gini Coefficient in Comparative Perspective, 2000–12*

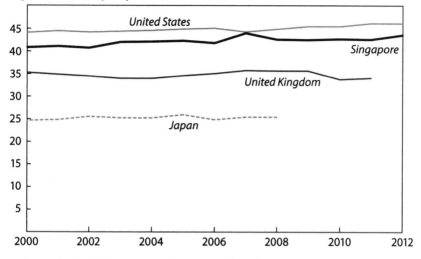

Higher = more inequality

Source: *Chartbook of Economic Inequality* (www.chartbookofeconomicinequality.com/).

scholars, policy analysts, and diplomats. American leaders dating back to John F. Kennedy and Lyndon B. Johnson, presidents at the time of Singapore's foundation in the early 1960s, have been similarly impressed.[66] Interestingly, it has also drawn praise from China's leadership for many, many years. From Chairman Mao onward, five generations of Chinese leaders enjoyed good relations with Singapore's remarkable first prime minister, Lee Kuan Yew, in particular. Among foreigners, only Henry Kissinger has commanded comparable personal standing with Beijing.[67]

In early November 1978 Deng Xiaoping visited Singapore on the very eve of his historic Four Modernizations proposals.[68] He quickly bonded with Lee Kuan Yew, whom he met several more times across the years, and was deeply impressed by Singapore's ability to combine economic growth and political stability.[69] Deng viewed the tiny city-state as both a useful model for his own reform program and as an indispensable intermediary for China with the broader global community.[70] Singapore's decision, for example, to actively participate in China's development through such steps as its Suzhou investment joint venture helped immensely in bolstering foreign-investor confidence in Deng's modernization program.

Deng dispatched numerous emissaries and study groups to Singapore to learn about planning, public management, and corruption control.[71] He also exhorted Shenzhen, Zhuhai, and other reforming special economic zones to learn from Singapore during his famous Southern Journey of early 1992.[72] Several other Chinese leaders have followed in Deng's wake. Most recently, Xi Jinping visited Singapore in 2010, just before assuming top-level leadership in Beijing, and returned on a state visit in November 2015 to commemorate the 25th anniversary of China-Singapore diplomatic relations. [73]

Over the past three decades, enthusiasm for Singapore's policy approaches has spread around the world. Major European business schools such as the Institut Européen d'Administration des Affaires (INSEAD) have established campuses there. Russia has actively encouraged emulation of Singapore, sending students from its best universities there while recently tapping Singapore expertise to build a multibillion-dollar e-government program over the coming decade.[74] The nations of the Persian Gulf rely on Singapore to manage their hotels, just as Rio de Janeiro engages Singapore to manage its airport, and countries ranging from Argentina to Vietnam call on it to handle their container seaports.[75]

Even the developing world is taking close notice. President Paul Kagame of Rwanda, one of Africa's most practical and activist reformers, is deeply impressed with the Singapore economic model and has dispatched his most trusted and able assistants to Singapore to study and report back in detail on how its example could inform Rwandan development. To Kagame, as to many visionary analysts in both the G-7 and the developing world, Singapore clearly is Number One. At Rwanda's annual Thanksgiving Prayer Breakfast in late 2012, for example, President Kagame explicitly held up the city-state approvingly as a model, noting that "we are not seeking to become Singapore, but we can be like Singapore. We must have a vision of where we want to go, and work harder to achieve [it]."[76] In a troubled world that values both growth and human freedom, how relevant is Singapore's experience? And what are the practices that provoke this spirit of emulation? These are issues taken up in the following pages.

Conclusion

In today's volatile globalizing world, the paradigms of the past are rapidly losing their normative and predictive value. No longer are nation-states the intrinsically dominant and autonomous actors that they have long been assumed to be. No longer are the technological frontiers and political-economic parameters clear enough for states to confidently and strategically plan in "developmental" fashion. With increasing urbanizing, the problems of energy, transportation, and environment are growing more serious, especially among the developing nations.

Yet neither national governments nor the global community are addressing these challenges effectively. As budget crises deepen around the world, the "entitlement" model is proving impractical in the social-welfare realm, and even morally suspect to some. Similarly, as markets open and volatile international transactions proliferate, the "developmental state" concept is growing decidedly passé in the world of economic development.

Singapore presents a puzzling challenge to fashionable classic paradigms of political-economic affairs—particularly the entitlement model of social welfare and the developmental-state approach to economic development. It is clearly succeeding by many measures—by its high levels of per capita GDP, rapid economic growth, political stability, public health, and environmental quality among them. Yet it is not following the policy prescriptions that have been standard for both industrial and developing nations. And there are undeniable questions, both at home and abroad, regarding its technocratic, technology-intensive, and rigorously neoliberal approach to public policy.

Why has Singapore so successfully swum against the tide, both of its challenging circumstances and of contrary opinion? How long can it continue to do so, and how? What do its successes, such as they are, suggest in a broader global context for how the world should deal with its pressing economic and social problems, both today and tomorrow? These are some of the key questions addressed in the pages to follow.

The Imperative to Be Smart
SMALL COUNTRY, FEW RESOURCES, VOLATILE SURROUNDINGS

We are the resource-poorest country in the region, and therefore we cannot afford to be other than honest, efficient, and capable if we are to stay out of trouble.

—LEE KUAN YEW (1998)

Singapore, as noted earlier, ranks surprisingly high on a global scale of both societal and governmental performance. It also plays a consequential, innovative role in international affairs. Yet it is not a large nation and lacks a powerful military. The question persists: why is Singapore so successful?

A broad variety of explanations have been offered for Singapore's success, particularly by sociologists and political economists. Many have pointed to the outstanding personal leadership of Singapore's founding father, Lee Kuan Yew, and to the values of pragmatism, meritocracy, and honesty that he inculcated in his colleagues.[1] Others have stressed the distinctive organizational structure of the Singaporean bureaucracy, while still others privilege social coalitions and socioeconomic organization of civil society.[2] Still others have emphasized the ability of Singaporeans to understand and respond to global market forces.[3] Some, however, are entirely skeptical of not only Singapore's economic achievements but also its social outcomes, which they consider the perverse results of its history of soft authoritarianism.[4]

This volume presents a holistic view of Singapore's distinctive success (as well as its few failures) based on research covering a broad range of socioeconomic parameters. Most of these reflect a striking ability to perceive and respond in a single-minded way to long-term trends in the global political economy, particularly the Digital Revolution. In other words, Singapore is successful fundamentally because it is smart in the way it handles challenges, both from within and from beyond its national boundaries. It governs, in short, efficiently and pragmatically.

In the 21st century, smart governance depends heavily on leveraging human intelligence and administrative capacity through information technology. It means creating a network of physical objects—devices, vehicles, buildings, and other items—embedded with electronics and software: an Internet of Things (IoT) that allows those objects to collect and exchange data.[5] Singapore is also rapidly becoming smart in this sense.

The "smart" concept can be applied illustratively in four specific contexts: nation-state, city, hub, and institutional, while ascribing the qualities to follow:

—*Smart states* are minimalist and enabling; they facilitate the smooth operation of society in a fluid global environment, rather than maintain dirigiste, hierarchical control.

—*Smart cities* adopt an integrated, holistic approach to management, by means of innovative technology.

—*Smart hubs* connect interactively across national boundaries, creating new ideas and pragmatically commercializing them, leveraged by the power of digitalization.

—*Smart institutions*, more generically, respond and act holistically over time and across interorganizational boundaries, tackling multiple problems through unified collective effort.

The explanation provided here incorporates some elements of previous analyses. It accepts and indeed emphasizes the catalytic role of Lee Kuan Yew and the crucial supportive role of Singaporean bureaucrats. But it looks beyond personal factors—distinctive as they may be—to the nature of the system that was created, its ability to deal flexibly with change, its unique linkages to the broader world, and its unusual ability to assimilate and capitalize on the latest technology. Moreover, the role of innovative electronics and communications technology receives special attention in giving government new, more perceptive, and more powerful roles.

The smart mechanisms that Singapore employs—"smart" in the sense that a "smart grid" or the guidance system of a "smart bomb" responds to outside stimuli—are outlined in chapter 3. First, however, one needs to consider *why* Singapore has been so driven to perceive and respond dynamically to the complex pressures of the changing, globalizing world when many surrounding nations or even small countries with similar factor endowments have not done so. The imperatives behind Singapore's actions in this regard fall into five categories: geography, demography, finance, politics, and technology.

The Profile of Geographical Paradox

Singapore's demonstrable successes in both public policy and international affairs are grounded in a distinct geographical paradox: this is one of the smallest and arguably most vulnerable countries in the world along many dimensions—domestic market size, resource base, and geopolitical positioning, to name but a few. Indeed, Singapore is so diminutive that it stretches the very definition of a modern nation-state. It has more in common politically with medieval Venice or city-state members of the Hanseatic League, whose geographical scale was also in sharp contrast to their commercial importance, than it does with the conventional idea of a nation in today's world.[6] Singapore, like its medieval counterparts, in this sense provocatively stretches conventional paradigms of city and state in international affairs.

Covering little more than 700 square kilometers, which is slightly less than four times the size of Washington, D.C., Singapore ranks only 191st among nation-states in land area. Its population of less than 6 million, which is roughly that of Minnesota in the United States, places it 183rd in this category. But that figure includes around 1.6 million guest workers and over 2 million foreigners in all.[7] To add to its challenges, population density is high: 7,737 people per square kilometer of area, versus 35 for the United States, 349 for Japan, and 517 for Korea.[8] Even on the GDP calculus, affluent Singapore ranks only 38th.[9]

Just as challenging for Singapore as its small scale is its related lack of natural resources. The tiny city-state has absolutely no domestic oil and gas. It produces virtually no food. And despite its tropical location and almost daily rainfall, it is even radically short of water, having to import 250 million gallons a day from neighboring Malaysia.[10]

Despite its relatively substantial population, Singapore is frequently short of locally developed human resources in various dimensions. It lacks sufficient computer programmers, and many of its financiers and other executives are expatriates. Overall, 21 percent of Singapore's white-collar workers are of foreign nationality.[11] Even more critically, blue-collar labor and service workers are in radically short supply.

Fully one-third of Singapore's local labor force is now foreign, with that share steadily rising: in 2015, 70 percent of total employment growth came from the increase in guest workers.[12] Since 1970 the proportion of citizens among Singapore residents has fallen from 90 to only 61 percent.[13] This trend has begun to generate social tensions and dislocations, especially at the blue-collar level, which present potential challenges to the continued viability of Singapore's remarkable economic story.

Domestic labor shortage may be a vulnerability, but like many of this resourceful city-state's deficiencies, it is *not* necessarily a weakness. Singaporeans themselves view such shortages as a challenge to innovation and improvement. As Prime Minister Lee Hsien Loong stressed recently, "We need to continue to welcome foreign talent, while encouraging employers to train and build up the local talent pool."[14] In the borderless, mobile political economy of the 21st century, where countries and companies must compete increasingly for talent transnationally,[15] Singapore fully intends to transform labor-shortage vulnerabilities into competitive strengths, through proactive training and recruitment policies (see chapter 3).

Singapore's High-Stakes Neighborhood

Given the pressing challenges and vulnerabilities related to its diminutive scale and lack of resources, Singapore naturally hopes for a stable, predictable environment beyond its shores. Yet its precarious geopolitical circumstances do not readily afford such a luxury. The tiny city-state is sandwiched among three of the four most populous nations on earth: China, India, and Indonesia (figure 2-1)—two of them nuclear armed, and all destined to be among the major powers of the 21st century.

Singapore also lies directly astride the Strait of Malacca, arguably the most economically and militarily important maritime chokepoint on earth—only 1.7 miles wide at its narrowest point.[16] The strait is the shortest sea route between the major oil and gas producers of the Persian Gulf and the rapidly growing economies of Asia (figure 2-2). It is traversed by nearly 80,000 vessels annually.[17] Every day over one-quarter of the crude oil that flows in international commerce, as well as an even higher share of the world's total trade by volume, flows before Singapore's doorstep, presenting tempting targets for terrorists or megalomaniacs intent on global control.[18] And surrounding nations in Southeast Asia have not been historically stable, generating

Figure 2-1. *Singapore's Densely Populated Neighborhood*

Population total (millions)

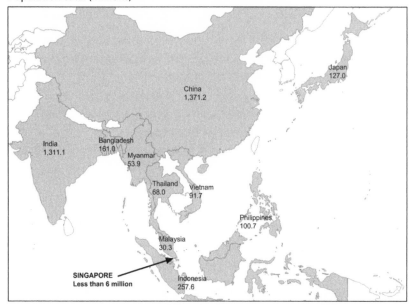

Source: Figure created by the author using the data from World Bank, "Population, total," *World Development Indicators* (2015).

Figure 2-2. *The Strait of Malacca*

Source: Ralf Brennemann, "Map of Strait of Malacca," *Atlas of the World*, RB-DESKART (www.welt-atlas.de/).

Table 2-1. *Singapore's Giant Neighbors: Danger Meets Opportunity*

Country	Population	Area (sq. km)	Total GDP (dollars billion)[a]	GDP/ capita (dollars)[a]	Active military personnel	Urban population (percent)
China	1,364,270,000	9,388,211	17,189	12,599	2,333,000	54.4
India	1,295,291,543	2,973,190	7,045	5,439	1,150,900	32.4
Indonesia	254,454,778	1,811,570	2,553	10,033	395,500	53.0
Singapore	5,469,724	707	432	78,958	72,500	100.0

Source: World Bank, *World Development Indicators* (2014), and International Institute for Strategic Studies, "Asia," in *The Military Balance 2015* (London: Routledge, 2015), pp. 207–302. For population, see http://data.worldbank.org/indicator/SP.POP.TOTL; land area, see http://data.worldbank.org/indicator/AG.LND.TOTL.K2; for GDP per capita (PPP), see http://data.worldbank.org/indicator/NY.GDP.MKTP.PP.KD; for urban population, see http://data.worldbank.org/indicator/SP.URB.TOTL.IN.ZS.

a: GDP figures are in constant "international dollars," denoting what could be purchased in the cited country with the comparable aggregate of goods and services that a U.S. dollar would buy in the United States. This term is used in World Bank purchasing-power parity calculations.

additional national-security challenges for Singapore, equaled only by those confronting Israel in the Middle East.

The Mixed Curse and Blessing of Singapore's Regional Positioning

Singapore's geo-economic circumstances are inevitably a double-edged sword. Given its affluence and strategic location, the much larger powers surrounding it—China, India, and Indonesia, in particular, all with substantial military potential and growing strength—have an unavoidable interest in Singapore. Yet in the economic calculus, these neighbors, with their huge populations and growth potential, could also be promising future markets. The three countries together have well over 2.5 billion people (table 2-1)—more than a third of the entire world's population.

Singapore's distinctive mix of vulnerability and strategic placement has an economic dimension as well. As a diminutive city-state lying amid larger powers, its economy is radically exposed, with the highest ratio of trade to GDP in the world, at 326 percent.[19] It has been badly wounded in past years by global economic downturns, such as the Asian financial crisis of 1997–98 and the Lehman crisis of 2008. Yet it can also benefit disproportionately from upturns, as during 2010–14. Despite foreign exchange reserves of nearly US$250 billion, 11th largest in the world, Singapore retains powerful stakes in the stability and prosperity of neighbors—and indeed, of the world economy as a whole.[20]

Singapore's location—sandwiched among potentially unstable yet rising powers of Asia, astride a globally strategic waterway—also provides it with inextricably linked diplomatic challenges and opportunities. Paradoxically, in this context its weakness and vulnerability can also turn out to be a major strength—but *only* if it is smart. Precisely because Singapore is so small and exposed, it is less threatening to large powers than many of their counterparts, thus giving it unusual potential as a mediator and an entrepôt center in a troubled region. Yet that potential must be intelligently grasped and nurtured in order to be realized.

Financial and Macroeconomic Vulnerabilities

Throughout its modern history, Singapore's economy has ranked as one of the most open in the world in terms of international trade and foreign investment. The city-state is a free port, with virtually all tariffs set at zero and total merchandise trade exceeding two-and-a-half times national GDP.[21] Inflows of foreign investment amounted to 22.3 percent of GDP in 2015.[22] Singapore's high degree of openness naturally leaves it vulnerable to periodic external shocks, of which the Asian financial crisis and Lehman shock were among the most serious, but by no means the only ones. Volatility transmitted from the international economy through capital and trade flows can dangerously confound a broad range of domestically relevant parameters in Singapore, including exchange rates, commodity prices, real estate values, and, of course, economic growth.

Owing to the domestic economy's small relative scale and high degree of international exposure, the annual growth rate of GDP fluctuates much more actively than that of the United States (figure 2-3). This problem is compounded by the volatility of capital flows in and out of a small exposed economy and the exchange rate implications thereof. In the years since the 2008 global financial crisis, as surrounding nations have grown more affluent, hot money inflows, combined with central bank policies condoning currency appreciation to temper inflation, have contributed to a substantial appreciation in the value of the Singapore dollar relative to its U.S. counterpart.[23]

Volatile capital flows and economic growth rates have meant volatile real estate and housing prices. Singapore property prices have risen by 74 percent since 2004 (figure 2-4a) and are up by 40 percent since 2009 alone. This situation has benefited existing property owners, of course, and the impact on average citizens is mitigated by the availability of affordable public housing. The

Figure 2-3. *Singapore's Volatile GDP Growth Rate, 1970–2014*

Percent

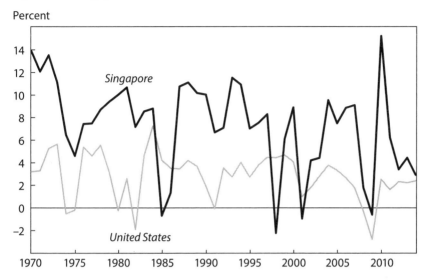

Source: World Bank, *World Development Indicators* (1970–2014).

Figure 2-4. *Singapore's Volatile Property Prices*

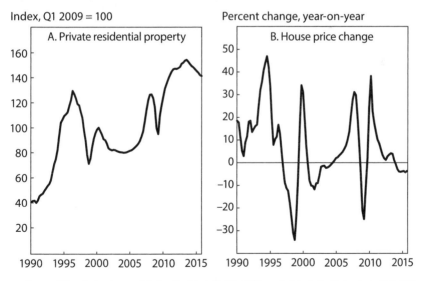

Source: Urban Redevelopment Authority, *Private Residential Property Price Index* (data.gov.sg/dataset/
private-residential-property-price-index-by-type-of-property).

impact of property price inflation has thus been felt most intensely by expatriates, offsetting some of the other substantial personal benefits in Singapore.

Appreciation in the exchange rate and real estate made Singapore in late 2015 the most expensive city in the world.[24] During financial crises, real estate pricing patterns typically move into reverse, making life chronically uncertain for even those with a tangible propertied stake in society. Housing prices varied from year to year by as much as 40 percent during the Asian financial crisis period, and by nearly 30 percent before and after the Lehman shock (figure 2-4b). In recent years the escalation has moderated, but rapid Asian growth would most likely reignite Singapore property prices once again.

Financial volatility, combined with large, rapid international capital flows, has also rendered Singapore vulnerable in another way: the value of its national financial holdings has fluctuated rapidly. Sovereign wealth funds, for example, experienced severe losses following the Lehman shock of 2008: Temasek's portfolio plunged by over US$40 billion (S$55 billion), or nearly 40 percent, between the onset of the crisis and March 2009.[25] GIC, Singapore's second fund, lost more than US$41 billion (S$59 billion).[26] Temasek and GIC were able to recoup their losses relatively quickly when global financial authorities began injecting massive liquidity to counter deflationary tendencies. Yet the vulnerabilities of Singapore's exposed position in the financial as well as the real economic arena were clear. Singapore's state needed to be smart to handle the multiple challenging tasks at hand.

A Heritage of Turbulent, Volatile Politics at Home and Abroad

Past experience has deeply ingrained in Singaporeans a sense of how fragile and volatile political environments can be. Lee Kuan Yew and his "old guard" comrades were virtually all graduates of the Raffles Institution, Singapore's first and most elite pre-collegiate educational facility. And they had struggled together under four distinct political regimes (British colonial rule, Japanese occupation, limited self-government, and unification with Malaysia) even before Singapore's independence in 1965. On Independence Day, the leadership faced a communist challenge, rampant unemployment, and ethnic nationalism within, together with the stirrings of the Vietnam War and the Chinese Cultural Revolution in close proximity abroad. Not long thereafter, Prime Minister Harold Wilson announced Britain's intention to withdraw Her Majesty's forces from east of Suez, leaving Singapore with an even further heightened national security challenge in the volatile world of Southeast Asia.

Since the late 1960s Singapore's domestic politics have stabilized, but they remain in peril because of uncertainties from the ever more integrated economies abroad. Developments of the past three decades—the Gulf War (1991), the Asian financial crisis (1997–98), "9/11," the Lehman shock (2008), and the global energy-price collapse (2014–16) in particular—reaffirm that the tiny city-state needs to be smart to survive and prosper.

Disruptive Technological Change: The Digital Revolution

The active and efficient way that Singapore has embraced the epochal developments of the Digital Revolution, centering on mobile telephony and the Internet, amply demonstrates that it should already be considered a smart state. The speed and ubiquity of its transition to a digital world are profoundly related to its other smart characteristics: pragmatism, long-term vision, and administrative sophistication.

Digitalization has spread around the world with blinding speed. The first mobile phone was created by Motorola in 1983; by 2015 there were more than 7 billion mobile phones in use around the world, up from less than 1 billion in 2000.[27] The World Wide Web became publicly accessible in 1991; today well over 3 billion people are using it. In 1984 less than 9 percent of Americans owned a personal computer; by 2015 the device had become virtually ubiquitous, with even more advanced and mobile tablet computers and smart phones actually exceeding PCs in Internet usage.

Now that the Digital Revolution has spread with full force in both the advanced industrial world and among the developing nations, it has generated immense new challenges for governments and civil society alike, requiring them to stay up to date and competitive in a rapidly changing global economy. At the same time, historic innovations in both computing and communications have created huge new potential for efficiency, speed, and transparency in addressing socioeconomic problems. By diffusing information broadly and rapidly, digital advances make it technologically easier for government agencies—at the local, national, or international level—to coordinate across jurisdictional lines. These developments in turn begin to flatten traditional hierarchies and empower more intense citizen challenge to government information monopolies.

Over the past 15 years the Digital Revolution has expanded beyond calculation and communication alone to the creation through sensors on physical objects of an Internet of Things (IoT). It is increasingly possible for objects to be sensed and controlled remotely across an existing network infrastructure. IoT has profound implications for such disparate fields as transportation logistics and medicine, which Singapore is working rapidly to realize.

Chapter 3 documents in detail how the Digital Revolution, including the IoT, helped to transform Singaporean decisionmaking processes and to create a distinctive smart state. Precisely because it enables transparency and collaboration across traditional bureaucratic lines, however, the Digital Revolution has even greater potential for creating smart states and smart cities in nations with a "holistic" approach to government and limited interministerial barriers and rivalries than in countries where those rivalries are strong. Thus small, unified nation-states like Singapore, or subnational units of government like cities, have less sociopolitical difficulty in becoming smart through cross-societal electronic integration than do larger national systems with complex and conflicting embedded interests, including agriculture and heavy industry, as in the case of Japan, China, or India.

A Powerful Stake in System Stability

Because of its geographical exposure and financial vulnerability, Singapore has a natural stake in system stability at both the regional and global levels, as well as intrinsic shared interests with status quo powers within and outside Southeast Asia. Singapore is thus, by virtue of its precarious circumstances, a natural catalyst for both neighboring states of the Association of Southeast Asian Nations (ASEAN), which desire political stability to facilitate their economic growth, and also for status quo powers beyond the region, such as Japan and the United States. To the extent that Singapore makes subtle common cause with both ASEAN and the United States, in particular, its leverage with the large and rising powers of Asia, such as China and India, is also enhanced.

It is sometimes argued that crisis is an important stimulant to economic and political innovation, by forcing leaders to be responsive to their surrounding political-economic environment.[28] The outstanding successes of Singapore public policy over the past half century provide clear support for this proposition. At critical junctures such as the transition to self-government (1959), independence (1965), and the period of the Asian financial crisis

(1997–98), Singapore demonstrated significant and generally far-sighted policy innovation.

Even during periods when the immediate political-economic uncertainties confronting Singapore have not been pronounced, as was broadly true across the 1980s, for example, the long-term existential challenges confronting that tiny city-state have not disappeared, nor has the endemic crisis consciousness of its far-sighted leaders. A deep sense of communal vulnerability and a realization that things could go badly wrong at any moment, whether domestically or internationally, have been a catalyst for Singapore's striking policy successes. Its facility in responding rapidly and efficiently to sudden challenges also owes much to embedded structural features and social practices, including a unicameral legislature, relatively limited bureaucratic rivalries, and a holistic approach to government. All of these features have interacted well with aspects of the Digital Revolution, including the Internet of Things phenomenon, to enhance information flows and transparency, giving Singapore unique potential for becoming digitally as well as politically smart.

Singapore's perilous circumstances thus dictate both crisis consciousness and activism, leveraged by technology, in domestic policies as well as diplomacy. If its leaders and their colleagues do not act effectively, the island state cannot feed and clothe itself, for it has few natural resources. Moreover, if its leaders do not act shrewdly, using all technical and policy tools available, Singapore cannot defend itself, particularly in a crisis. Nor can it magnify its otherwise miniscule role in world affairs. The chronicle of Singapore's success over the past half century is thus unavoidably linked to the historic challenges it has faced and the visionary, activist leadership with which it has smartly met those challenges and built technologically sensitive institutions in response.

3

How Singapore Became Smart

No army, however brave, can win when its generals are weak.

—LEE KUAN YEW (1998)

Singapore's geography and lack of resources, as suggested in chapter 1, are innately challenging. And its national history has been likewise difficult, from the very inception in the mid-20th century. The saga of Singapore's first two decades, in particular, illustrates clearly why Singapore needed to be smart, in the sense of being strategically yet pragmatically responsive, long before the opportunities to become smart in a narrower cybernetic sense began to arise. Singapore's early history also shows how proactive leadership was crucial to creation of the city-state's distinctively open and holistic institutional architecture, collaborative policy style, and willingness to learn from abroad. All those qualities, embedded long before the Digital Revolution, later made embracing smart ICT possible. The difficult history of those founding years also shows why crisis consciousness remains so deeply ingrained in both Singaporean political leaders and in their bureaucratic counterparts even today, driving them continually toward far-sighted policy innovation.

More recent developments—the Gulf War, the Asian financial crisis, 9/11, and the Lehman shock in particular—reaffirm that perils persist for a small city-state exposed to a turbulent world. Like earlier crises, these have profoundly shaped local institutions, configuring them to be flexible, adaptive, market-conforming, and responsive to new technological options. History and a perpetually strong consciousness of its varied political-economic perils thus continue to exert a powerful impact on the evolution of Singapore public policy, even in the IoT era. Perpetual crisis consciousness and flexible institutional structure render Singapore's institutions resilient, and its leaders resourceful, in the face of strong, volatile outside forces.

Singapore has been blessed with visionary leaders across its short but turbulent history. Yet a tiny band of individuals, no matter how capable, cannot singlehandedly manage even a small nation-state in the modern world with precision. In the long run, it is well-configured institutions, rather than philosopher kings, that enable nations to meet challenges with enduring strategic responses. As this chapter makes clear, a full understanding of Singapore's smart state must take note of how those key institutions emerged and flourished.

This chapter recounts chronologically the emergence and evolution of Singapore's smart institutions and smart group dynamics. That is best done by observing how its ministries, statutory boards, and para-public firms—in a word, its leadership—have grown increasingly skilled over the past half century in perceiving and responding to their political-economic environments, first by applying pragmatic common sense, and later by employing technology. It is thus essential to examine the impact of people, organization, the rule of law, and finally technology in making Singapore responsive to its pressing domestic and international challenges.

This chapter chooses the lens of crisis and response as an organizing concept for understanding how smart-state capabilities historically evolve. It focuses especially on how particular crises led to innovative responses that in turn enhanced Singapore's ability to be smart in a pragmatic yet strategic sense. It explores further whether states have grown smarter in iterative fashion, due to the enormous magnitude of the challenges that they faced at critical junctures; the quality of their leadership at such junctures; and the capacity of institutions and technology to assist in perceiving and responding to subsequent challenge. To understand creative responses to crisis that result in institution building, it focuses on the interaction among leadership, institutions, and policymaking processes.

This analysis further argues that positive leadership practices serve as a key catalyst for inclusive organization. They create a sense of community that makes teamwork—and ultimately innovation—much easier. The framework and operating procedures established by insightful leaders continue to benefit a nation, however, only as long as the parameters they create persist in adjusting to their evolving outside context, and continuing to align with new group dynamics brought about by succeeding generations of leadership.

In each leadership era of its short history, ever since attaining self-government in 1959, Singapore has faced distinctive challenges. Each leadership tenure roughly symbolizes an era in the evolution of the smart state:

—Under Lee Kuan Yew, it was the age of independence and state formation (1959–90).

—Goh Chok Tong oversaw an era of greater relaxation and experimentation, as the information revolution proceeded, with transnational interdependence deepening (1990–2004).

—Lee Hsien Loong faced an age of full-scale globalization, digitalization, and presentation of the Singapore model to the broader world (2004–present).

Singapore's political history can thus be divided along the lines of national leadership, with the latter two linked through a common challenge of global interdependence, although the shadow of Lee Kuan Yew casts itself across all three eras.

Throughout the three formal leadership tenures, Singapore public policy has remained flexible and creative, thanks to consistently smart institutions, updated with the latest technology and responding effectively to changes in domestic, regional, and global environments. A unicameral legislature, for example, in contrast to the more complex American, European, and Japanese systems, has no doubt made effective leadership easier, and probably smarter in the sense of being more perceptive of and more responsive to outside social forces. So have Singapore's major specialized statutory boards, especially the Housing and Development Board (HDB), Central Provident Fund (CPF), and Economic Development Board (EDB), which focus on housing, finance, and foreign investment challenges, respectively. This chapter will explore the role of leadership in configuring these distinctive outcomes, and how it critically aided in creating the smart Singaporean state, in both its pragmatic and its technologically sophisticated dimensions.

An empirically based analysis of the subject cannot proceed, however, without first examining the conceptual meaning of smart institutions and the varied ways that they can help to remedy common organizational pathologies. With that foundation, it becomes clear that Singapore's government became smart in two distinct phases, largely in response to dual stimuli: political-economic crisis and technological change. The concept of critical juncture is used here to delineate periods of particular fluidity and decisive institutional transformation.[1]

For theorists such as Max Weber, bureaucracy is the apotheosis of organizational forms and the bureaucratic state is intrinsically "smart"—so there is little need to evolve in that direction.[2] Revisionist literature, however, has pointed out at least four pathologies that can affect the performance of bureaucratic states in the real world:

—*Clientelism:* George Stigler finds that the regulated have strong incentives to coopt their regulator.[3]

—*Routinization:* Anthony Downs notes that as bureaucracies expand, they become preoccupied with internal coordination rather than external response.[4]

—*Vertical communication:* In Michel Crozier's view, bureaucracies often grow stalemated owing to pathologies in top-down information flow and incentives.[5]

—*Inadequate Institutionalization:* Samuel Huntington adds that state structures may be inadequately configured to accommodate rising popular desires for political participation.[6]

All of the foregoing analysts seriously question the actual performance of actual nation-states in some parts of the world, in the course of their theoretically guided investigations. Yet the ills of governance they describe have been effectively avoided or largely countervailed in Singapore, demonstrating its unusual capacity to operate as a smart state in the pragmatic/strategic sense and creating the analytical puzzle that inspires this research.

In neutralizing the classical pathologies of governance outlined above, smart institutions in Singapore exhibit three notable operational traits that enhance their effectiveness.

First, Singapore's smart institutions pursue an integrated approach to challenges. They think and act holistically, not only over time (integrating the short and long term) but also across interorganizational boundaries. They tackle multiple problems, in short, with a unified approach, or through collaborative effort.

Second, they recognize the importance of the group dynamic within their smaller subunits. They invigorate individual ministries, statutory boards, and other public organizations by recruiting high-quality young participants. And they enhance the communications potential of those bodies by nurturing strong vertical, cross-generational networks. The incentive structures that smart institutions in Singapore create thus help to motivate efficient and ambitious individuals to join the government institutions being reconfigured. Smart states and cities also confer responsibility on younger, able individuals, rather than allocating posts solely on the basis of seniority. Singapore seems willing to risk bringing fresh people with new perspectives into high-profile meetings and training them for greater responsibility.

Third, smart institutions are also less prone to clientelism, because transparency and distance from political bodies are embedded in their architecture, as well as in their environment. Singapore's powerful statutory boards, which report to ministries rather than to politicians, are a clear case in point. In keeping with the leadership's strong insistence on continuous innovation to keep abreast competitively with developments elsewhere in a changing world, the structure of such technocratic bodies comes under continuous, systematic review by knowledgeable arbiters, subject to sunset provisions that weed out seemingly ineffective approaches.

In short, Singapore smart institutions avoid pathologies classically ascribed to the bureaucratic state, while retaining positive aspects of "embedded autonomy." From a historical perspective, their evolution in this regard can be divided into two distinct eras: an early phase and a later phase, differentiated by the salience of globalization. The following analysis considers how smart institutions have evolved in Singapore itself, noting where relevant any notable contrasts to evolutionary patterns elsewhere. Historical comparison provides a more refined understanding of just what makes the Singaporean smart state and smart city distinctive, and worthy of consideration elsewhere as policy paradigms, which future chapters propose to do.

Early Phase: Challenges during the 1960s

During the early postwar years (1945–55), before self-government, Singapore was rocked by multiple sociopolitical challenges, as were other transitioning states in Asia, including India, China, Burma, Malaysia, and Indonesia. This turbulence reached a particular pitch in the mid-1950s (figure 3-1), against a backdrop of painfully high unemployment—it was nearly 14 percent when Singapore attained self-government in 1959. The fledgling polity also faced complex ethnic tensions, such as the Hock Lee bus riots (April 1955) and the Chinese Middle School riots (1956), as well as pervasive labor unrest. Neither the high unemployment nor the endemic social tensions were to fully subside for nearly a decade.[7]

Amid this unrest and unease, consolidating regime stability and neutralizing ethnic unrest were political challenges that helped catapult the People's Action Party (PAP) to power, less than five years after its founding in November 1954. With the PAP winning 43 of the 51 seats at stake in the 1959 general election, victory made Lee Kuan Yew chief minister at the tender age of 35.[8] The PAP victory was met, however, with broad dismay among

Figure 3-1. *Number of Strikes and Work Days Lost, 1946–2016*[a]

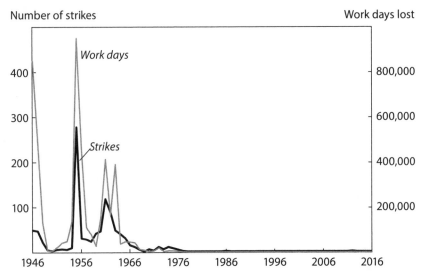

Source: Chong Yah Lim, *Singapore's National Wages Council: An Insider's View* (Singapore: World Scientific Publishing, 2014), pp. 151–52. Number of strikers in 2012 SMRT strike from Cheryl Sim "SMRT Bus Drivers' Strike," 2015 (http://eresources.nlb.gov.sg/infopedia/articles/SIP_2015-03-11_162308.html).

a. Over the past four decades (1976–2016), Singapore has experienced only two strikes: the 1986 Hydril strike (122 work days lost) and the 2012 SMRT bus drivers' strike (518 work days lost).

multinational firms, which saw the party as radical and dominated by communists. In protest, several of these firms moved their headquarters from Singapore to a more congenial and conservative Kuala Lumpur.

As it struggled to consolidate power, the PAP too faced multiple, interrelated domestic challenges—from the unions, the left, and the forces of Chinese nationalism. A major concern was the rising strength of communists within both the party and broader Singapore society, especially in the unions. In August 1961 the PAP split, with 13 pro-communist PAP assemblymen breaking off to form the Barisan Sosialis.[9] As many as 30 percent of the Singapore electorate in the early 1960s were estimated to be communist sympathizers, with a special concentration at Chinese schools such as Nanyang University.[10]

Emotional identification with the Chinese revolution, coupled with frustration at the lack of job opportunities for non-English speakers amid high general unemployment in Singapore, made local Chinese particularly susceptible to leftist appeals. More conservative Chinese nationalist groups, such as the Singapore Chinese Chamber of Commerce (SCCC), also opposed the PAP's efforts to dominate Singapore politics by propounding a broad,

ethnically inclusive, and cosmopolitan concept of national identity. The eth-
nics in particular resented being charged with "Chinese chauvinism" by the
PAP's solidly ethnic-Chinese leadership, viewing this as political opportun-
ism and a betrayal of Sinic solidarity.

To address these issues, the PAP initially opted for force but eventually
found merger with Malaysia to be more practical, until the federation's even-
tual collapse in 1965 triggered another social challenge and political crisis.
While stressing its own socialist character, the PAP-led government moved
first against the radical unions with the passage of the 1960 Trade Union
Act, which allowed it to deregister many of these unions. Then it played the
racial card, criticizing groups educated in ethnic schools such as Nanyang
for championing the cause of exclusivist education and for advocating special standing for the Chinese language in Singapore. Similarly, in February
1963 the government's security forces launched Operation Cold Store. In one
night, nearly 150 journalists, student leaders, labor activists, and opposition
politicians were detained without trial or charges under the Internal Security Act. In many instances, the detentions were not even acknowledged by
the government.[11]

The government then sought to consolidate all legitimate union activities in corporatist fashion under its own state-led National Trades Union
Congress (NTUC). Eventually, the PAP sought stability in federation with
Malaya, rather than through further local institution building, in order to
dilute its pronounced domestic difficulties and external challenges. In July
1963 Singapore, Malay-dominated Sarawak, and peninsular Malaya formally
merged, creating a new, ethnically hybrid state that was 53 percent Malay,
37 percent Chinese, and 10 percent Indian.

Confederation with Malaya and Sarawak did not solve Singapore's internal political problems, however. Nor did it provide broader opportunities for
Singaporean influence within a larger, multiethnic state, as Lee Kuan Yew
and others had initially hoped. Lee's PAP did not do well in either the late
1963 "Malaysian Malaysia" campaign or the ensuing 1964 Malaysian general
elections, only winning one out of nine contested seats.[12] Lee also refused to
grant ethnic Malays, who were politically dominant in peninsular Malaya,
the same preferential treatment in Singapore, to which Malays felt they were
entitled, as the largest ethnic group in the Malaysian federation as a whole.[13]

Ethnic tensions thus began building in both Singapore and Malaysia,
despite their nominal unity within the Malaysian state of the day. Singapore
experienced two more serious race riots in 1964—one in July that resulted in

23 deaths, 454 injuries, and 3,568 arrests; and a second in September that led to another 13 deaths, 106 injuries, and 1,439 arrests for rioting and curfew breaking.[14] The first was provoked by Muslim radicals following a mass rally on Singapore's Padang to commemorate the prophet Muhammad's birthday, while the second was triggered by the murder of a Malay trishaw driver, ostensibly at the hands of local Chinese.

Along with domestic ethnic tensions, an international factor called into question the viability of the nascent Singapore-Malaya union: undeclared war (*Konfrontasi*) from Indonesian president Sukarno. Just across the Strait of Malacca, Bung Karno (Comrade Karno) fiercely opposed and vowed to destroy the fledgling union as a "neo-imperialist tool" of the British and other allegedly nefarious powers. This *Konfrontasi* consisted of not just pitched jungle battles in Sarawak and Kalimantan, but also sabotage, including 29 bombings within Singapore itself. In the most egregious incident, perpetrated in March 1965, Indonesian commandos bombed MacDonald House in Singapore (home of Hong Kong and Shanghai Bank), the local Australian High Commission, and the Japanese Consulate. These assaults resulted in three deaths, including that of the assistant to the Hong Kong and Shanghai Bank branch manager.

Singapore's leaders, including possibly Lee Kuan Yew himself, realized well before its actual breakup that the Malaysian federation might not endure.[15] Eventually, on August 9, 1965, the Malaysian parliament voted to formally expel Singapore from the Malaysian union. And also on August 9, Singapore declared its own independence. With its PAP government confronting high unemployment, a housing crisis, Indonesia's *Konfrontasi,* and a deepening challenge from communist unions, not to mention the rapidly expanding Vietnam conflict steadily deepening less than 700 miles (1,100 kilometers) to the northeast, prospects for the fledgling city-state did not look bright, to put it mildly.

Increasingly on its own in facing domestic and international troubles, Singapore sought innovative responses, which in turn fostered the creation of smart institutions. On the domestic front, this approach was applied to high unemployment, a lack of infrastructure, and a housing crisis, as well as tensions between ethnic and ideological groups. On the international front, security became a deepening challenge with the escalation of the Vietnam War following full-scale U.S. intervention (February 1965) and the gradual outbreak and intensification of the Chinese Cultural Revolution between late 1965 and May 1966.[16] Also fatefully important was Harold Wilson's January

1968 decision to withdraw British forces from east of Suez. By October 31, 1971, all of Britain's forces had left Singapore, after more than 150 years of sustained presence, apart from World War II. The Lion City-State faced a deepening security challenge, with the Vietnam War raging nearby and the Chinese Cultural Revolution in full bloom.

Response to Early Challenges: A Cohesive, "Smart-State" Leadership Team Emerges

These domestic and international challenges placed Singapore at a critical juncture in its early days—it was a period of fateful indeterminacy, lasting more than a decade (1959–71), in which leadership decisions had the scope to exert a profound and creative impact on the city-state's still-malleable future.[17] Those decisions owed much to the key leaders and the decisionmaking structure in place at the time. The leaders were few in number and diverse in background. Yet their early actions played a central role in establishing internationally distinctive institutions that configured Singapore public policy along lines that persist to this day and that continue to enhance its smart-state capacities. The broad network of associations and information exchange spawned by their informal ties gave rise, in turn, to a holistic policy approach that has augmented the quality of governance in Singapore. In later years this holistic approach also facilitated Singapore's rapid response to the Digital Revolution and the Internet of Things, further amplifying Singapore's ability to cope with rapid socioeconomic changes, both at home and abroad.

Despite diversity of background, Singapore's early leaders, who worked closely together through important formative experiences, shared important common personal characteristics and approaches to problem solving. This commonality was a key prerequisite for the collegiality and lack of sectionalism that were to become a hallmark of Singapore policymaking in future years. All were risk-takers who also took an integrated, holistic approach to the issues they confronted. All had served in a broad variety of policy roles and refused to let bureaucratic rivalries stand in the way of a pragmatic, common approach to Singapore's substantial domestic and foreign challenges. Known commonly as the Old Guard, this tightly knit group displayed a strong mutual commitment to collective welfare, synergistic with their diversity of backgrounds and personalities, that inspired both the development of smart, flexible institutions and a common cosmopolitan pragmatism that has greatly aided Singapore's globalization.

The central player on this team was of course Lee Kuan Yew, the young, formidable, and pragmatic new chief minister. Of Hakka and Hokkien ancestry, Lee was a labor lawyer with a Cambridge education who had cofounded the ruling People's Action Party in 1954, in an expedient alliance with pro-communist trade unionists. Influenced profoundly in his early days by both Fabian socialism and Arnold Toynbee's notion of "challenge and response," Lee believed that change was constant in world affairs, and that existentially exposed Singapore needed to continually innovate in order to survive.[18] Moreover, its innovations had to combine broad and eclectic concern for social welfare with a hardheaded appreciation of the virtues of self-help. From the very beginning, Lee's strong belief in a holistic approach and specialized, case-specific expertise—the "helicopter quality," as he put it—left a lasting imprint on Singapore's pragmatic policies and dynamic decisionmaking processes.[19]

Among the Old Guard were Goh Keng Swee, Lim Kim San, Toh Chin Chye, and Sinnathamby Rajaratnam—each playing distinct, versatile roles in creating an economically vibrant, socially stable, politically consolidated, and internationally savvy—as well as smart—Singapore. Goh spearheaded the Economic Development Board, and Lim the Housing and Development Board—two cornerstones of the Singaporean smart state, which variously addressed emerging economic and social challenges in highly concrete and pragmatic fashion. Toh played a similar role at the People's Action Party, which mediated political pressures to ensure stability for half a century, through an eclectic blend of low-cost government and broad social coverage that cuts across left-right divisions in Europe and the United States. Rajaratnam drafted an oath of allegiance that served as a pillar of support for multiethnic solidarity and political stability. Several of these individuals, especially Rajaratnam, helped to build the smart state in the international arena as well.

Deeply trusted by Lee, Goh Keng Swee was the mediator and innovator of Lee's early leadership team, often acting as his intermediary on delicate controversial missions. Born in Malacca to a Peranakan family, Goh was a man of unusual decisiveness and creativity.[20] After serving as Singapore's first minister of finance—initiating the smart EDB, as well as the Jurong Industrial Estates during his term at this post—Goh became first minister for the interior and defense (1965–67) following independence, tasked with building a local defense force, and at this time introduced the concept of compulsory national service. He again held the position of minister of defense in

1970–79, following Britain's fateful decision to withdraw from east of Suez, and later also served twice as minister of education (1979–80 and 1981–84). Ultimately Goh was deputy prime minister to Lee from 1973 to 1980, before retiring in the latter year.

Lim Kim San, first chair of the Housing and Development Board (1960–63), was the Old Guard's organizer and planner. He brought the dreams of others down to earth and realized them in brick and mortar. A businessman who commercialized a unique machine to produce sago pearls cheaply, he grew wealthy by his mid-30s and went on to become the director of several banks. Like Goh, Lim was trusted implicitly by Lee Kuan Yew.

After decisively addressing the chronic housing shortage, which had left 400,000 people in squatter conditions during the early 1960s, Lim was assigned to various ministerial posts: national development (1963–65), finance (1965–67), defense (1967–70), education (1970–72), national development once again (1975–79), and environment (1979–81). He also served as chair of the Public Utilities Board (1971–78), in which capacity he oversaw the development of new water reservoirs; and as chair of the Port of Singapore Authority (PSA, 1979–94), during which time Singapore became the world's number one container port.[21] Its successor, PSA International, has grown to become arguably the world's smartest global port operator, with business at 29 ports in 17 countries.[22]

Toh Chin Chye, noted for his persuasive skills, was the political operative on Lee Kuan Yew's early team. The two met in London when Toh was chair of the Malayan Forum, an anticolonial Southeast Asian student group. Toh collaborated with Lee for nearly 30 years (1954–81) as chair of the People's Action Party, one of the most durable ruling parties in the world. In that capacity, Toh cast the deciding vote for Lee in the initial party election for prime minister in 1959 and led the fight thereafter against leftist elements in the PAP. Toh held several key government posts, including deputy prime minister (1959–68), minister for science and technology (1968–75), and minister of health (1975–81). He also chose "Majulah Singapura" as Singapore's national anthem and headed the team that designed Singapore's coat of arms and flag.

Sinnathamby Rajaratnam, Lee Kuan Yew's early foreign-policy confidant, helped to build an ethnically integrated nation that reconciled the non-Chinese communities to Han dominance. Born to a Tamil family in Jaffna, Sri Lanka, the cosmopolitan Rajaratnam was raised in Malaya and educated at Singapore's elite Raffles Institution, then at King's College in London, returning to Singapore after World War II as a journalist. After a stint at *The Straits Times*, he cofounded the PAP together with Lee Kuan Yew and others, becoming minister of culture in Lee's first cabinet (1959). Following independence from Malaysia, Rajaratnam served as Singapore's first foreign minister (1965–80), then as minister of labor (1968–71), and deputy prime minister (1980–85). Rajaratnam negotiated Singapore's entry into the United Nations (1965) and the Non-Aligned Movement (1970), while also serving as one of the founding fathers of ASEAN, when it was established in 1967. A strong believer in multiracialism for Singapore, he drafted the Singapore National Pledge in 1966 stressing the nation's multiethnic character and solidarity, only two years after the serious 1964 race riots and in the immediate aftermath of independence itself.[23]

Clearly, Lee Kuan Yew had assembled an extraordinary group of advisers—with an unusual degree of camaraderie, owing not just to the fact that they had all studied overseas in London but also to their common commitment to the subsequent independence struggle. Ezra Vogel has labeled this clique a "macho meritocracy"—a group so able and incorruptible as to generate a special aura of speculative awe providing "a basis for discrediting less meritocratic opposition almost regardless of its arguments."[24] This elite group possessed exceptional esprit de corps and highly complementary personal traits that enhanced the efficiency of their leadership as a whole.[25] They also had an uncanny sense of the importance of institution building, as well as a striking understanding of global best practice and of effective policy implementation.[26] The Old Guard and their well-coordinated policymaking practices were, in a word, ideally suited to their historic role as the architects of new smart institutions.

Building the Smart State: Crafting Its Logic and Overall Design

These gifted members of the Old Guard laid the institutional cornerstones of Singapore's smart state—the ministries, the PAP, and statutory boards such as EDB and HDB—during the long tenure of Lee Kuan Yew as their formal leader (1959–90). Many of these individuals, and most of their technical subordinates, were engineers—particularly systems engineers. As discussed earlier, smart states and cities typically have an integrated, engineering-style approach to challenges, approaching them holistically, to provide single solutions for multiple problems with both short- and long-term relevance. This penchant for holistic thinking has been pronounced in Singapore, as the cases of the EDB and HDB illustrate, in part because of this common engineering background. Smart institutions, including those embedded in ethnic communities, such as the People's Association, recognize that positive internal group dynamics within subnational groups can give scope and incentives to able recruits from a diversity of age and ethnic backgrounds.[27]

To formulate, implement, and sustain policies capable of meeting the formidable challenges confronting their fledgling state, Lee Kuan Yew and his Old Guard colleagues recognized that they needed a policy apparatus sensitive to issues on the horizon, but sufficiently insulated from political pressures and cumbersome administrative procedures to respond intelligently and flexibly to them. Achieving that dual capability meant creating both a distinctively stable political environment for policymaking and also a set of governmental institutions capable of formulating intelligent responses. After outlining from a comparative standpoint the recipe for a smart state that Singapore devised in general terms, this chapter will proceed to show more concretely how the past architects of the smart state—both Lee Kuan Yew and his two able successors—went about building this edifice.

Overall Configurations. Operating within a formally democratic political context of one-party rule, Singapore has relied on the People's Action Party to provide top leadership ever since independence. The National Assembly is unicameral, with the PAP continuously holding more than two-thirds of all seats. This arrangement, which allowed the PAP to unilaterally revise the constitution with its two-thirds majority, has provided stability to the policy-making process and predictability to policies themselves. It has, however, also intensified the dangers of clientelism, against which Singapore's leadership has been forced consciously to fight.

The architecture of Singaporean government institutions is distinctive in comparative context: unique structural elements, together with a holistic orientation, enhance its ability to both perceive problems and respond rapidly to them. Apart from Singapore's simple and distinctive political institutions, such as a unicameral legislature, the city-state also features narrowly focused ministries oriented to addressing perceived social needs. Under their general jurisdiction, it has distinctive statutory boards and para-public firms that implement policies in remarkably dynamic fashion, more insulated from political pressures than is typical of bureaucracies in most parts of the world. To prevent stovepiping, a cohesive elite administrative service without strong countervailing ministerial loyalties unifies the bureaucracy at the top.

As in most nations, Singapore has ministries to perform the classical functions of government—supervising finance, trade and industry, defense, transport, communications, and so on. Among its 16 ministries, however, Singapore also features some unusual configurations, rarely found in other parts of the world, which enhance the efficiency of policymaking. These include a Ministry of Environment and Water Resources, which directs Singapore's unusual and strategically important approach to water issues; a Ministry of Manpower, which coordinates the city-state's distinctive focus on human resource development; and a Ministry of Culture, Community, and Youth, which works to systematically weld the unusually diverse ethnic mixture within Singapore into a coherent nation.[28]

Among Singapore's major ministries, two deserve special mention for the important role they play in supervising other highly dynamic semi-governmental bodies, while insulating them from political pressures that could distort their operation. One is the Ministry of National Development, which supervises the Urban Redevelopment Authority (URA) as well as the Housing and Development Board. These are the key bodies implementing Singapore's highly distinctive and successful housing policies—a linchpin of socioeconomic progress and political stability. The second is the Ministry of Transport, which oversees the Land Transport Authority (LTA) and the Public Transportation Council (PTC). These organizations are responsible for highly successful mass-transit policies that have enabled Singapore to control air pollution and traffic congestion, even as it has worked to decentralize economic activity and to create a sense of spaciousness in its living environment.

The Key Role of Statutory Boards. While Singapore has a relatively conventional ministerial structure, it is distinctive in the powerful role that it accords to the subordinate implementation bodies, the statutory boards. These are autonomous agencies of government established by acts of parliament and overseen by government ministries. They are not staffed by civil servants, so have somewhat more operational flexibility and frequently broader technical expertise than the ministries. They also draw in many employees as well as some directors from the private sector, enhancing the sensitivity of the boards to broad market trends.

The boards thus give the working-level officials that lead them a clear, specific mandate for action, allowing those officials to sidestep the cross-ministerial bureaucratic politics that often complicate implementation elsewhere in the world. The boards also shield operating officials from the political accountability prevailing in ministries themselves, rendering bureaucratic action in Singapore unusually technocratic and impervious to politically inspired and budget-busting patronage politics. The statutory boards have the added final merit of devolving policy decisions to small organizations with clear oversight responsibilities, giving such bodies the ability to take quick and effective action when needed.

Under colonial rule, statutory boards were relatively inconspicuous, with static functions. Yet since 1959 they have proliferated and grown rapidly to become the key instruments of Singapore public policy and smart government. The nation's 65 statutory boards also have the politically significant role of efficiently delivering needed public services.[29] Their importance is boosted by Singapore's lack of an elected local government that is autonomous from the national government.[30] Together with para-political organizations like the community centers and town councils, the statutory boards thus constitute a sensitive yet nominally apolitical mechanism for identifying mass public needs and efficiently satisfying them.

Imbued with a persistent sense of crisis owing to Singapore's turbulent history and fragile international position, its leaders have focused on innovation as a guiding principle of governance. As Prime Minister Lee Hsien Loong put it in August 2012, "In a rapidly changing world, Singapore must keep on improving, because if we stand still, we're going to fall behind . . . if we adapt to changes and exploit new opportunities, we will thrive."[31] The functionally oriented, technocratic, and implementation-focused statutory boards are institutionally configured to meet this imperative for managing the affairs of state efficiently and flexibly, particularly in support of rapid socioeconomic development in troubled times.

The statutory boards are attractive to Singaporean leaders for two other major reasons.[32] First, they reduce the workload of Singapore's career civil service, thus allowing it to remain smaller, more exclusive, and more capable of flexible, rapid response than would otherwise be the case. In addition, since statutory board salaries are often better than those of the civil service, and working conditions more flexible, the boards also reduce the brain drain from government-related institutions into the purely private sector, putting Singapore's best minds to work on its most pressing socioeconomic problems.

Although Singapore's statutory boards are quite unique in comparative context, especially in the way they are used to sidestep politicization of public policy, they do have some rough equivalents elsewhere in the industrialized world. One rough parallel is the independent commissions of the United States, such as the Securities and Exchange Commission, Federal Trade Commission, Interstate Commerce Commission, and so on. Independent regulatory bodies in Europe and Japan, such as the Federal Financial Supervisory

Authority (Ba Fin) in Germany and the Financial Services Agency (FSA) of Japan, also have some similar functions, centering on the supervision of banks, insurance companies, and financial-service institutions, as well as investor protection. The Singapore statutory boards, however, administer as well as regulate and are much more salient in the overall national-policy apparatus than in major industrialized nations elsewhere. They also enjoy greater continuity of key personnel, owing to the high salaries and favorable working conditions provided to their key employees.

The Smart State in Its Human Dimension: Minimalist Government, Bureaucracy, and Its Meritocratic Recruiting Practices

To reiterate, the perceptiveness and responsiveness of Singapore policymaking are by and large products of four key factors: (1) an apt organizational structure; (2) high-quality personnel; (3) predictable regulatory parameters, especially the rule of law; and (4) timely technical innovation, such as e-government. The first three qualities prepare the ground for the fourth— the essence of smart government as it is conventionally conceived of late. Holistic decisionmaking mechanisms such as the statutory boards evolved in the early postcolonial days. They would be ineffective today, however, if the Singaporean smart state had not learned to recruit and use able personnel to staff them and the ministries that supervise them.

The overall structure of Singapore's bureaucracy, as well as its recruitment practices, greatly augments the Singapore leadership's ability to efficiently manage a complex, ambitious policy process at relatively low cost and with limited manpower. Despite originating in the colonial civil service, more recent incarnations are far more focused on both social needs and efficiency—the result of five decades of fine-tuning. The Public Service Commission (PSC) is a case in point: although established by the British in 1951, the PSC's merit-based recruitment system was created in 1961, only two years after self-government, with many of the statutory boards also founded or restructured around the same time. Today, after more than five decades of curbing bureaucratic expansion, the country has less than 141,000 public officials, who constitute only 4 percent of the workforce.[33] They are divided into two categories: "civil" servants, numbering 82,291 in 2014, who man the 16 government ministries; and "public" servants (58,574), who serve with the 65 statutory boards.[34]

This clear administrative division allows the government to differentiate in its recruitment and compensation practices between those who perform the formal tasks of government and those who conduct more politically charged and commercially related functions. To inhibit corruption—a bane of the developing world—Singaporean civil servants operate under extremely severe behavioral constraints and reporting requirements. They are, however, compensated with high salaries, those for high-level officials reaching well over S$1 million annually.[35] Public servants at the statutory boards are recruited from broader backgrounds, often including the private sector, and operate under somewhat different, generally more market-oriented, incentive systems than their erstwhile bureaucratic colleagues.

To secure the very best candidates for both the civil service and the statutory boards, Singapore's government leaders spare little effort. Able candidates are typically identified as they finish secondary school, at around 17–18 years of age, just before their A-level examinations. They are then offered all-expenses-paid scholarships to the best universities in the world, conditional on admission, in return for bonded 6- to 8-year commitments to government service. Upon graduation from Princeton, Harvard, Cambridge, and other elite universities in the world, these able young people are tested in Singapore government departments and agencies before being talent-spotted by supervisors. The successful candidates enter Singapore's elite administrative service, consisting of only about 270 career officials. There they constitute the administrative core of the smart state, supervising bureaucrats affiliated with the government ministries and organs of state, as well as the employees of the statutory boards.[36]

Creating Small, Responsive Administrative Bodies with Broad Policy Concerns. Some concrete examples illustrate not only the integrated, holistic response of Singapore's smart state, through the statutory boards, to outside developments, but also the creativity of its design. To address political-economic challenges, especially those arising from a lack of infrastructure, inadequate housing, and ethnic tensions, the Housing and Development Act was drafted and implemented in 1960. That law authorized the HDB and led to a sweeping transformation of Singapore's housing situation. Whereas in 1959 less than 10 percent of Singaporeans owned their own homes, today that share exceeds 90 percent, with the overwhelming proportion of new homes having been built by the HDB itself.[37]

This board has also pursued an integrated approach to addressing a broad range of other social problems, not only the housing crisis but ethnic tensions as well. Its housing policies have not only generated a stake in society for Singaporeans through home ownership, for example, but they have also enhanced acceptance of ethnic diversity through measures that bring people of different backgrounds together as neighbors. Holistic Singaporean smart-state policies also provide citizens with individual Central Provident Fund (CPF) savings accounts that they can tap to buy homes.

When Singaporean authorities mandate the building of actual living spaces, they move beyond abstract thinking about policy to *holistic* planning and implementation that focus on how overall communities will realistically evolve. They design living spaces with multiple functions, making housing complexes self-contained and thus reducing energy consumption and time expended in commuting.

In addition to the HDB, Lee's early team also created the Economic Development Board (1961), during a turbulent critical juncture that gave birth to the Singaporean smart state. The flexible and creative EDB developed a dynamic program of foreign investment incentives, going far to address the initial misgivings of multinational firms about Lee Kuan Yew's fledgling PAP government. For more than half a century, the EDB, even now with less than 600 employees, has facilitated the systematic transformation of Singapore's economic structure from labor-intensive manufacturing to high value added services. That key pillar of Singapore's smart state, the entrepreneurial minister of finance, Goh Keng Swee, proposed the EDB and powerfully endowed it with a S$100 million budget,[38] while Singapore's per capita GNP still remained less than US$320 a year.[39]

During the 1970s, the EDB was instrumental in bringing Texas Instruments to Singapore, thus facilitating the emergence of a powerful local electronic-components manufacturing industry.[40] Within a few years, the EDB was also spearheading the structural transformation from manufacturing to services, promoting Singapore as a "Total Business Center," in which services were central. During the 1980s the EDB co-established institutes of technology and technological manpower training with German, Japanese, and French organizations, while also soliciting technology-oriented apprenticeships for Singaporeans with such global firms as Philips, Rollei, and Tata.

The EDB's staff, drawn from the best of Singapore's top bonded-scholarship recipients, is seasoned through extensive overseas on-the-job training at 21 international offices in 12 key countries worldwide.[41] Its deployment often follows advanced graduate work in the best business and law schools of the world.[42] The staff is organized into project teams, working intensively on priority cases, with a performance-oriented culture and incentive structure similar to those of U.S. consulting and investment banking firms like McKinsey or Goldman Sachs.

Smart government, as already discussed, not only builds new, socially and economically responsive institutions but also recognizes the importance of group dynamics within the subnational components of the state, such as Singapore's EDB, HDB, and other statutory boards. It works to refresh important organizations by bringing new faces into key roles within them, as catalysts for change, instead of following more static seniority-based promotion systems. At the same time, smart government fosters networks between the vigorous young and their knowledgeable seniors.

Vertical Networks: The Principal Private Secretary System. Another distinctive Singaporean practice that has augmented the effectiveness of core leadership and enhanced the smartness of governance more generally is Lee Kuan Yew's system of principal private secretaries (PPS). From the early days of his prime ministership and throughout his leadership career, Lee handpicked young, energetic officials whom he considered particularly promising and mentored them personally as members of his private staff. Then Lee sent these talented "leaders in embryo" out into a variety of strategic and challenging positions across the government, often in a variety of fields, to hone both their general management skills and their holistic consciousness. Lee continued to interact with his PPS alumni personally and to follow their development once they left his staff. Heng Swee Keat, for example, served first as managing director of the Monetary Authority of Singapore (2005–11), and subsequently as minister of education (2011–15), then as minister of finance (2015–16).[43] Leo Yip, Lee's PPS during 2000–02, served as permanent secretary of the Ministry of Manpower (2005–09) and chair of the Economic Development Board (2009–14) before becoming permanent secretary for home affairs in 2014.[44] Such personal protégés of top leadership, and the relationships they build, are the very sinews of a state based structurally on institutions, but augmented by intricate personal networks linking and transcending those organizations themselves.

Building a Smart Foreign-Policy Structure

Astute foreign-policy responses to early challenges from abroad, such as developing close but not exclusive diplomatic relations with the United States, were crucial in building the institutional framework of Singaporean smart government. In doing so, Singapore conformed to Joseph Nye's admonition that smart power should include both "hard" and "soft" power in complementary dimensions.[45] On the hard side it developed a highly trained and well-equipped military, while on the soft side it stressed public diplomacy, exchange programs, development assistance, disaster relief, and military-to-military personal contacts.

The international challenge that Singapore's leaders faced on independence in August 1965 was an existential one for their fledgling nation, coming just months after U.S. combat troops began pouring into South Vietnam. That challenge was compounded by domestic fragility, including stubbornly persistent double-digit unemployment. Upon independence, Singapore thus faced a critical juncture abroad, as at home—indeterminacy amid crisis, with institutions still fluid, in circumstances where leadership decision was crucial.

Response from Lee and his colleagues was not wanting. And it came in a characteristically pragmatic and nonideological form, on both the international and the domestic fronts, that took the perceived reality of a dangerous, changing world as a disturbing given. Lee persistently used Toynbee's "challenge and response" concept and his own "survival motif" to cajole Singapore's trade unions into cooperating with his policy design.[46]

Overseas, Singapore strengthened its ties to regional neighbors, to Israel, and ultimately to the United States, even as it proclaimed itself a member of the nonaligned movement. Domestically, Lee and his team aggressively pursued economic growth. They did so particularly through a neoliberal agenda of low taxes and foreign-investment incentives, while also intensifying their high-tempo program of public housing expansion.

Emulating Israel. The progression of Singapore foreign policy immediately after independence clearly illustrated both Lee Kuan Yew's pragmatism and some important divisions among his subordinates, which ironically enhanced the country's tactical flexibility. Singapore's first overtures in political-military relations abroad were to neutralist Egypt and India, championed by Foreign Minister Rajaratnam, but they were rejected. In short order, Singapore approached Israel, whose strategic circumstances Lee himself regarded as quite parallel to Singapore's own.[47] Both, he noted at the height of *Konfrontasi* in the mid-1960s, were small nations, surrounded by larger, implacable foes.

Confronted with a hostile regional environment, Israel had "leapfrogged" its region to align with Europe and America. Lee believed that Singapore needed to perform a similar strategic feat, adding Northeast Asia to its range of prospective interlocutors as well. Tactically and operationally, Singapore needed to turn itself into a "poisonous shrimp," too tough and heavily armed to be easily digestible by neighboring adversaries, including Sukarno's Indonesia.[48]

Given Lee's strategic vision, Goh Keng Swee, who on independence had volunteered to move from finance to defense minister, quietly contacted

Mordecai Kidron, the Israeli ambassador in Bangkok, for help. On August 9, 1965, only days after the breakup with Malaysia, Kidron flew into Singapore from Bangkok to offer Israel's assistance with military training.[49] Over the ensuing years, Israel provided invaluable assistance to the Singaporeans, arming them with Soltam mortars and other weapons while advising them on combat doctrine (the "Brown Book") and military-intelligence structure (the "Blue Book").[50] Its advice included a valued threefold prescription for military manpower recruitment: mass conscription for national service, plus a professional military and a large ready reserve.[51]

Characteristically, the leaders of Singapore's smart state kept their strategically important relations with Israel discreet while simultaneously exploring potential alternatives. Singapore did not conclude formal diplomatic relations with Israel until 1969 and never established a full mission in either Tel Aviv or Jerusalem.[52] Meanwhile, Lee's foreign minister, Rajaratnam, continued to cultivate Afro-Asian neutralists, many of them bitter opponents of Israel, and even formally affiliated Singapore with the nonaligned movement in 1970.[53]

Behind this complex, two-track approach to Israel and the Islamic world were very real differences among Singapore's top leadership, which in combination with Lee Kuan Yew's pragmatism ironically enhanced the country's tactical flexibility. Foreign Minister Rajaratnam was vocally critical of Israel and sought internally to have Israel condemned for its attack on neighboring Arab states during the June 1967 Six-Day War.[54] Defense Minister Goh Keng Swee, by contrast, strongly opposed that gesture, warning that the invaluable Israeli defense advisers would leave. It fell to Prime Minister Lee to resolve the differences by quietly overruling Rajaratnam.[55]

Multipower Diplomacy. The pragmatism and division of responsibility among Singapore's leadership showed clearly in early dealings with regional powers, the United States, and ultimately China—the three long-term focal points of Singaporean diplomacy. As *Konfrontasi* with Indonesia subsided in the wake of Sukarno's 1965 overthrow, Singapore began actively approaching its noncommunist neighbors, with Foreign Minister Rajaratnam, of Tamil origin, being one of the early catalysts for the formation of ASEAN in 1967.[56] Prime Minister Lee, whose strong views had alienated many neighbors, stayed in the background, and all Singaporean leaders pointedly avoided associations with China.

Following independence, Singapore's formal security ties were with the Five Power Defense Arrangements (FPDA) nations, including Britain, Australia, New Zealand, and Malaysia.[57] Given Lee's anticolonialism, his delicate ties with Malaysia, and Harold Wilson's disinterest in Asia, however, this multilateral partnership could not satisfy Singapore's fundamental security needs. Following Wilson's 1968 decision to withdraw British forces from east of Suez, the strategic logic of close ties to Washington was clear, and Lee himself pursued it brilliantly, at a highly personal level.

Lee encouraged Richard Nixon to talk with China, in the hope of a breakthrough.[58] Meanwhile, Nixon's quest for gradual redeployment of U.S. forces away from Southeast Asia, without full withdrawal, coupled with enhanced American dialogue with the People's Republic of China, paralleled Lee's own strategic thinking.[59] And Lee continued a tradition of direct personal diplomacy—invaluable for Singapore's global standing—with every succeeding U.S. president through Barack Obama.[60] Little Singapore, with less than 6 million people, has consequently enjoyed some of the most unfettered and productive Oval Office access over the past half century of any nation in the world.

Lee Kuan Yew's Personal Touch. Lee's personal diplomacy also forged invaluable ties with China, Singapore's other major interlocutor, in an era when suspicion of China in Southeast Asia was high. Lee invited Deng Xiaoping to Singapore in October 1978—a fateful meeting that helped lay the groundwork for Deng's historic Four Modernizations, and for the positive development of Sino-American relations following the Carter administration's normalization with China in January 1979.[61] Singapore was not to normalize its relations with China until late 1990—a month after Indonesia did so, honoring a commitment to its ASEAN colleagues to be the last to establish ties with Beijing. Yet the personal ties that Lee developed with Chinese leaders were invaluable. Lee continued this pattern in personally helping to bring Chinese vice president and presumptive future leader Xi Jinping to Singapore at a crucial stage in Xi's career during 2010.

Second-Phase Challenge: Surviving and Thriving in a Knowledge-Intensive Global Economy

The first phase of Singaporean smart-state evolution (roughly from 1959 to 1990) had centered on state formation and consolidation: on building the basic, holistically oriented infrastructure of both smart government and the broader economy. As the years of Lee Kuan Yew's long formal stewardship over this period drew to a close, an elemental new challenge for Singapore was emerging that demanded smart capacities in a different sense. Revolutionary changes in telecommunications and finance, followed by the waning of the cold war, gave rebirth to a truly global political economy for the first time in nearly a century. The volatile, complex, technically sophisticated, and rapidly changing world presented an extraordinary mix of danger and opportunity that made capitalizing on the Digital Revolution indispensable to Singapore's survival and prosperity. The escalating pace of technical and geopolitical change created its own new dangers alongside fresh opportunity. Thus in the second phase of Singaporean evolution the leadership faced the difficult task of updating and refining the Lion City's institutions and strategies in order to confront the digital age.

In responding to these new challenges, Singapore chose to become knowledge intensive—both economically and in terms of state structure. To this end, it pursued the "postindustrial" socioeconomic paradigm, popularized by sociologist Daniel Bell and based on the principle that knowledge and ideas generate more wealth than the conventional manufacturing-based economy.[62] Industry still did have some place, but in a more information-intensive form. Automation, cybernetic feedback systems, and computer-aided processes were growing increasingly important as an era of the Internet of Things began to dawn.

During the 1960s, 1970s, and 1980s, the political-economic challenge for Singapore's founders was clear: devising institutional frameworks suitable for an industrial age (see table 3-1). With this given framework and infrastructure, Goh and Lee Hsien Loong, Singapore's second and third prime ministers, were able to refine the smart institutions created under Lee Kuan Yew and to recondition them for a knowledge-intensive and more thoroughly globalized new era. Although the challenges of the 1990s and 2000s diverged from those of previous years and required different policy responses, Singapore now had in place a basic framework of smart institutions, with their open, holistic bias, that had generated the more technically oriented policies and ensuing economic success of the 1970s and 1980s.

Singapore's later leaders shared a common institutional ethos with its founders: featuring a pragmatic and quick response to challenges, collaboration, and a willingness to assume substantial risks in order to realize long-term reward. The new leaders also saw the importance of stable, consistent parameters for business activity, including respect for the rule of law. In redefining and adjusting their institutions along these lines, Singapore's leaders ensured that their paradigms remained relevant in the 21st century.

After an extraordinary 31 years at the helm of government, Lee Kuan Yew retired formally as prime minister in November 1990, to be succeeded

Table 3-1. *Singapore's Economic Transformation and the Evolving Challenges*

1960s (labor intensive)	*1970s (skill intensive) and 1980s (capital intensive)*
Develop basic industrial facilities, infra-structures, and amenities	Clean and light industries: factories developed within residential areas
Industrial development located away from residential areas	Workers in residential areas tapped to support industrial activities
Heavy industries do not affect the population significantly	Minimal travel for workers because of integrated work-residential complexes
1990s (technology intensive)	*21st century (knowledge intensive)*
R&D focus	Knowledge industries
Mixed-use development	Clustering and integration
Technology/science parks created to facilitate research, develop prototype, and enhance market reception	Sectoral focus on biomedical research, IT, and multi-media development (for example, Biopolis, Medianopolis, and Fusionopolis)
	Work, live, play, and learn environment: ex- one-north, create land use intensification; ex-urban farming, multistory factory complexes, underground space usage

Key factors for success?

Ability to

—Initiate and implement *multiprong, interministerial economic strategies and policies in integrated, pragmatic, and effective fashion*

—Develop necessary infrastructure and facilities to respond quickly to new requirements

—Identify new economic drivers quickly

—Identify and rapidly adapt to emerging challenges, utilizing stable, transparent legal parameters

Source: Er Tang Tak Kwong, CEO and president of Jurong International, "Sustainable Industrial Development in Singapore," presentation at the World Bank, October 7, 2010 (http://siteresources.world bank.org/INTURBANDEVELOPMENT/Resources/336387-1286571882293/Tang.pdf).

by his trusted deputy, Goh Chok Tong. Lee nonetheless continued his direct involvement in policymaking, first as senior minister (1990–2004), and then as senior minister mentor (2004–11), continuing to help build Singapore's smart state. As Lee ceded formal authority to Goh, Singapore entered a significantly different leadership era, marked by a changing, increasingly volatile political-economic world.

Goh approached the new challenge of leadership with a deeply ingrained sense of duty and integrity. When he was nine, his father died of tuberculosis, and Goh played a key role in raising younger brothers and sisters, in support of his widowed mother.[63] He spent more than eight years in the private sector, at Neptune Orient Lines, which honed his pragmatic sense; there he associated with many wealthy entrepreneurs, such as Y. K. Pao of Hong Kong. Yet Goh was never corrupted by their flamboyant lifestyle and served as a paragon of the able, principled, and at the same time self-sacrificing young official aspiring with other early leaders to build the smart state.[64] Indeed, young Goh's life story and clear ability so attracted Prime Minister Lee Kuan Yew on Goh's return from graduate study in the United States (Williams College) that Lee actively recruited Goh as his principal private secretary.[65]

Goh's Tenure and the Smart State's Evolution: Provoking Innovation, Improving Citizen Access, and Inhibiting Clientelism

To Goh Chok Tong, a fundamental task of government was to be socially responsive. Focusing on popular needs, he allowed fresh ideas and people to freely enter politics, short-circuiting the rigidities and distortions of personal gain, thereby enhancing direct citizen access to the mechanics and output of state power. Electronic government, with the transparency it spontaneously provided, coupled with anticorruption provisions codified in law were central elements in this new equation.

Introducing Electronic Government. One of Singapore's smartest moves, illustrating its responsiveness to new technology, was to wholeheartedly embrace electronic government during the 1990s and 2000s. Today almost every government service is provided online: driver's licenses, export-import authorizations, and documents establishing corporations, just to name a few. And these services are provided quickly and transparently—one key hallmark of an authentically smart state.

Electronic government in Singapore has one of the longest pedigrees of any such service in the entire world, dating back to 1982 with the advent of the Civil Service Computerization Program.[66] E-government's journey in Singapore began just as the global information revolution itself was dawning, with the goal of transforming Singapore's government into a world-class user of information technology.[67] Thereafter e-government proceeded in three phases, gaining particular momentum and strategic orientation during the 2000s.

The late 1990s saw the technical convergence of information technology and telecommunications, which naturally transformed the concept of service delivery in Singapore. This epochal technological transition paved the way for the e-Government Action Plan (2000–03), focusing on rolling out as many new government online services as possible.[68] Among those now consolidated on the e-Citizen website are passport applications, school-fee payments, changes in personal Central Provident Fund allocations, income and property tax payments, information on Battle of Singapore historical sites, and even a portal to help parents monitor their children's homework.[69]

The initial e-Government Action Plan was succeeded by a sequel (2003–06) that concentrated on improving the service experience of customers. Then came the i-Government 2010 Master Plan (2006–10) built on the foundation of its predecessors, which focused on mobile services, as well as on creating an integrated government that would work seamlessly behind the scenes to serve customers better. By 2015, 97 percent of Singaporean citizens and businesses expressed satisfaction with the general quality of these e-services.[70]

Over the past five years, Singapore's e-government advances have won numerous international accolades. In 2015, for example, Singapore topped the Waseda University Institute of e-Government's global rankings as it had for most of the previous decade.[71] During 2014 it also ranked third in the United Nations E-Government Development Index, and second for online service delivery thanks to its new e-citizen portal, its on-inbox secured platform for receiving government electronic letters, and its continuing upgrades to mobile government.[72]

Capitalizing on these successes, Singapore has turned e-government into an export industry. A key element of this transition involved privatizing e-government activities under the auspices of a new para-public firm called Crimson Logic. The genesis of this new and important entity came in 1988 through a Singapore government initiative to develop TradeNet, one of the world's first single-window systems to facilitate trade.[73] Crimson Logic continued to grow and diversify into other areas of e-government, including health care and legal services, and into commercially based international operations in over 30 countries (for further e-government details, see chapter 6).[74]

Process Innovations. Goh also introduced important procedural innovations in Singapore's political process, designed to enhance government responsiveness and thus to enhance smart government institutionally, as well as technologically. These changes included a system of nominated members of parliament, designed to introduce intellectual gadflies into the political process; group representation constituencies, intended to enhance the role of well-defined subnational communities; government parliamentary committees; and grassroots governing bodies (mayors and community development councils) to bring government closer to the people.[75] A constitutional amendment providing for direct election of the president, while strengthening this individual's prerogatives to include a review of possible abuses of power under internal security and religious-harmony laws,[76] as well as corruption investigations, also enhanced political pluralism and the vibrancy of internal political debate.[77] This change became effective shortly after Goh took office, so significantly influenced the politics of Singaporean policymaking during his tenure as prime minister and helped make the Singaporean state smarter in its response to civil society.

PAP candidates for election to parliament have traditionally ranked among the key leadership networks in Singapore. These people have been carefully vetted by senior Singapore officials, including prime ministers themselves, in a top-down process that leaves little to chance. Goh Chok Tong introduced a system of nominated members, not subject to election, to broaden the ranks of prospective parliamentarians, bringing academics and others with distinctive skills into leadership ranks, as already mentioned.

Nurturing Smart Institutions to Stay Globally Relevant and Competitive. In response to the globalization challenge, Goh Chok Tong's policies gave birth to the National Computer Board; the major e-government one-stop portals; the CPF Edusave, Medisave, and Medifund programs; and the SIJORI Growth Triangle concept. A new Ministry of Information and the Arts was also introduced (1990) in keeping with Goh's vision of making Singapore a "world-class Renaissance city" and "a nation of ideas" capable of staying globally competitive and relevant in the 21st century.[78] In a departure from his predecessor's more austere approach, Goh also supported establishment of a Speakers' Corner in Singapore, modeled after London's Hyde Park, quietly applauding "little bohemias" of this nature.[79]

With his quiet yet principled ability to lead, Goh efficiently navigated through the volatile global environment of the 1990s and early 2000s. He rallied Singaporeans during the Asian financial crisis of 1997, in the aftermath of the 9/11 attack on New York and Washington, and during the SARS epidemic of 2003. Goh left an enduring legacy for his city-state in the global arena—"a culture of greater openness and public engagement, as well as a higher international profile for Singapore."[80] He was assisted in these efforts by Senior Minister Lee Kuan Yew, who focused on projecting Singapore upon the broader world stage, capitalizing on his formidable range of international contacts while staying out of domestic issues and Southeast Asian regional affairs.[81] Meanwhile, Deputy Prime Minister Tony Tan—a previous defense minister, Lee's personal choice for prime minister, and Singapore's future president—concentrated on both security issues and, anomalously, education policy.[82]

Lee Hsien Loong's Efforts to Vitalize the Smart State Stress the Counterintuitive

On the wall of Lee Hsien Loong's prime ministerial office at the Istana hangs an elegant scroll, as noted earlier, that bears the ancient Tang dynasty admonition: *Ju an si wei, jie she yi jian* (Watch for danger in times of peace. Be thrifty in times of plenty).[83] It reflects perhaps the most important characteristic of the younger Lee's leadership over the past decade and more: his persistent and systematic efforts to renew the smart state. He has done this by reexamining existing assumptions and reconfiguring even well-established and well-regarded policy approaches for the new century, with a special emphasis on technology. Although the elder son of Lee Kuan Yew, and one who clearly holds his father's remarkable tenure in high personal regard, the younger Lee has adopted strikingly different approaches to governance and has been extremely successful in implementing his own novel approach.[84]

Lee Hsien Loong's approach rests on the concept of mindset change. As Lee puts it, "We have to see opportunities rather than challenges in new situations, we have to be less conventional, we must be prepared to venture, and you've got to do this as individuals, we've got to do this as a government, and I think we have to do it as a society."[85] Toughened by years of military experience, he appears to be highly disciplined. Lee is also clearly pragmatic and attuned to following a realistic rather than an ideological course, in keeping with the traditional pattern of Singapore's smart state.

The younger Lee has applied his penchant for counterintuitive thinking even to long-held tenets of his father's policy approach. Where the elder Lee stressed unity and sacrifice, his son, despite his extended military background, has emphasized diversity and compassion for the less educated, the elderly, and the disabled.[86] While his father was often regarded as authoritarian, Lee Hsien Loong has emphasized teamwork, while manifesting empathy to those of different, less privileged backgrounds.[87] From the early days of his involvement in grassroots politics during the mid-1980s, he has been known as a reformer, alert to the dangers of popular disaffection with the sort of "macho-meritocracy" that Singapore was becoming.[88]

When he succeeded Goh in 2004, Lee Hsien Loong also explicitly stressed global competitiveness and positioning Singapore as a knowledge hub for the high value added segment of the world economy. This approach helped make Singapore an attractive destination for able, innovative foreigners, whom the younger Lee's administration attempted to nurture with ambitious global cooperative projects and Singapore-based international research centers. Like his predecessor Goh Chok Tong, Lee gave strong priority to information and to the arts through such technically oriented vehicles as the Infocomm Development Authority of Singapore.[89]

Lee Hsien Loong's emphasis on staying competitive by treating the challenge of globalization as an opportunity has enabled Singapore to survive and even thrive in a globalized era. Singapore strives today to achieve structural transformation toward a knowledge-intensive economy by enhancing its own role as a global knowledge hub and as a connector and catalyst among globally prominent institutions in its areas of special research priority.

The National Research Foundation (NRF), established in January 2006, less than two years after Lee Hsien Loong came to office, plays a key role in implementing this strategy. It provides appropriate research environments for entrepreneurs and researchers from throughout the world who are talented in creating ideas and inventions. The NRF seeks to translate the resulting research and inventions into commercialized products, by investing heavily in priority sectors and companies, leveraged by para-public firms like Temasek.

Various government bodies, including both the NRF and Temasek, work strategically to foster this future potential through diverse tools uniquely suited to their own state of development. At each stage of innovation and enterprise, entrepreneurs are provided access to a substantial level of support. Proof-of-concept grants (from the NRF) and technology-gap funding (by Exploit Technologies Pte., Ltd. [ETPL], for example) have been established to help entrepreneurs with conceptualizing ideas and prototyping. Government support continues into the early and volume-expansion stages of the product life cycle through programs such as the Sector Specific Accelerators Program and Early Stage Venture Funding schemes.[90] The government also strives to create a base level of innovative capacity through programs such as the University Innovation Fund for Entrepreneurial Education, supported by the NRF. The overall goal is to promote a steady progression from the conceptualization to the commercialization of ideas, and then to economic growth. Ultimately, the micro-level objective is to prepare firms for initial public offerings and conclusive judgment by the financial markets.

Beyond his research and development emphasis, the younger Lee worked to integrate Singapore more deeply into the global economy by strengthening the global free trade regime and thus crafting a larger market in which

Singapore could grow. Goh Chok Tong, to be sure, concluded the landmark U.S.-Singapore free trade agreement, just before leaving office in 2004. But it was Lee who subsequently concluded free trade agreements with some of the largest economies in the world, including India (2005), China (2008), and the European Union (2012). He also successfully managed a major economic crisis when the Lehman shock of 2008 sent Singapore's economy into a tailspin, imposing painful losses on the city-state's global investments.

Lee's initiatives to stay globally competitive have worked to make Singapore an attractive destination for foreigners across many facets of the economy. Lee even authorized the opening of two new casinos in 2005, merely a year after taking office. Pointing out that there were already 13 casinos on and around the nearby Indonesian island of Batam, just 45 minutes from Singapore by high-speed ferry, with many more in Malaysia, Macao, and other neighboring areas, he asked pragmatically why Singapore should reject an activity attracting so many wealthy Indian and Chinese tourists.[91] At the same time, he did respond to criticism by religious leaders and others by insisting on a prohibitively high entry fee, which discouraged gambling among those of modest means who might otherwise waste hard-earned family income on this activity.[92] Lee's pragmatic, open style was also reflected in his willingness to introduce F-1 auto racing into Singapore: in 2008 the narrow streets of Singapore became the site of the first nighttime F-1 race in the world.[93]

The Smart State as Provider of Stability and Social Protection

During its early days, the central responsibility of Singapore's nascent smart state was twofold: to provide a stable framework of rules for economic development, and to supply low-cost yet enabling forms of social protection. This hybrid approach continued under succeeding leaders, as it had under Lee Kuan Yew. Both Goh Chok Tong and Lee Hsien Loong pursued pragmatic policies that cut across the left-right ideological divides that have so polarized Western welfare states.

As prime minister, Goh introduced a broad range of creative policies focused on combining improved economic efficiency with broad social-welfare coverage. These innovations he labeled his "Next Lap" initiatives and, in an updated format, "Singapore 21."[94] Among the novel yet socially sensitive approaches were Edusave, a tax-advantaged savings program to aid with education expenses, including enrichment programs; Medisave and Medifund, to help both average citizens and the needy with medical payments;[95] the Vehicle Quota System for controlling overcrowding on the highways; and important upgrades to the HDB housing program.[96] In international affairs, Goh undertook important initiatives in East Asian regional relations, including the SIJORI free economic zone Growth Triangle agreement with Indonesia and Malaysia (1994); the Suzhou industrial park agreement with China (1994); and free trade agreements with Japan, New Zealand, Australia, and ultimately, in April 2003, with the United States.[97]

Singapore's Distinctive Leadership Style, and the Evolving Smart State

From the early 1960s to the present, Singapore has confronted numerous challenges to stability and prosperity both from within and from overseas. These challenges can be reduced to two basic variants. From self-government in 1959 and independence in 1965 until roughly the end of the cold war in 1990, Singapore's major task was to ensure stability at home and security abroad. The institutions required to qualify as a smart state engaging smoothly with its socioeconomic environment were minimalist yet enabling social-welfare providers like the Housing and Development Board and the Central Provident Fund, as well as economic-development catalysts like the Economic Development Board. The leadership Singapore needed—and got—was austere, and verging on soft authoritarian.

This period was marked by effective and creative leadership, abetted by the close personal ties among Lee Kuan Yew's Old Guard colleagues. Goh Keng Swee, S. Rajaratnam, Lim Kim San, and Toh Chin Chye, for example, had all known each other for decades and fought together in myriad political battles over the years. Their shared formative experiences enhanced the intimacy and efficiency of their cooperation, allowing also for a specialization of functions that minimized bureaucratic conflict.

Since 1990 Singapore has faced a new challenge emanating from integrated global markets and rapid technological change and calling for a different set of smart institutions and a different sort of leadership. Expanding on the institutional framework inherited from their Old Guard forbearers, subsequent leaders created a hybrid smart state that deployed electronic government to simultaneously promote economic development and social welfare. Their policies envision Singapore as a global knowledge and network hub—a center of technological innovation and of knowledge creation that draws on global contacts to nurture high value added industries and wealth creation at home, through worldwide transactions in global markets.

Singapore's vulnerable position as a tiny yet globally interactive player in a volatile world political economy has made good leadership all the more important and thus strengthened the hand of high-quality subordinates. Macho-meritocracy could retain neither its rationale nor its legitimacy in a less precarious world.[98] Intermittent critical junctures such as the advent of self-government, the dissolution of Malaysia, the Asian financial crisis, and the Lehman shock all served as catalysts leading able, self-confident leadership to create or renew apt domestic institutions, while also leaving their diplomatic mark.

Those achievements have by no means been the work of only three men, however, or of a technocratic decisionmaking process insulating them as prime ministers from perverse political processes. The distinctive character of Singapore's broader leadership networks, a crucial informal element of the smart state, has also played a large role, as have the design of subnational organizations, meritocratic personnel policies, the rule of law, and responsiveness of government to the immense potential inherent in technological change.

Conclusion

Singapore began life as a self-governing community with a set of static colonial institutions, competently but passively administered, that conspicuously failed to address many emerging sociopolitical problems of the day. Unemployment was at 14 percent, economic growth was stagnant, and only 1 in 10 Singaporeans owned his or her own home. Ethnic riots were frequent, and pessimism about the future abounded.

The social turmoil of the period, chronicled earlier in these pages, caused a critical juncture in Singapore's evolution that demanded new institutions and policy approaches. In response, the incoming government of Lee Kuan Yew created a range of new institutions, including the EDB, while reconfiguring others, such as the CPF and the HDB. The new leaders, who proved remarkably collaborative, pursued their ends in ways that provided enabling social benefits to a large number of citizens at very low public cost, while forging specialized institutions within a holistic framework. This was the beginning of smart government, marked by the emergence of smart institutions that facilitate both an efficient, comprehensive understanding of their environment and an efficient, holistic response.

All this sprang from the visionary yet pragmatic initiatives of Lee Kuan Yew and his Old Guard, epitomized in pioneering statutory boards with a decidedly hybrid character—they were socially responsive yet technocratic, holistically oriented, and shielded from political pressure by their lack of direct parliamentary accountability. The efficacy of public administration was enhanced by embedded structural features of Singapore politics, like the unicameral legislature, and by innovations such as the nominated member of parliament system.[99] Meritocratic recruitment of bureaucrats, through measures like the bonded scholarship system, helped raise the quality of government, as did systematic support for the rule of law. And technological changes, like the Digital Revolution and the Internet of Things, facilitated by the holistic approach to policy pursued since the 1960s, enabled Singapore through e-government to enhance governmental responsiveness still more. As a result of these successive pragmatic reactions to sociopolitical crisis and technological change, Singapore's city-state today has one of the most flexible and responsive governmental systems in the world, which is examined in detail across the chapters to follow.

4

Singapore as Smart State
MINIMALIST, ENABLING GOVERNANCE

We are not Britain. We cannot be Britain. Remember that.

—LEE KUAN YEW (1976)

This chapter explores the smart-state concept and its specific applicability to Singapore by considering how smart states perform three central roles that nation-states in general classically play: (1) providing social protection, (2) facilitating economic development; and (3) conducting foreign relations. This effort strives to integrate an understanding of the state's varied roles and to suggest a new paradigm of state behavior, embodied in the concept of "smart state: minimalist and enabling governance." This involves both of Singapore's core smart capacities: pragmatism and technological sophistication.

There has been much literature elaborating each specific state functional role enumerated above. John Micklethwait and Adrian Wooldridge, for example, have stressed the rising costs of entitlement systems.[1] Thomas Friedman and Michael Mandelbaum have pointed to the constraining impact of entitlements on foreign policy as well.[2] In relation to this debate, the central question raised here is: how can the state sustainably provide social protection consistent with the implicit social contract with its citizenry? This chapter presents a perspective sensitive in particular to the deepening challenges for social policy arising out of demographic change.

A second question of special concern will be how the smart state handles economic development. For 30 years and more, the relationship of governmental design to economic growth and social stability has been a central concern of social science. In the view of Chalmers Johnson, for example, ambitious "plan-rational developmental states," such as that of Japan during the 1950s and 1960s, could dynamically transform the societies within which they were embedded, promoting rising, high value added sectors and directing resources away from less promising areas.[3] Refining this argument, Peter Evans highlighted the special role that state officials—especially bureaucrats—could play when "embedded autonomy" insulated them from parochial political intervention.[4] Peter Hall, in a broader review of state structures in varied cross-national and cross-temporal contexts, affirmed the importance of state institutions in configuring policy outcomes, as have Theda Skocpol, Stephan Haggard, and others.[5]

Concept of the Smart State

In contrast to the developmental state, the smart state as conceived here does *not* necessarily aspire to state-led structural transformation of the domestic political economy. In the volatile, open global economy of the 21st century, the political-economic future is less predictable, the political resources of bureaucracy less potent, and the technological frontiers more uncertain than three decades ago, when Chalmers Johnson wrote. Dirigiste efforts at structural transformation can be either ineffective or counterproductive to growth in a globalizing world, where capital flows are volatile and selective. The smart-state concept reflects that emerging reality. The emphasis under this new paradigm is much more on state adaptability, access to information flow, facilitation of global networks, and responsiveness to market incentives than on state-directed transformation.

These features can be illustrated not only in the smart state's approaches to social welfare and economic development but also in its shrewd management of foreign policy. The role of government on the international stage has long been a fertile subject for scholarly debate. Classical realist theory suggests that state size and "power resources" are the key determinants of influence in international affairs.[6] State involvement in alliances is also generally esteemed for its role in enhancing both systemic stability and national influence.[7]

Virtually all of the classic studies of state behavior in both domestic and international contexts fail, however, to consider the impact of globalization and deepening interdependence on state functioning and efficacy. Neorealist approaches, such as the work of Joseph Nye and Robert Keohane, do, it is true, factor in the emergence of transnational relations and supranational structures. Yet they focus more on subnational civil society and on supranational forces than on the operation of the nation-state itself.

Although each theory summarized here has contributed to the understanding of state behavior in general terms, these approaches, coined years ago, are inadequate to explain state behavior in the fluid context of the rapidly changing 21st century. To better understand the actual role of nation-states in the volatile and truly global political economy now emerging, there is need for a new concept: that of the smart state. There is a particular need for an understanding of the varied prospective roles of the state outlined above, within the context of the contemporary global political economy. An integrated concept like that of the smart state—a government entity that perceives and responds rapidly, pragmatically, strategically, and empathetically to changes in its external environment, as well as to domestic pressure within—is very much needed, both normatively and empirically.

In policy and structural terms, it is argued, a smart state manifests two central traits. First of all, it is *minimalist*, in that it strives to reduce budgets and personnel, preparing its citizens and market actors and institutions to be self-reliant. In contrast to the developmental state, a smart state assumes a mediating rather than a dominating role in sociopolitical affairs. The smart state remains on the periphery of social interactions, performing a low-profile but indispensable role. This low posture leaves citizens and market institutions at the center of decisionmaking as suits them best. This arrangement allows the state to provide a social safety net, and to effectively meet social expectations for economic growth, without excessive use of taxpayer resources.

Second, the smart state is also *enabling*. Since it is configured to handle only fundamental roles, as the minimalist prescription provides, the smart state imbues citizens and market actors with resources, guidelines, and information. This arrangement helps participants, in theory, to make their own decisions and to confidently maneuver through the rapidly changing world equipped with a predictable framework of rules to provide stability and predictability. Meanwhile, the state provides the resources and information (through state-sponsored education, vocational training, and entrepreneurship start-up grants) to enable private actors to achieve socially acceptable personal objectives. Smart-state enabling expenditures are thus quite different in character from conventional welfare spending, which generates little economic value when disbursed. This enabling scheme, like public investment, generates value by "catching two birds with one stone"—enabling social actors to become honestly self-reliant, as active participants in economic life, and simultaneously helping them to promote social stability.

The Smart State in Action

This overall pattern of minimalist, enabling governance is a typical expression of smart-state behavior. The way this policy paradigm operates can be aptly illustrated in Singapore, which epitomizes the smart state in action.[8] Its distinctive patterns of government-business relations make strategic use of civil society and private institutions that have distinctive advantages in maneuverability, as well as sensitivity to change. Note, however, that Singapore's government by no means shrinks from intrusive intervention in the life of individual citizens. Local government institutions are ambitious and often seek to transform society. Many are functionally specific, creatively designed, and oriented toward pragmatically realizing broad national interests, although not necessarily through developmental transformation.

Singapore's location, state structure, and policy portfolio also make it uniquely equipped to address the historic challenges of economic development and social-welfare provision that have recently become so salient in world affairs. Its manageable size and efficient structure absolve it of the complex bureaucratic and interest-group politics that plague most larger states and facilitate adoption of the latest technologies. Singapore's example thus has potential global application as a veritable policy laboratory of best practice, with implications far beyond its own neighborhood. The salience of the state in Singapore's socioeconomic life makes this an excellent place to test arguments about the relationship of government to economic and social performance. Aside from remarkable leadership, the highly distinctive role of government in this city-state's social and economic life is probably its most defining trait, and largely responsible for the Lion City's spectacular success over the years.

Singapore's smart state thus plays three key functional roles in the national political economy: (1) social protection, (2) economic development, and (3) national security. Its work in each area has two dimensions: minimalist and enabling. Singaporean policy profiles in these areas, in terms of the distinctive minimalist and enabling parameters, demonstrate how a small smart state successfully adapts to the formidable challenges of today's volatile, globalizing world, characterized by rapid and disruptive technological change.

1. The Smart State as Agent of Protection and Social Stability

One of the quintessential functions of modern government—in both advanced industrial nations and in developing societies—is to ensure the social welfare of citizens. Indeed, ensuring that citizens have access to a humane level of health care and security in old age is increasingly considered central to the implicit social contract between state and citizens that underlies social stability in the modern world.

Nations perform this vital social welfare function in a broad variety of ways. The classical Western paradigm, at least since the Great Depression of the 1930s, has been to provide fixed entitlements to citizens, largely commensurate with their social needs. The alternative paradigm, to which Singapore subscribes, is *minimalist* and *enabling*: instead of providing expensive government entitlements, administered by an expensive government bureaucracy, it prepares its citizens to face sickness, retirement, and other life cycle challenges. In addition, Singapore's smart state empowers citizens with the analytical tools and infrastructural support that not only help them achieve personal self-reliance but also enhance growth and stability in society as a whole.

The following pages explore how the smart Singaporean state employs minimalist, enabling governance to ensure basic social security for its citizens, in an inclusive yet also cost-effective fashion. After documenting the limited scale and budget of Singapore's formal government, this chapter shows how the Central Provident Fund (CPF) assists citizens to save for their own health care and housing. It also shows how extensive education, vocational training, use of technology, and entrepreneurship-support programs, reaching down to the grass roots, help citizens to live more comfortably, intelligently, and productively.

Sustainable Yet Minimalist Mechanisms for Social Protection: Health Care and the CPF

The distinctive and persistently economical minimalist aspect of Singapore's government is clear from the low ratio of government employees to the national workforce, which is less than 5 percent (figure 4-1). In the United States, by contrast, over 10 percent of all workers are in government employ, while in Britain the public employment ratio reaches 16 percent.

Equally notable, Singapore's government consumes only about 10 percent of national GDP, compared with over 14 percent in the United States and more than 20 percent in Japan (figure 4-2). Moreover, the share of government

Figure 4-1. *Government Employees and the National Workforce: A Cross-National Comparison, 2014*

Percent of labor force

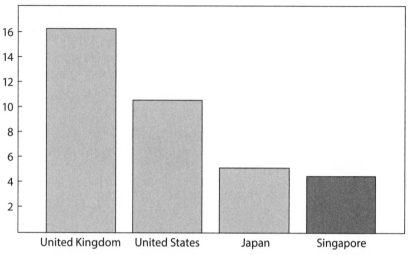

Sources: For labor force size, see World Bank, *World Development Indicators* (2014). For public sector employment in the United Kingdom, see Office of National Statistics, "Public Sector Employment: Q4 2014" (www.ons.gov.uk/employmentandlabourmarket/peopleinwork/publicsectorpersonnel/bulletins/public sectoremployment/2015-03-18); United States, see U.S. Census Bureau, "2014 Annual Survey of Public Employment & Payroll" (www.census.gov/govs/apes/); Japan, see www.jinji.go.jp/hakusho/h26/0-4a. html; Singapore, see Department of Statistics–Singapore, *Yearbook of Statistics Singapore 2015* (www.sing stat.gov.sg/docs/default-source/default-document-library/publications/publications_and_papers/reference/yearbook_2015/yos2015.pdf).

expenditures in Singapore GDP has declined over the past 40 years, in contrast to the substantial increases in the United States, Japan, Britain, and even that laissez-faire bastion, Hong Kong.

Minimalism, in the sense of cost-effective service delivery, is certainly a hallmark of the government's social programs. Despite their modest scale and expenditures, these programs still perform a broad range of socioeconomic functions. In the field of health care, for example, Singapore's approach neutralizes the powerful fiscal pressures that have caused the scale of government in the Western industrialized world to spiral so precipitously of late, especially with the rapid aging of the populations there.

Minimalist government has allowed Singapore to minimize the painful trade-off so common in the advanced industrial nations and those that have imitated their practices between social coverage and expenditures.[9] Spending per beneficiary under Singapore's social protection programs (as a percent

Figure 4-2. *Singapore's Minimalist Government Reflected in Public Expenditure/ GDP Patterns in Singapore versus Other Major Economies, 1970–2014*

Percent of GDP

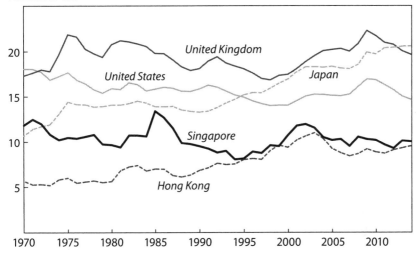

Source: World Bank, *World Development Indicators* (1970–2014), "General Government Final Consumption Expenditure" (http://data.worldbank.org/indicator/NE.CON.GOVT.ZS).

of GDP per person) is strikingly low—at the level of India or Thailand, which are much poorer nations, and significantly less than in the Philippines, Pakistan, and Malaysia (figure 4-3). Yet the percentage of the Singaporean population actually covered by government social protection is extremely high—around 80 percent of the city-state's eligible citizenry.

Singapore's approach to social welfare is now being pursued by several other major Asian nations, including notably China and South Korea (figure 4-3). This pattern contrasts sharply with the classical Western welfare state pattern, which typically provides generous per capita entitlements, but often with sharply varying levels of coverage in such critical areas as health care. The resulting combination of high costs and intermittent inequity makes that Western model unattractive to many Asian policymakers, especially when compared to its more economical—and in many ways more equitable—Singaporean alternative.

Health Care in Comparative Perspective. Health care is a realm that clearly illustrates the contrasting approaches pursued under the Western welfare state and the Singapore minimalist, enabling governance paradigm. To understand concretely how Singapore is able to keep public spending on

Figure 4-3. *Depth and Breadth of Major Asian Countries' Social Protection Programs*

Spending per beneficiary as percent of GDP per capita

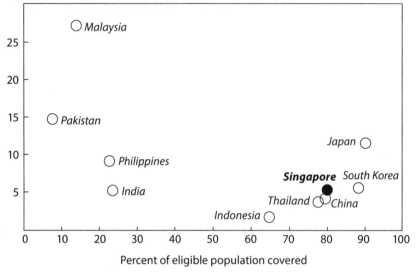

Percent of eligible population covered

Source: Asian Development Bank, "The Social Protection Index Database: Assessing Results for Asia and the Pacific," Manila, 2013, pp. xii–xiii (https://spi.adb.org).
Note: Depth and breadth indicators are interpreted as "spending per beneficiary as percent of GDP per capita" (y-axis) and "coverage of percentage of eligible population" (x-axis), respectively.

social programs relatively low, while still achieving high coverage ratios, it is instructive to look in some detail at its health care programs, from a comparative perspective. Like Britain and Japan, and the United States since the advent of the Affordable Care Act, Singapore has a broadly universal public health care system, in terms of coverage. Yet the governmental share of health care spending has been less than half of levels in Britain or Japan, and only 65 percent of levels in the United States—*even before the Affordable Care Act began to expand American health care coverage toward levels that Singapore had already achieved* (figure 4-4).

The Importance of Coverage System Design. All of the nations in question now have close to universal health care coverage. Yet Singapore's public costs are somewhat less than those prevailing in Western industrial democracies and in Japan (figure 4-4). Singapore achieves a distinctive combination of broad health care coverage and limited governmental health care spending through three key practices: (1) making basic care affordable, as well as simply administered; (2) differentiating subsidy levels according to the patient's

Figure 4-4. *Public Spending on Health as a Share of National Health Expenditures*

Percent

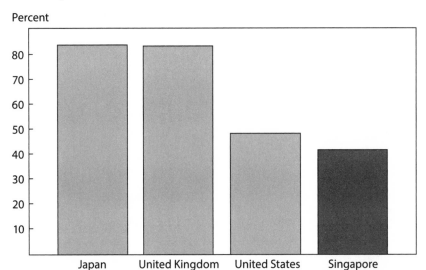

Source: World Bank, *World Development Indicators* (1970–2014) (http://data.worldbank.org/indicator/SH.XPD.PUBL).

choice and ability to pay, while avoiding categorical entitlements; and (3) preparing citizens to pay relatively high co-payments through mandatory individual saving accounts.

The difference between Singapore and other cases lies in the design of coverage systems. The U.K., U.S., and Japanese variants are based on the notion of entitlement—which implies that recipients have an innate right to broad levels of care based on universal ascriptive characteristics, such as citizenship or age. Singapore's system limits entitlements much more radically, on a means-tested basis guided by the concept of enablement. That is to say, the underlying principle is to help individuals help themselves, through tax-advantaged insurance and savings programs that support desired increments above the most fundamental levels of care. Entitlement above these basics is granted only to the destitute and the disabled, as well as the pioneer generation that founded Singapore.

The contrast between Singaporean and Western welfare-state health care programs is evident most starkly in the differences between Singapore and Britain. In Britain the National Health Service provides "a comprehensive service, available to all, irrespective of gender, race, disability, age, sexual

Table 4-1. *Providing Both Liberty and Equality
in the Singapore Health Pricing System*

Monthly income of patient (Singapore dollars)	Class C subsidy for citizens (percent)	Class B2 subsidy for citizens (percent)
3,200 and below	80	65
3,201–3,350	79	64
3,351–3,500	78	63
3,501–3,650	77	62
3,651–$3,800	76	61
3,801–3,950	75	60
3,951–4,100	74	59
4,101–4,250	73	58
4,251–4,400	72	57
4,401–4,550	71	56
4,551–4,700	70	55
4,701–4,850	69	54
4,851–5,000	68	53
5,001–5,100	67	52
5,101–5,200	66	51
5,201 and above	65	50

Source: Singapore Ministry of Health, "Healthcare We All Can Afford," n.d. (www.moh.gov.sg/content/dam/moh_web/Publications/Educational%20Resources/2009/MT%20pamphlet%20(English).pdf); and Singapore Ministry of Health, "Revised Healthcare Subsidy Rates for Permanent Residents," 2012 (www.moh.gov.sg/content/moh_web/home/pressRoom/pressRoomItemRelease/2012/revised_healthcaresubsidyratesforpermanentresidents0.html).
Note: Classes C and B2 represent lower and higher quality of facilities, respectively.

orientation, religion, belief, gender reassignment, pregnancy, and maternity or marital or civil partner status."[10] Such coverage is free, as a citizenship right. Singapore, on the other hand, provides subsidies only to make the most basic health care universally affordable. Co-patient responsibility for a citizen averages 61 percent, with the level of government subsidy *depending on patient choice, monthly income, and quality of service provided.* This variation introduces both a redistributive and a personal-choice element into the health care equation (table 4-1), while also economizing on overall government public health expenditures.

In the case of Japan, health care is not free, but subsidy levels are much higher and co-payment much lower than in Singapore. In 2009, for example, patient co-payment averaged only 14 percent of total medical costs, as opposed to 61 percent in Singapore.[11] Japanese national health insurance premiums conversely paid almost 49 percent of total medical bills along with 37 percent provided by public subsidy, as opposed to less than 32 percent categorized under Singapore government national health expenditure, along with 7 percent "subsidy" withdrawn from individual Medisave and Medishield CPF accounts.[12]

In contrast to Singapore, Japan's central criterion for co-payment is patient age: those 75 or older pay only 10 percent of expenses, whereas those between 7 and 69 years old pay 30 percent.[13] Singapore instead uses economically linked criteria—income level, along with individual choice—to determine a patient's expected contribution to medical expenses.[14] Not surprisingly, the government ends up paying 81 percent of total health care costs in Japan—a slightly lower share than Britain's 84 percent, but far in excess of Singapore's 32 percent.[15] Japan's low co-payments lead to heavy deficits in the national health insurance system that the government ultimately must finance through social security.

U.S. public spending on health care is much larger than in either Japan or Singapore. Only 48 percent of health care spending in the United States is publicly financed, it is true, compared with an average of 62 percent for countries of the Organization for Economic Cooperation and Development (OECD).[16] The United States spends more heavily, however, on entitlements for the elderly and for lower-income groups. Medicare, Medicaid, and the Affordable Care Act, otherwise known as Obamacare, all involve high levels of subsidy and absorb large and rising shares of U.S. GDP.[17]

Singapore's patient co-payment rates are higher than in Japan or the United Kingdom; the patient, in other words, absorbs a higher share of the burden of medical costs than in these other industrial nations. This does not mean, however, that the Singapore government neglects its citizens. Indeed, it enables them, with options such as Medisave, Singapore's enforced medical savings account system, which can be used to pay medical bills. The pages to follow discuss the Central Provident Fund (CPF), within which Medisave is a central but not exclusive element. Particular attention is devoted to Singapore's smart method of providing social protection through this CPF—a comprehensive compulsory individual savings account that enables participants to cope with diverse social challenges: health care, housing, and retirement among them.

Key Role of the Central Provident Fund. At the heart of Singapore's minimalist yet enabling social-protection program, both philosophically and operationally, is the Central Provident Fund. Based on a national philosophy of self-reliance, this comprehensive—and compulsory—savings scheme provides for three essential elements of financial security: health care, home

Figure 4-5. *Singapore Becomes a Consistent Saver, 1960–2014*

Percent of GDP

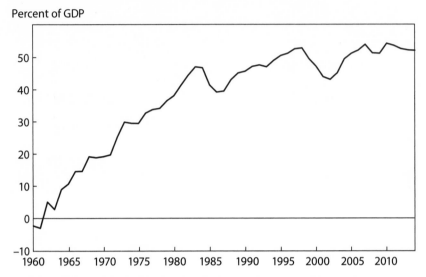

Source: World Bank, *World Development Indicators* (1960–2014) (http://databank.worldbank.org/data/reports.aspx?source=world-development-indicators).

ownership, and retirement. As discussed earlier, Medisave accounts prepare Singaporean citizens to cover relatively high co-payments with personal savings. The health care savings and insurance affiliates—known as Medisave and MediShield—are also key components of the national health care system, supporting the provision of quality medical care to Singapore's people.[18] The CPF has also enabled Singapore to become a nation of home owners, thus giving everyone a Lockean stake in society.[19] Furthermore, the CPF helps its members to provide for their retirement needs through regular savings.

Established in 1955, the CPF is an atavistic remnant of British colonial self-help policies, intended to ensure that outlying parts of the empire did not burden the metropole unduly with their local social challenges. Originally the CPF was a simple mandatory savings program. After 1965, however, it came into the hands of an ambitious PAP government headed by Lee Kuan Yew and was transformed into the most innovative and most effective savings program in the world, playing a key role in the sharp rise of Singapore's savings rate during the first three decades of independence (see figure 4-5).

The CPF has also become a powerful multipurpose tool of social engineering, macroeconomic management, and industrial policy, helping to reinforce the enduring political stability that Singapore has enjoyed under democratic

Figure 4-6. *Building Savings over a Lifetime—Changing CPF Roles of Employer and Employee*

Employee age

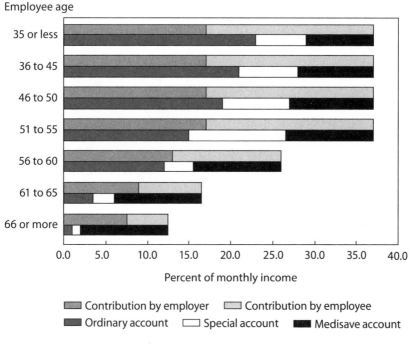

Percent of monthly income

■■ Contribution by employer   ⊏⊐ Contribution by employee
■■ Ordinary account   ⊏⊐ Special account   ■■ Medisave account

Source: Central Provident Fund Board, "CPF Contribution and Allocation Rates," tables A1, C1 (January 1, 2016 (www.cpf.gov.sg/employers/employerguides/employer-guides/paying-cpf-contributions/cpf-contribution-and-allocation-rates).
Note: Contribution rates are effective from January 1, 2016, for private-sector employees and public non-pensionable employees with monthly wages greater than or equal to S$750, who are (a) Singaporean citizens; (b) permanent residents from the third year of obtaining SPR status; or (c) permanent residents during the first two years of obtaining SPR status, but who have jointly applied with employer to contribute at full employer and full employee rates.

governance for half a century. The CPF's defined individualized accounts are jointly funded by workers and employers—in 2016 workers under 55 contributed 20 percent of their income, and employers an additional 17 percent.[20] Employers pay a larger share when workers are young, to help them build assets (figure 4-6), but it slowly falls over time through workers' own efforts as they become more affluent. Currently the CPF has nearly 2 million active members, including 90 percent of Singapore's resident labor force.[21] The assets are invested in commercial fashion, at the discretion of individual CPF members.[22]

The CPF's Central Features. Member contributions to the CPF are credited to three separate accounts: an ordinary account (OA) that can be used for the purchase of a home, investment, or other approved purposes; a special account dedicated to retirement and the purchase of retirement-related financial products; and a Medisave account (MA) to meet personal or family hospitalization expenses. Under a formula fixed by the government, gross contributions to an individual account shift automatically over the life cycle, going first to savings, then housing, and finally medical expenditures. Members are obligated to amass a minimum sum in their special and Medisave accounts by the time of their 55th birthday, to provide for contingency expenditures.[23] This minimum sum is invested in special Singapore government securities, which are nontradable bonds issued specifically to the CPF Board, Singapore's national pension fund, and guaranteed by the government.[24] Once that minimum commitment is made, however, members who have accumulated more than that amount are free to invest a portion of their remaining balances in riskier assets, such as equities or even gold, through the CPF ordinary and special accounts, so as to target a higher rate of return.[25]

Every employed person making over S$750 a month must save a fixed portion of his or her pre-tax income in a tax-advantaged CPF account, with the proportion declining inversely with age (figure 4-6). Employers must also contribute to an account for all employees earning over S$50 a month, with their share declining as the age of their employee rises. The age-dependent contribution structure is designed to help younger people build a nest egg that will utilize the power of compounding to help them build savings most efficiently over the years.

Singapore's Central Provident Fund is arguably the most successful savings program in the world and simultaneously a powerful policy instrument of wide relevance owing to the following six traits:

—It makes employee savings mandatory and requires employers, as well as the government, to support the process.

—It reduces risks for the elderly by forcing participants to set aside minimum amounts for medical and retirement expenses, while providing lifetime annuities as an additional option.

—It is sensitive to life cycle requirements in that it facilitates heavy savings by young people, helps young families and maturing individuals purchase housing, and encourages medical savings for older people.

—Unlike social security programs in the major Western industrial nations, it avoids redistribution.

—Beyond these requisites, it encourages citizens to acquire a stake in society by facilitating home ownership.

—It allows those who have amassed sufficient savings for retirement to attempt to improve rates of return through riskier investments, including equities and even gold.

Precisely how the CPF concept might be applied elsewhere in the world is a promising issue for future policy research.

Minimalist Mechanisms for Social Stability:
Housing Policy and Diversity Management

A central feature of Singapore policymaking is its *holistic* character. Singapore's leaders, in short, strive to hit multiple policy targets at the same time and are cross-trained across ministries to be conscious of how diverse policies fit together. Singaporean housing, finance, and diversity policies clearly illustrate this holistic approach in action.

One of the distinctive features of ordinary Singaporean CPF accounts—and a vital one in political-economic terms—is their versatility. These accounts provide tax-advantaged savings for retirement, medical care, education, and, most important, housing investment. Preparing citizens responsibly for home ownership is a key element of smart minimalist government: it indirectly shifts the burden of social security, in the fullest sense of the term, from entitlements, which involve large government expenditures, to home equity, which does not. Home ownership in Singapore is also enabling, both in helping citizens to build assets that make them more socially secure and in encouraging them to develop a sense of community, within the unusually diverse ethnic environment in which they live.

Privileging home ownership and home equity has been a traditional supplementary element of social security in many industrialized nations, including the United States. In recent years, however, traditional practices like the American home mortgage deduction are losing their effectiveness in promoting financial security for many citizens, especially urban dwellers, owing to rising housing costs and volatile financial markets. These transformations not only reduce the supply of affordable housing but also make it harder for average citizens to save efficiently to finance a home. Singapore addresses the core problems that are generating long-term housing crises for the middle class elsewhere, both through the CPF and through the activities of its distinctive public housing institution, the Housing and Development Board (HDB).

Housing Policy and Creating a Stake in Society. Housing is a quintessential core element of Singapore's unconventional approach to welfare. Government does not give housing to citizens or declare it an entitlement. Instead, it systematically builds public housing on a large scale and then provides citizens with attractive opportunities to buy it, through personal savings generated in CPF accounts. Housing, for government strategists, has value both in enhancing social security without expensive entitlement payments and in simultaneously promoting political stability, while also muting ethnic tensions.

Today most Singaporeans own their homes. About 82 percent of all Singaporeans live in public housing, with nine-tenths of HDB inhabitants owning the flats in which they live, and more than 94 percent of households reportedly satisfied with those flats.[26] HDB homes are not gated at the lobby or the block, so visitors are free to come and go right up to the front door. However, security is preserved through closed-circuit CCTV monitoring. Through its extensive public housing programs, Singapore has thus become a nation in which virtually all citizens have a concrete "stake in society" in the form of public flats built by the HDB and financed through CPF accounts.

When Singapore achieved self-governance in 1959, it had chronic housing problems, stemming from massive World War II damage, low construction rates, and large-scale squatting. Less than 10 percent of its people owned a home.[27] Housing was understandably the first priority of fledgling leader Lee Kuan Yew. And it has been a hallmark of Singapore's unconventional approach to welfare ever since, owing to its crucial role in promoting public well-being, social stability, and consequently a positive environment for far-sighted, economically rational public policies.

Lee spearheaded the Housing and Development Act of 1960, which created the Housing and Development Board. That in turn cleared up the squatters and slums of the 1960s and efficiently resettled residents into public housing provided by the HDB. Home ownership was thus effectively broadened and promoted.

In 1968 the HDB's revised home ownership scheme allowed workers to use their CPF to purchase and own the homes.[28] Government financing and tax benefits supporting home ownership were steadily enhanced thereafter. In 1989, for example, the right to own HDB flats was broadened to include Singapore permanent residents as well as citizens. In 1991 single citizens at least 35 years old gained the right to own flats. In 1994 housing grants became available to married couples for the purchase of flats from the resale market. And since 2004 eligible singles as well as married people of any age have been able to purchase flats in any location.[29]

Along with this expansion of housing prerogatives, low-cost home protection insurance, such as the Home Protection Scheme, also ensures that families will not lose their home if the insured member passes away or is permanently incapacitated before the age of 65. In the event of premature disability or death, Singapore's CPF Board contracts to pay the outstanding housing loan, based on the amount insured under the Home Protection Scheme.[30]

These practices enhance social and political stability by creating expanded opportunities for citizens to hold substantial housing-related stakes in society. As a consequence, overall satisfaction with the HDB has been consistent at high levels in recent years, reaching 93 percent in 1997 and over 91 percent in 2013.[31]

A Holistic Approach to Ethnic Diversity. As Samuel Huntington and others have pointed out, and as recent history has confirmed in nations ranging from Syria and Iraq to Ukraine and Russia, Myanmar and Bangladesh, ethnic conflict is one of the most serious sociopolitical challenges to confront the post–cold war world.[32] Southeast Asia itself, including Singapore, has experienced this explosive problem in full measure. However, Singapore has made great strides in diffusing ethnic conflict and in nurturing a sense of national identity in an environment where that sentiment does not come naturally. Indeed, its national pledge of 1966 vows, "One united people, regardless of race, language, or religion." And the mechanisms it has employed to this end avoid the elaborate ethnic compensation, affirmative action entitlement, or ethnic quota schemes that are common in many nations. Singapore's minimalist, holistic, and enabling government efforts, and the concrete policies behind them, merit serious consideration in the broader world.

Singapore starts domestically with a social pluralism that is unusually pronounced, both by the standards of relatively homogeneous nations like Japan and even ethnically plural nations like the United States. Singapore's largest ethnic group, the Chinese, constitutes only about 74 percent of the city-state's total population (figure 4-7). That is far less than the 98 percent share of the dominant Japanese ethnic group in Japan, or the 91 percent share of the Han in China.

Singapore's ethnic pluralism is not limited to the fact that its overseas Chinese majority is less dominant demographically than its counterparts are in many nations. The city-state also plays host to several relatively large minority groups. The Malay community, for example, constitutes 13.3 percent of the total population, and Indians 9.2 percent (figure 4-7).[33] This pattern of three relatively sizable ethnic groups presents potentially severe domestic political challenges. These do not occur in any of Singapore's Asian neighbors and are only replicated in a few Middle Eastern, Pacific, and African nations with severe ethnic tensions, such as Iraq, Fiji, and South Africa.

Figure 4-7. *Singapore's Strong Ethnic Pluralism*

Percent of population

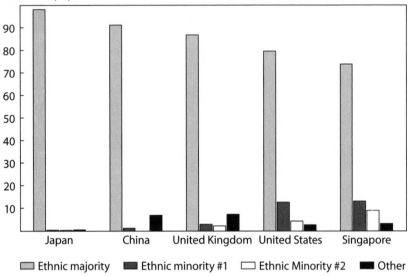

Japan   China   United Kingdom   United States   Singapore

☐ Ethnic majority   ▮ Ethnic minority #1   ☐ Ethnic Minority #2   ▮ Other

Sources: For Singapore, see Department of Statistics–Singapore, "Population Trends 2015," p. 5, and Central Intelligence Agency, "Field Listing: Ethnic Groups," *World Factbook* (www.cia.gov/library/publications/the-world-factbook/fields/2075.html);
Note: Ethnic minorities 1 and 2 denote Singaporeans of Malay and Indian background. Singaporeans of Chinese origin form the ethnic majority.

Ethnic tensions at one point posed a serious threat to Singapore's domestic cohesion and stability. As noted in chapter 3, two serious race riots occurred in 1964—one provoked by Muslim radicals following a mass rally to commemorate the prophet Muhammad's birthday, and a second triggered by the murder of a Malay trishaw driver, reportedly at the hands of local Chinese. Singapore and Malaysia both experienced serious race riots again in 1969.

Singapore's government also experienced a second sort of ethnic challenge—from ethnic zealots whose intracommunal activities, including ethnic schooling, threatened to generate broader national tensions. Ironically, the stiffest challenge to Singapore's Chinese-led government came from within the Chinese community itself, which had its own elaborate network of Chinese-language schools and mass media organizations. Many in this group were sympathetic with the 1949 communist revolution on the Chinese mainland.

This support contrasted with the broad hostility to mainland China both in the United States and elsewhere in Southeast Asia during the 1950s and 1960s and placed Singapore's government in an awkward position, with strong incentives to inhibit the links between its overseas Chinese compatriots and China. This felt imperative to constrain ethnic nationalism within the Chinese community was intensified by the Cultural Revolution and the Vietnam War and continued from Singapore's independence in 1965 right down into the 1980s. Significantly, Singapore, despite its large ethnic Chinese population, was the last ASEAN nation to recognize China in 1990, a quarter century after Singapore's own independence.

As recent scholarship has increasingly emphasized, national identities are far from fixed and primordial.[34] Those that are strongest are typically forged, like strong states, in the fires of war and revolution.[35] Singapore did not emerge with that degree of turbulence, however, and manifests a strong underlying ethnic diversity that acutely complicates the establishment of a coherent national identity. To make matters worse, the constituent ethnic groups represent ancient civilizations and powerful nations—China and India, in particular—with powerful traditions of their own.

To retain its own coherence in the face of powerful centrifugal ethnic forces, Singapore fell back on a classic tool of fledgling polities in crafting a nation-state: "invented tradition."[36] To give citizens a consciousness of common identity—which for many had not existed previously—the smart state emphasized common struggles for independence and development in school curricula, reinforced by museums, monuments, and even tourist attractions. To enhance social stability, the government extensively used housing and language policies.

Minimalist Yet Holistic Strategies for Managing Diversity. Singapore's efforts at managing diversity reflect a minimalist yet holistic approach to social stability—that is to say, both *national institutions* and *residential patterns* are configured to reinforce ethnic integration and thereby reduce prospects for ethnic conflict, with lesser reliance on direct legal constraints. This constitutes an indirect approach to reconciliation among Singapore's complex and once fractious ethnic groups, relying on public housing arrangements to accomplish this objective. Unlike many developing nations, including neighboring Malaysia, Singapore's smart state has refrained from employment quotas or preferential treatment at public corporations. Instead, it has sought to neutralize ethnic tensions in three creative ways: (1) through statutory boards, including the Housing and Development Board as well as People's Association (PA); (2) through education that creates sympathetic understanding of ethnic diversity, as well as contrasting ethnic experience; and (3) through initiatives providing diverse symbolic representation within national institutions.

Statutory boards—autonomous agents of government, established by acts of parliament and overseen by government ministries—are a major and distinctive structural feature of Singapore public policy. Although the system originated under colonial rule, its boards have come to assume much more dynamic roles in economic life since independence. They are not staffed by civil servants, so have somewhat more operational flexibility, and broader technical expertise in many cases, than the ministries, drawing in many employees from the private sector.

The boards thus give the operating officials that lead them a clear and specific mandate for action, allowing those officials to sidestep cross-ministerial bureaucratic politics that often complicate implementation elsewhere in the world. Statutory boards also shield these officials from the political accountability prevailing in ministries themselves, rendering bureaucratic action in Singapore unusually technocratic and capable of avoiding politically inspired and budget-busting patronage politics. The boards have the added merit of devolving policy decisions to small organizations with clear oversight responsibilities, giving such bodies the ability to take quick and effective action when needed.

Two Singaporean statutory boards were configured specifically, in part, to manage diversity. Such efforts began only months after the PAP came to power in 1959 and were explicitly designed to be synergistic with other social policies. Indeed, the very first two statutory boards established in Singapore after self-government—the Housing and Development Board, initiated in February 1960, and the People's Association, established only five months later (July 1960)—were created to aid the integration process.[37] They have continued to play a central role in managing diversity ever since.

The key diversity-related initiative that the HDB took was housing integration. Through the HDB, Singapore's government has over the years provided public housing to its citizens, with attractive options to purchase; more than 80 percent of the population lives in public housing today, as already mentioned. Since 1989 the Ethnic Integration Policy has explicitly promoted racial integration in housing through the use of ethnic quotas. To prevent social stratification that might lead to communal conflict, the housing of different ethnic and income groups has also been mingled together in housing estates and new towns.[38] The HDB also provides these complexes with extensive common spaces, including recreational facilities, where Chinese, Indians, Malays, and others of varied ethnic and social backgrounds can interact in athletic and other social activities.

The principal tool that the PA employed to promote diversity and simultaneously neutralize potential ethnic conflict was grassroots organization. The physical and regulatory efforts of the HDB in this regard have been, by design, deeply synergistic with the PA's activities, which many observers see as Singapore's answer to the traditional mass-mobilization tactics of communist parties around the world.[39] Starting at its foundation in 1960 with 28 community centers, the PA today boasts more than 1,800 grassroots organizations.[40] Most are based in and integrally related to the public housing complexes that shelter the vast majority of Singapore's population. The PA manages its relationship with member grassroots organizations through platforms such as citizens' consultative committees (since 1965), women's executive committees (since 1995), residents' committees and community development councils (since 1997), and community sports clubs (since 2006).[41]

Together these nongovernmental organizations (NGOs) provide a rich, diverse mosaic of grassroots social activities that utilize the extensive common spaces built purposely into Singapore's omnipresent public housing. The neighborhood committees (since 1998) extend the concept of intense grassroots organization into private housing estates as well. All of these group activities are promoted on an integrated basis, as a key tool for managing diversity and providing two-way communication with the government regarding public needs and aspirations. Supported by its large grassroots network, including five community development councils, the Social Development Service, and other organizations, the People's Association is in a position to understand public aspirations and concerns in a way that few other Singapore organizations can.

Singapore's leaders have also clearly recognized that managing diversity has an *educational dimension*, and to that end have created an elaborate set of institutions to promote deeper consciousness of the city-state's rich and diverse ethnic heritage. Coordinating these bodies is the National Heritage Board (NHB),[42] with an annual budget of over S$100 million.[43] Significantly, the NHB was not founded until 1993, more than three decades after the HDB and the PA. Its evolution illustrates how Singapore's diversity policy worked to first build community through sociopolitical action, before addressing more directly such delicate issues as history and the promotion of ethnic pride.

Over the past two decades, however, the NHB and related institutions have done an elaborate job of chronicling the distinctive aspects of Singapore's experience and communicating them in a balanced way to the broader public. Museums have been a major element of that effort—Singapore today has a well-developed National Museum, with a strong emphasis on ethnic history; an Asian Civilizations Museum; a Peranakan Museum; a Sun Yat-sen Nanyang Memorial Hall; and heritage centers representing the three major ethnic communities of the city-state (Indian, Malay, and Chinese). In September 2014 Prime Minister Lee Hsien Loong participated in the formal inauguration of the S$110 million Singapore-Chinese Cultural Center project, scheduled to be completed by 2017, adding another dimension to the increasingly public expression through institutions of Singapore's diverse cultural heritage.[44]

The Singaporean state also took a series of more positive and globally transferable steps to dilute ethnic pressures and to promote national consciousness. Many of these, such as inauguration of a national anthem sung only in Malay, were explicit concessions to important minority groups. Singapore's complex calendar of national holidays, with special recognition of five discrete cultural traditions, was another such reaffirmation of diversity (see table 4-2).

In its effort to manage diversity, the Singapore government also apportions key governmental positions along lines of ethnic balance. Since independence the prime ministership has consistently been held by members of the Chinese majority—two of the three incumbents since 1965 being the able father-son combination of Lee Kuan Yew and Lee Hsien Loong. Four of the seven presidents, however, have been non-Chinese, including Malay, Eurasian, and Indian individuals, while a fifth was Peranakan (Malay Chinese); the prospect of more formal rotation is substantial. The cabinet has been similarly diverse (see table 4-3), although selection has been based on merit rather than deliberate racial policy. The foreign minister, however, is typically of Indian origin.

The Distinctive Stability Strategy of a Minimalist Smart State

To reiterate, smart states like Singapore use minimalist, rather than entitlement or compensation, strategies as a primary means of ensuring political stability. In this sense, they differ sharply from older industrialized nations, ranging from Britain and the United States to Japan, which rely much more heavily on entitlements and other compensation-based approaches.[45] Singapore thereby hopes to avoid the deepening fiscal crisis of the welfare state that currently afflicts other members of the G-7.

As previously noted, Singapore's approach to stability has two dimensions. First, it gives high priority to helping citizens create a tangible "stake

Table 4-2. *Singapore's Diverse Calendar of National Holidays*

Public holidays	Dates (in 2016)	Tradition observed
New Year's Day	January 1	Global
Chinese New Year[a]	February 8, 9	Chinese
Good Friday[a]	March 25	Christian
Labor Day	May 1	Socialist/communist
Vesak Day	May 21	Buddhist
Hari Raya Puasa[a]	July 6	Islamic
National Day	August 9	Singaporean
Hari Raya Haji[a]	September 12	Islamic
Deepavali[a]	October 29	Hindu
Christmas Day	December 25	Christian

Source: Ministry of Manpower (www.mom.gov.sg/employment-practices/public-holidays).
a. Dates change by year.

in society" through extensive housing construction, mandatory savings, and home-finance programs that enable them to safely and rapidly build home equity and personal savings. Second, it neutralizes ethnic tensions that would otherwise threaten stability through housing, education, and government appointment policies designed to reduce the danger of communal conflict. Both strategies minimize government expenditures on welfare and security, while giving private business and civil society concrete incentives to adopt the national goal of social stability as their own. Another important and smart aspect of Singaporean strategy, to be considered in the following section, is its emphasis on enabling governance. Like minimalist government, it aspires to address social needs, while restraining public expenditures.

Smart Governance Enables Self-Reliance in Civil Society

Singapore's smart state may be lean and minimalist, but it is definitely not the laissez-faire institution of Darwinian or contemporary arch-conservative lore. Reflecting its founders' complex neo-Confucian and Fabian socialist intellectual pedigree, Singapore's government has from its earliest days accepted the responsibility of helping citizens to grow and progress personally, even as it systematically minimizes state welfare expenditures. Its leaders have viewed education, practical job training, entrepreneurship, and the nurturing of domestic skills as a *positive* variety of welfare. They have viewed these activities as productive investments in individual citizens, helping them to build a more efficient, secure, and dynamic nation, rather than as an unproductive

Table 4-3. *Singapore's Diverse Cabinet, 2016*

Position	Name	Ethnic background
Prime Minister	Mr LEE Hsien Loong	Chinese/Hakka
Deputy Prime Minister and Coordinating Minister for National Security	Mr TEO Chee Hean	Chinese/Teochew
Deputy Prime Minister and Coordinating Minister for Economic and Social Policies	Mr Tharman SHANMUGARATNAM	Sri Lankan Tamil Hindu
Coordinating Minister for Infrastructure and Minister for Transport	Mr KHAW Boon Wan	Chinese/Hokkien
Minister for Trade and Industry (Trade)	Mr LIM Hng Kiang	Chinese/Teochew
Minister for Manpower	Mr LIM Swee Say	Chinese/Teochew
Minister for Communications and Information	Dr YAACOB Ibrahim	Malay
Minister for Defence	Dr NG Eng Hen	Chinese/Hokkien
Minister for Foreign Affairs	Dr Vivian BALAKRISHNAN	Chinese/Indian
Minister for Home Affairs and Minister for Law	Mr K Shanmugam	Indian/Tamil Hindu
Minister for Health	Mr GAN Kim Yong	Chinese/Hokkien
Minister for Trade and Industry (Industry)	Mr S Iswaran	Indian
Minister for Finance	Mr HENG Swee Keat	Chinese/Teochew
Minister for Culture, Community and Youth	Ms Grace FU Hai Yien	Chinese/Hokkien
Minister, Prime Minister's Office	Mr CHAN Chun Sing	Chinese/Cantonese
Minister for Social and Family Development	Mr TAN Chuan-Jin	Chinese/Hainanese
Minister for National Development	Mr Lawrence WONG	Chinese/Hainanese
Minister for the Environment and Water Resources	Mr MASAGOS Zulkifli	Malay
Acting Minister for Education (Schools) and Senior Minister of State for Transport	Mr NG Chee Meng	Chinese
Acting Minister for Education (Higher Education and Skills) and Senior Minister of State for Defence	Mr ONG Ye Kung	Chinese/Hokkien

Source: Prime Minister's Office Singapore, The Cabinet—Effective from 1 October 2015 (www.pmo. gov.sg/cabinet).

Figure 4-8. *Public Spending on Education, 2011*

Percent of government expenditure

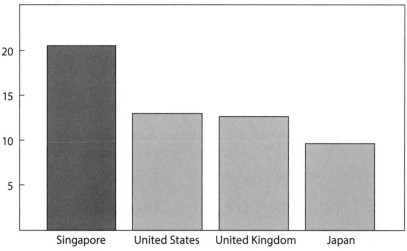

Source: World Bank, *World Development Indicators* (2011) (http://data.worldbank.org/indicator/SE.XPD. TOTL.GB.ZS).

sunk cost like welfare entitlement. Even housing policy and the CPF savings program are viewed as an enabling investment—while neutralizing ethnic conflict, both also enhance political stability and social protection.

Support for Educational Opportunity: Pathway to a Productive Workforce. In keeping with Singapore's bias toward "opportunity, not entitlement," the government places great emphasis on quality education, especially for the city-state's best and brightest. In 2014 it spent an extraordinary 21 percent of its national budget in that field—almost as much as the 25.6 percent that it allots to defense, and roughly five times the share that it devotes to government administration.[46] Singapore's strong support for education amounts to roughly double the budget share prevailing in Japan, and half again as much as in Britain and the United States (figure 4-8).[47] Through such support for educational opportunity, Singapore prepares its citizens to become more self-reliant while also enhancing their prospective role as skilled workers in a high value added economy.

Support for Conventional Education. Much of Singapore's educational spending is institutional—directed toward building world-class universities and technical institutes that nurture global competitiveness. A substantial portion of that spending, however, also indirectly supports public welfare—by opening the door of educational opportunity to all young people, and by encouraging both students and the schools they attend to nurture excellence at the primary and secondary levels. The heart of this smart-state effort is the Edusave program, which can be studied with profit around the world.

Edusave is a financial support program applicable to Singaporeans between the ages of 7 and 16 who study full-time at schools, institutes of technical education, or special education schools. Established in 1993, the Edusave Endowment Fund that supports it is built from various Singapore government contributions. Singaporean children are automatically given an Edusave account at the time of their admission to regular, vocational, or special education schools, into which they receive a minimum government contribution of about S$200 annually.[48]

There are various reward programs for students who meet certain academic rankings as well, including programs targeted at low-income households. These include the Edusave Scholarships, Good Progress Award, and Edusave Awards for Achievement and Good Leadership and Service (EAGLES).[49] Singapore also offers a Post-Secondary Education Account co-savings scheme. Under this program, the government will match family contributions for higher education up to a given level, with unspent funds transferred to a child's personal CPF account when he or she reaches the age of 30.[50] Since 2008 all Singaporean children between the ages of 7 and 20 have received a post-secondary account upon turning 7.[51]

Staying Employable: Emphasis on Job-Training Programs. In contrast to classic Western welfare states, Singapore rejects the concept of unemployment insurance, with its expansionary implications for both government budgets and governmental scale. Instead, it stresses lower-cost training, productivity, and employment-information programs designed to create good jobs and efficiently inform potential employees as to where those jobs are. Distinctively among major nations, Singapore has a Ministry of Manpower and under that ministry has established both a National Productivity Council and a Singapore Workforce Development Agency.

To raise worker skills and productivity, the Ministry of Manpower has developed a nationwide system of continuing education and training campuses, which trains 50,000 people annually.[52] Workers can also sign up for programs and courses under the Singapore Workforce Skills Qualification system to upgrade their skills and enhance their employability.[53] The Ministry of Manpower publishes a labor-market guide compiling executive and nonexecutive jobs expected to be in demand across various industries. And the government runs a National Productivity Fund, currently totaling over S$2 billion, to support firms in developing centers of expertise and implementing productivity improvements.[54]

The Fruits of Educational Investment. Singapore's educational support—financial, cultural, and otherwise—has opened the door of educational opportunity to its young citizens with striking results, simultaneously enhancing national welfare and national competitiveness. In the 2012 competition of the Program for International Student Assessment, for example, Singapore narrowly bested South Korea in overall performance, while placing second worldwide in mathematics, and third in both reading and science.[55] Its results were well above the average of the OECD advanced industrial nations.[56] In another even more fundamental dimension of education—problem solving—Singaporeans ranked number one as well.[57] Singapore thus ranks highly in the most rigorous areas of education—even in the English language, which is not native to most Singaporeans.

With the intensifying stress on all dimensions of education since the 1960s, the city-state's skilled labor pool has steadily expanded. Between 1985 and 2001, the share of workers with university degrees increased from 5 to 17 percent. The share with some postsecondary education or vocational diplomas nearly doubled, from 11 to 21 percent.[58] Thus, as the 21st century dawned, well over one-third of Singaporean workers had skilled-worker qualifications—more than twice the share of a generation previously.

Fostering Entrepreneurship: Leverage for Creativity, Innovation, and Economic Growth. Beyond education, a key enabling priority of Singapore's smart state is fostering entrepreneurship. As Senior Minister Indranee Rajah recently remarked, "Entrepreneurship is vital for our economy as it contributes to innovation and problem-solving. It also nurtures the values of self-reliance, resilience and perseverance"[59] The state contributes directly to that process, but the spark actually begins within the educational process. In 2013, for example, Singapore's Ministry of Education, in collaboration with the Action Community for Entrepreneurship, launched a S$15 million three-year entrepreneurship program for secondary schools.[60] This now gives more than 600 students at least some exposure to entrepreneurship training. The government is also providing extensive start-up funds for promising new businesses through SPRING Singapore, an enterprise development agency under the Ministry of Trade and Industry, through programs such as the Business Angel Scheme.[61]

A Modest Core of Entitlement Assistance. Although Singapore emphatically favors enablement over entitlement, primarily through education and housing, it does not ignore the question of direct support for the chronically poor or disabled entirely. One example, a supplement program for low-income workers, gives them assistance in finding a job for up to three months.[62] Singapore also provides cash grants, medical aid, and assistance with rent and utility payments to the aged destitute, as well as to those medically unfit for work, and to widows with children under 12 years of age. In synergistic entitlements that are also enabling, the workfare system and the Digital Inclusion Fund provide both financial support and special access to computers, as well as Internet services, to low-income households.[63] Similarly, the government provides cash gifts of up to S$8,000, as well as co-savings (dollar for dollar matching) up to S$12,000, for the first to fourth children of young families, as an incentive for family formation.[64] The authorities have also dedicated capital sums of close to S$4 billion to Medifund and Medifund Silver to finance the health care costs of means-tested, certifiably needy patients, and since 2014 it has altered the pioneer generation package.[65] In all of these programs, the emphasis is on creating a broad yet cost-effective social safety net.

2. The Smart State as Agent of Economic Development

Social welfare is, in sum, a more substantial dimension of Singapore governmental activity than often supposed, although its minimalist, enabling paradigm contrasts sharply with the entitlement approach of the classical Western welfare state. Yet in the final analysis the central focus of smart state activities is clearly economic development. In this area too, Singapore follows minimalist and enabling principles—with an eye to facilitating and empowering private activities while limiting government budgets and personnel, often through privatization and corporatization.

In its first quarter century of independence (1965–90), Singapore relied heavily on public corporations and government statutory boards as agents of economic development, as Taiwan, Malaysia, and many other developing economies did.[66] In recent years, however—owing to increasing volatility and uncertainty in the global economy—Singapore's smart state has shifted to a lower profile. It has engaged in massive corporatization—which refers to the conversion of state enterprises into private firms.

By downsizing the direct public role in economic life, the state is confining itself increasingly to supplying a framework of rules. This provides a stable and predictable environment for market actors—both domestic and foreign—who then operate adaptively in rapidly changing global markets. Sovereign Singaporean interests are represented through various para-public firms, such as Changi Airport International, PSA, Jurong International, and Singapore Airlines. In all of these, the Temasek government-owned investment company infuses funds—substantially on a market-oriented basis.

Courting Markets by Corporatizing Government-Linked Companies

Corporate governance, a powerful tool for harnessing human incentives to public purpose, is a major dimension of Singapore public policy. Such policy is emphatically market-oriented, with a decidedly minimalist public sector, in terms of both government spending and personnel. As the preceding pages have demonstrated, however, Singapore's approach is by no means laissez-faire. The city-state's leaders have a clear strategic conception of where they want their country to go, and they seek to employ tools of public purpose such as housing, land-use, and transportation policy to get there.

To resolve the natural tension between public purpose, with its inevitably arbitrary character, and underlying market forces, Singapore employs a decentralized approach quite different from the more dirigiste and unified orientation of classical developmental states. Singapore's smart state relies not only on ministries and statutory boards but also on government-linked companies (GLCs). These are hybrid enterprises manned at the top by trusted current and former public servants, in which government has a substantial direct or indirect equity stake, but which are subject to market discipline.[67] Although GLCs may obtain governmental start-up support, or temporary sustenance amid abnormal global circumstances, such as financial crises that are not of their making, these firms are expected ultimately to stand or fall on the basis of their market viability. The GLCs are expected to be efficient and profitable; they are not supposed to receive special privileges or concealed subsidies; they are free to recruit staff in the open market on competitive terms; and they should be allowed to fail if they lose money.[68]

GLCs with minority state ownership, such as PSA and Jurong International, have become increasingly important since the 1990s. During that decade, a major wave of privatizations took place, reducing the state's formal ownership role and allowing the Singapore government to focus on its core responsibility of policymaking and regulation.[69] The imperatives of technological change, the need to raise capital for infrastructure development, and a desire to conclude free trade agreements with major market economies, including the United States, were major drivers of these privatization and corporatization trends. The result was GLCs with enhanced confidence, financial strength, and competitive dynamism, together with policy experience and technical expertise.

The evolution of Changi Airport, recently considered to be one of the most efficient major airports on earth, illustrates the evolution of Singapore's minimalist yet enabling economic development approach, and the sharp contrasts to Chalmers Johnson's dirigiste developmental state model. Previously run by a public corporation, Changi was corporatized in 2009 to enhance its operational efficiency. Its shares were transferred from the government balance sheet to that of Temasek Holdings, Singapore's business-oriented, government-owned investment company. Before corporatization, the Civil Aviation Authority of Singapore (CAAS) had both regulatory and operational responsibility for the airport. Since 2009 those functions have been separated, with a restructured Civil Aviation Authority playing only a regulatory role.

Since corporatization, Changi has grown more entrepreneurial, greatly expanding its global shopping center and affiliated industrial and service parks, while engaging in active marketing promotions.[70] It has encouraged facilities suitable for medical tourism, which have begun to expand around the airport complex.[71] The airport corporation has also competed actively in high-quality international management, attracted by the substantial compensation it is now able to provide, and expanded its international advisory role, capitalizing on success in Singapore itself. Changi Airport Group worked with Russian authorities, for example, to plan and construct Sochi International Airport, opened just before the 2014 Sochi Winter Olympics.[72]

A second concrete example of Singapore's minimalist approach to economic development—avoiding direct state management in favor of a lower profile—is the Temasek Holding Corporation. Incorporated under the Singapore Companies Act of 1974, Temasek is a commercial investment company tasked with managing assets held by the Singapore government on a market-oriented basis. The objective, as described on Temasek's own website, was "to free the Ministry of Finance to focus on its core role of policymaking and regulations, while Temasek would own and manage these investments on a commercial basis."[73]

Temasek reportedly views itself as an "Asian investment house headquartered in Singapore," rather than a sovereign wealth fund. It does not make non-equity investments or buy debt, in contrast to many sovereign wealth funds.[74] Although Temasek's operations by no means resemble those of the developmental state institutions in the Japan or Korea of the 1960s and 1970s, they do have positive significance for the Singapore political economy, in conformity with a more market-oriented smart-state paradigm.

Operating with a small but multinational staff of just over 500 people, Temasek manages a net portfolio of over S$240 billion, of which only 29 percent is invested in Singapore.[75] Temasek invests 27 percent of its assets in North America, Europe, Australia, and New Zealand, as well as 42 percent elsewhere in Asia. Former World Bank president and U.S. trade representative Robert Zoellick, an outspoken free trade advocate, joined the board in 2013, where he interacts with a range of distinguished business and former government leaders.[76]

Although Temasek operates on a commercial basis, its assets are typically invested in sectors of importance for Singapore's future: financial services, telecommunications, media and technology, transportation, life sciences, real estate, natural resources, and energy.[77] Through its investment activities the firm is thus able to accumulate valuable information on global market conditions and microeconomic competitive trends that can be of use to Singaporean firms as well. As a strategically placed holding company, it is capable of playing multiple supportive roles to the GLCs, not to mention the government itself.

Temasek's substantial Singapore-based investments must, as noted earlier, compete for the firm's attention and favor with investment opportunities elsewhere in the world on an internationally transparent basis. This approach is designed to provide diversification for Singapore's small and internationally exposed economy, and also discipline for the Singapore-based firms held in Temasek's portfolio. If the companies in question do not perform on a market-oriented basis, they in principle face the danger of their shares being sold in favor of more competitive enterprises.

The major government-linked firms that Temasek to some extent supervises are concentrated in service sectors. There they provide, in effect, public goods for the local economy as a whole, in furthering its role as a global economic center. Their government linkage, typically coming in the form of equity participation by Temasek, reputedly yields them a premium of about 20 percent on interest charges in financial markets.[78] GLCs in which Temasek holds an interest include Keppel Shipyard, which absorbed the assets of a colonial entity (the Tanjong Pagar Dock Board) when the United Kingdom withdrew from Singapore; Neptune Orient Limited, the shipping line that Goh Chok Tong helped bring to prominence; Development Bank of Singapore; Singapore Airlines; Changi Airport Group; PSA International (formerly Port of Singapore Authority); and Jurong International.[79]

Although these government-linked firms have heretofore been preoccupied with drawing foreign investment to Singapore and making the local economy more competitive, over the past decade they have grown more global. They are, indeed, an increasingly major, albeit minimalist and market-oriented, conduit in Singapore's emergence as a policy laboratory for the broader world. Singapore's move over the past two decades toward corporatization contrasts sharply with the dirigiste, bureaucracy-led approach of Japan's MITI during the post–World War II years and is a major reason that the small city-state has been able to capitalize so smoothly on the globalization process.[80]

Key Institutional Expressions of Enabling Governance

Singapore's smart government is configured in small efficient units, such as the statutory boards, which are responsive to the general logic of their political-economic environment. These maneuverable units are, however, strategically detached from clientelist political pressures that might distort their operation and bloat their work force by their subordination to ministries, which are in turn the governmental unit directly responsible to parliament.[81] This detachment creates a sort of ideal embedded autonomy for the statutory boards and the GLCs—isolating them from politics but not markets and thereby shielding elite technocrats operating within an at least nominally democratic system. Through this structural isolation, Singapore's minimalist government achieves maximum return for a given expenditure of resources and thus enables economic development. The next section explains how one of the most effective such minimalist yet enabling institutions—the Economic Development Board—actually operates.

Singapore's Globally Oriented Risk-Taking Organizer: The Economic Development Board. As the lead agency for enhancing Singapore's role as a global business center, and thus for enabling private interests in the economic development process, the Economic Development Board (EDB) is arguably Singapore's most important statutory agency. It is formally charged with "delivering solutions to create value for companies and investors, while also creating, for Singapore, sustainable economic growth, with vibrant business and good job opportunities."[82] The EDB has a formidable global presence, comprising 21 offices in 12 countries.[83]

The EDB plans and executes strategies for sustaining Singapore as a global business hub, providing for its priority clients what amounts to one-stop service in setting up their Singapore-based operations. That service can include support in selecting a location, finding employee housing, and recruiting staff, as well as providing financial incentives. The EDB is able to open doors flexibly, especially for major multinationals, owing to its extraordinary network of local connections. Among its alumni are the minister in charge of the Prime Minister's Office; the chair of Temasek Holdings, Singapore's preeminent investment company; the CEO of Singapore's preeminent industrial location firm; and the CEO of the Central Provident Fund, to name a few.[84]

The EDB's unique influence and effectiveness flow from the fact that, despite its extensive network across Singapore's establishment, the board is isolated from party politics, but not from markets. From a microeconomic standpoint, this felicitous situation is due to its statutory-board structure, which shields elite technocrats within an at least nominally democratic political system. Although the EDB is a statutory board playing a strategic role in Singapore's political economy, it is entirely shielded from direct legislative review, and hence politicization, unlike parallel organizations in ostensibly developmental states like Japan. The EDB does provide parliament with general information on its activities, but only through the ministries directly responsible for particular projects. This sort of "embedded autonomy," also enjoyed by other strategic statutory boards, allows the EDB to operate much more flexibly and efficiently than most economic-development bodies in the West, or even elsewhere in East Asia, and to serve as a key pillar of minimalist, enabling government.[85]

The EDB's global orientation is reinforced not only by its extensive overseas branch network and the cosmopolitan training of its staff, but also by the configuration of its board of directors. The chair is a medical doctor and EDB veteran with a quarter century of consulting and administrative experience, ranging from biomedical sciences to industrial restructuring, who also recently served (2012–14) as permanent secretary of the Ministry of Law.[86] Membership of the board has a strong private-sector component (consisting of 8 of the 12 members), which is also highly international (7 of the 8 private representatives are foreign).[87] Significantly, however, the NTUC (Singapore's principal labor union) also provides a board member, giving the board a socially inclusive cast much more typical of continental European than U.K. and U.S. multinationals.

Apart from its board, the EDB has an International Advisory Council consisting of a cabinet minister and 13 CEOs of global corporations.[88] This intensifies the EDB's global orientation still further. The council meets

Figure 4-9. *The EDB "One-Stop Shopping" Network*

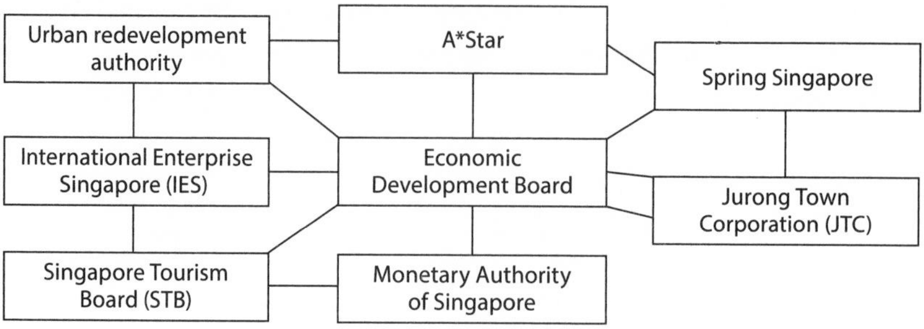

Source: Sree Kumar and Sharon Siddique, "The Singapore Success Story: Public-Private Alliance for Investment Attraction, Innovation, and Export Development," *International Trade and Integration* 99 (March 2010): 20.

annually and provides critical inputs into Singapore's growth strategy. The 2013 council meeting, for example, generated concrete recommendations on how Singapore might intensify efforts to become a global city by building a strong local talent base, improving the local climate for entrepreneurship and innovation, and becoming the advanced manufacturing and digital communications hub of Asia.[89]

Since the establishment of its investment subsidiary in 1991, the EDB itself has become a risk-taker, by assuming ownership stakes through its subsidiary in entrepreneurial new ventures. EDB Investment (EDBI) was set up to provide equity in projects that expand Singapore's cluster of key industries, in partnership with local companies, multinational enterprises, or both. This funding, in the form of so-called strategic direct investments, is intended to spur new projects that will ultimately be self-sustaining; the EDB exits the project in question once it has achieved its operating objectives. An additional EDBI affiliate, EDBV Management, works closely with domestic and international co-investors on operational issues, to enhance success prospects of the ventures in which EDB Investment acquires a stake.

The EDB's Market Sensitivity in Its Multifaceted Yet Integrated Approach. Operationally, the EDB leverages its influence by its detachment from local politics, and also through its synergistic ties to other key government organizations. The EDB lies at the heart of a public policy complex composed of eight major organizations, including the EDB itself. (figure 4-9). All are devoted to supporting in various complementary ways the EDB's mission of vitalizing the Singaporean economy by attracting high-quality foreign investment. The services they provide to foreign firms range from housing and conferencing facilities to finance. The EDB's ability to present persuasive support packages for attractive potential investors is powerfully aided by the backing of these diverse agencies. This holistic organizational macrostructure thus operationalizes the EDB's ordained role as a one-stop shopping window for global firms. Developmental states elsewhere in the world—including even Japan, Korea, and France—have simply never been able to replicate this pattern owing to their endemic internal bureaucratic rivalries.

Both the support agencies themselves and the synergistic way in which they interact under EDB guidance are unique, when seen in comparative context. The smooth and efficient allocation of functions within a broader system inhibits bureaucratic rivalries as well as duplication and is a major contributing factor to minimalist government. In maximizing sensitivity to foreign investor requirements, this structure has become a major reason for Singapore's strong and rising global competitiveness.

The EDB's offer of one-stop shopping allows multinational firms to negotiate customized incentive packages with it that are aligned with their own global production networks and strategic plans. Those packages typically include tax incentives, infrastructure, and even arrangements for corporate housing provided by other Singapore organizations such as the Housing and Development Board, with which the EDB coordinates. Through these arrangements the EDB naturally strives to create spinoffs for local enterprises, as in the "SPRING Singapore" program. As the national standards and accreditation body, this spinoff in the 1970s from the EDB focuses specifically on helping local Singapore enterprises grow, and on building trust in Singapore products and services. The ultimate objective, however, is to encourage world-class manufacturing and especially service companies to invest in Singapore, and to bring their key headquarters and management functions to the tiny but efficient city-state.[90]

Over the past decade the EDB has increasingly stressed a synergistic approach of co-developing problem solutions together with industry partners from around the world, while also promoting Singapore as a home for business, innovation, and talent. The EDB's current sectoral priorities include biomedical sciences (pharmaceuticals, health care services, and medical technology), informatics, and logistics/transport (including aviation, maritime transport, and supply-chain management). The EDB also focuses on the development of ecosystems that foster enterprise development, in such areas as venture capital, corporate incubation, and intellectual property protection.[91]

The EDB as a Catalyst for Broader Cooperation. The EDB's integrated approach can also be seen in its cooperation with other statutory boards, for which it serves as linchpin. The EDB cooperates with the National Arts Council and the Singapore Tourism Board, for example, to organize Singapore Art Week, and to use that nine-day annual event to position Singapore as Asia's leading arts destination. The EDB also worked with the Monetary Authority of Singapore to establish the FinTech Office, opened in May 2016, to promote Singapore as a financial technology hub.[92] Meanwhile, International Enterprise Singapore promotes international access for prospective Singapore-based investment, as well as insights into prospective product markets, thanks to its large database on international tariffs and standards.

Through EDB introduction and even equity participation through subsidiaries, a potential investor can also explore relationships with A*STAR, otherwise known as the Agency for Science, Technology, and Research, in such promising areas as biomedical science. A*STAR provides "intellectual, human, and industrial capital" for new ventures entering Singapore, with a focus on manpower training, especially in the areas of science, engineering, and technology.[93] A*STAR's activities are complemented by those of the Urban Redevelopment Authority,[94] which provides customized housing and office space, as well as the Jurong Town Corporation, which manages industrial estate development and provides customized infrastructure to priority investors.[95]

The EDB, not to mention the government behind it, of course hopes to generate spinoffs from foreign investment that benefit local firms. Driven by rising local criticism that government policies benefit foreigners at the expense of Singaporeans themselves, spinoffs have of late become an increasing priority of the EDB and its affiliate organizations. In April 2002 such pressures led to the creation of SPRING Singapore—nominally the Standards, Productivity, and Innovation Board. This was actually a restructured version of the Products and Standards Board established in 1996, but with a special new function of promoting creativity and entrepreneurship among Singaporeans, including local small businesses. It helps such firms improve productivity, tap innovation, and upgrade capabilities so as to stay competitive in the global market. The long-term efficacy of this effort in a socioeconomic environment where large multinationals have major advantages remains unclear, however.

More than a static, free-standing organization, Singapore's Economic Development Board is in reality a synergistic coordinator. It provides venues and platforms for both foreign and domestic firms to connect with one another. It also helps with logistics, so that market actors can focus on strategy, internal operations, and innovation. Manned by a small elite staff, led by dynamic leaders close to Singapore's leadership, and supported by prominent international corporate advisers, the EDB coordinates the activities of related and complementary sister organizations. In its entirety this group is clearly more than the sum of its parts owing to the EDB's ability to effectively promote itself and to stimulate broad systemic efficiencies through inter-organizational coordination.

Singapore's smart state obviously plays a significant role in local economic development, but it does so largely indirectly and in minimalist fashion, in that it operates on limited budgets and with a small cadre of government officials. It works through small, market-sensitive statutory boards—preeminently the EDB—and corporatized yet public-linked firms, in which Temasek, the government's sovereign wealth fund, typically holds a significant stake. These government activities leverage the private sector, thus playing an important enabling function for both locally led and international Singapore-based firms that enhances their global competitiveness.

3. The Smart State and Foreign Relations

Today's world is an incessantly turbulent one—wracked by ongoing international crises in Ukraine, Syria, Iraq, and the South China Sea, not to mention more domestic security challenges like ethnic conflict and terrorism. For a tiny city-state like Singapore, sandwiched among ravenous and growing nations in the most populous corner of the globe, today's world—and likely tomorrow's to an even greater degree—is also a starkly Malthusian realm of food and resource scarcity. Given the high degree of trade and financial interdependence in this globalized world, and the consequent sensitivity of its markets to developments thousands of miles distant, even minor political-economic uncertainties can easily magnify Singapore's dual soft and hard security challenges.[96]

Security, in both these dimensions, is thus a rare and much sought-after commodity, especially in developing nations like those surrounding Singapore. And Singapore has much to teach—not only to its neighbors but also to nations throughout the world. The Lion City's experience is also relevant to local authorities, and to ambiguous political entities that, like Taiwan or Kurdistan, function as remarkably independent actors, but without the broad international recognition typical of most nation-states.

The following pages examine the details of Singapore international security policy, in its hybrid soft and hard configurations, that are of special relevance to the world in three dimensions: (1) political-military relations; (2) classical diplomacy; and (3) international networking and agenda-setting. In all three areas there is much in little Singapore's approach that is strikingly relevant even to much larger nations. The analysis will also consider Singapore's food and resource-security policies, together with the relevance that Singapore's implicit comprehensive security approach has for other nations, as well as their key subnational units.

Overall, Singapore's approach to foreign relations is remarkably parallel to the way its smart state approaches questions of social welfare and economic development. Both public policy and national institutions are in a very basic sense *minimalist*—characterized by remarkably low budgets, limited legal constraints, and limited personnel staffing, considering the scale of the challenges involved. At the same time, policy is *enabling*, as well as minimalist—that is, in the foreign-policy sphere, it enhances Singapore's national interests in a multi-directional, global sense, without excessive commitment of financial or human resources.

The Political-Military Dimension

Despite being a tiny nation-state located astride the highly strategic Malacca Strait—through which more than one-quarter of the world's foreign trade routinely passes, including the bulk of Northeast Asia's energy supply—Singapore has no formal alliances with any of the major world powers, including the United States. Nevertheless, Singapore considers itself secure and is trusted not only by Washington but by many nations with which the United States has delicate ties, including China. As a city-state with a broad, ambiguous, and nontransparent political persona, Singapore has also been able to maintain substantial political-military ties with such unorthodox actors in international affairs as Taiwan and even one-time pariah states (Myanmar and Vietnam during the early 1990s, for example) long before they were reintegrated into respected international society.

What is the secret of Singapore's paradoxical ability to gain substantial dividends in its political-military relations with the broader world without incurring what are normally considered to be inevitable related costs? The answer appears to be fourfold: (1) its low profile; (2) robust and highly operational defense capabilities, however discreetly obscured; (3) careful network cultivation; and (4) substantive contributions on the international scene. This configuration could be considered a "Singapore model" of political-military relations, potentially applicable elsewhere in the world.[97]

Singapore is not, it should be emphasized, without significant domestic military capabilities. Indeed, like Israel, after which it has quietly patterned

Figure 4-10. *Singapore's Military Spending in Comparative Perspective, 2012*

Percent of government expenditure

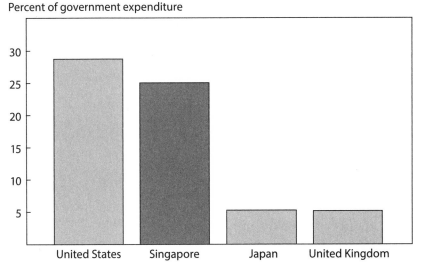

Source: World Bank, *World Development Indicators* (2012) (http://data.worldbank.org/indicator/MS.MIL. XPND.ZS).

its geopolitical approach of fostering both "out-of-region" friendships and significant local rapid-reaction defense capabilities, Singapore devotes nearly as large a share of its budget to defense as does the United States, and almost five times the shares prevailing in Britain or Japan (figure 4-10). Singapore also spends quantitatively more on defense than any other nation in Southeast Asia, despite being the smallest nation in terms of land area by a decisive margin.[98] Indeed, with a defense budget of US$10 billion, Singapore spends well over twice what Vietnam does on national security.[99]

Singapore's principal political-military partner is the United States, with which the city-state has a low-profile yet substantive relationship. It rests on no formal treaty, unlike U.S. security ties to Japan and South Korea.[100] Like those other cases, however, U.S.-Singapore security ties do involve the local presence of American military personnel, who play substantive and valuable yet inconspicuous functions. U.S. forces are extremely limited in number: they total less than 350, including less than 200 uniformed personnel. Furthermore, American forces do not occupy a formal U.S. military base. Their activities center on logistical support for the U.S. Seventh Fleet, including planning the resupply of food, ordnance, and fuel, and ship repairs.[101] In addition, the U.S. government runs significant accounting operations out of

Singapore for U.S. official facilities throughout the Pacific, down to the issue of paychecks and reimbursements for taxi receipts.

Other aspects of Singapore's low-profile yet substantive pattern of military cooperation with the United States include:

—*The provision of first-class infrastructure,* prepared carefully to meet demanding U.S. technical specifications. In March 2001 Singapore completed, at its own expense, the construction of a deep-draft pier at Changi Naval Base capable of servicing, and if necessary repairing, U.S. aircraft carriers, with the USS *Kitty Hawk,* based formally at Yokosuka, Japan, being the first of many U.S. ships to use the facility. The Singapore government's considerable alterations to accommodate U.S. forces doubled the prior physical size of the preexisting naval base at the same location, making it the only facility capable of major repair work on U.S. Navy ships between Japan and Diego Garcia in the Indian Ocean.[102]

—*Discreet American use of Singapore transit facilities.* More than 100 U.S. Navy ships a year call at Singapore, and U.S. fighter aircraft regularly deploy there. Singapore was a transit point for U.S. aircraft, troops, and ships before and during the Gulf War, for example, while Singapore's Paya Lebar Air Base supported U.S. airlift operations to first Somalia and then Saudi Arabia. Since 2012 the United States has also deployed U.S. littoral combat ships such as the USS *Freedom* and the USS *Fort Worth* on rotation to Singapore.[103]

—*Joint training and exercises.* Singapore began training bilaterally with U.S. Army Pacific units in 1981 and has continued to do so ever since, through exercises Tiger Balm and Lightning Strike.[104] It currently also trains bilaterally with the U.S. Navy in the context of the CARAT series, and multilaterally with the United States in RIMPAC, Cobra Gold, and other exercises.[105] Similarly, Singapore's military engages extensively with the U.S. Air Force. It does so both in Singapore, through bilateral exercises like Commando Sling, initiated in 1990, and reciprocally in the United States at Luke Air Force Base in Arizona, through Peace Carvin II, which has been running continuously since 1993.[106] Through its annual exercise at Luke, Singapore's Air Force rigorously trains both its F-16 pilots and its support engineers in close cooperation with American counterparts. It also engages with the U.S. Air Force multilaterally in such exercises as Red Flag (since 1976, redesignated in 2006) and Cope Tiger (since 1994).[107]

—*Equipment pre-positioning.* Singapore provides facilities to the U.S. military in Singapore, based on a 2005 bilateral strategic framework agreement for storing heavy equipment, ordnance, and supplies, so as to enhance the speed and effectiveness of rapid deployment, to deal with unexpected contingencies in Southeast Asia or surrounding areas.[108]

—*Intelligence cooperation.* Singapore and the United States reportedly engage in a periodic exchange of information with respect to such issues as terrorist threats in Southeast Asia.

Since Singapore's security cooperation with the United States is substantive, realistic, and flexibly granted, it elicits a uniformly high evaluation from American counterparts. One former high-level U.S. intelligence official, for example, considered Singapore's cooperation in his area of expertise more useful than that with any formal American ally in the Pacific other than Australia. Another former defense official informally praised Singapore for the quality of its logistical cooperation with the U.S. Navy, and the speed with which it closed the gap in U.S. repair and resupply capabilities created by Philippine refusal in 1991 to renew its base agreement with the United States.

Singapore also fills an important post–cold war geographical void in U.S. global basing structure. Although the United States has important bases in Northeast Asia (Korea and Japan), as well as at Diego Garcia in the Indian Ocean and at Guam in the Western Pacific, it has no other major air presence between Okinawa and the Persian Gulf (figure 4-11). Thus it very much needs either Singapore or the Philippines, if not both, for a combination of logistical and strategic reasons.

Since Singapore's security cooperation with the United States is informal, it finesses the political difficulties that have historically plagued U.S. military relations with all three of its current formal allies in the Pacific. It avoids the haggling over base rentals that cost the United States its bases in the Philippines and the bitter negotiations over host-nation support and base relocation that have periodically soured ties with Japan and South Korea.[109] Singapore's informal, low-profile approach has also sidestepped the operational rigidities due to local political constraints regarding force deployment that have traditionally plagued U.S. military operations in and out of Japan, thus making operational ties between the U.S. and Singaporean militaries unusually positive.

Multidirectional Security Diplomacy

Singapore's low-profile approach to security cooperation with the United States also helps to preserve its broad diplomatic interaction with other governments of the Asia-Pacific region, including many of America's past and present adversaries. For more than three decades Singapore has conducted

Figure 4-11. *Singapore's Strategic Location in the U.S. Global Basing Context*

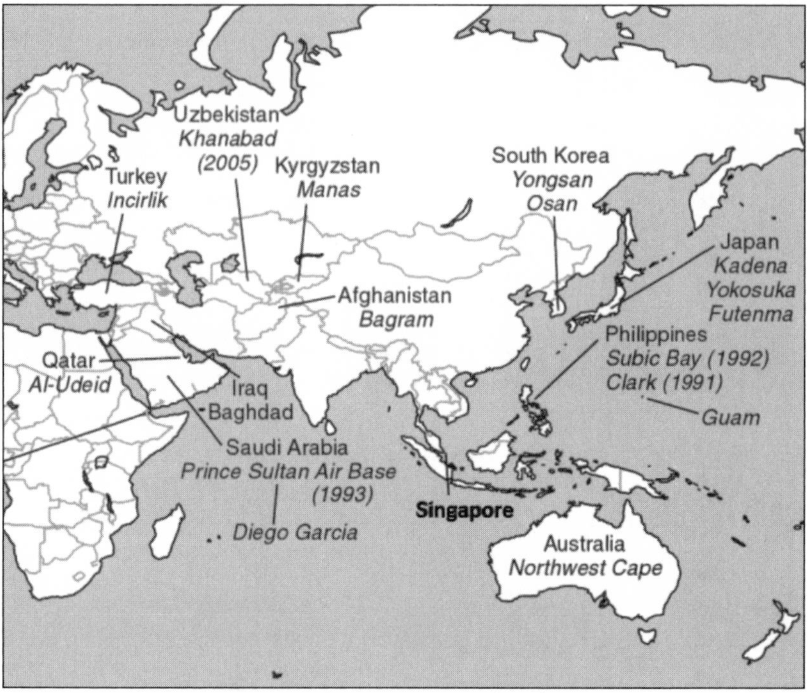

Source: Kent E. Calder, *Embattled Garrisons: Comparative Base Politics and American Globalism* (Princeton University Press, 2007).
Note: Dates in parentheses indicate year of base closure, if any.

far-ranging, top-level security dialogues with China, even as it also conducts military training and joint military drills, code-named Operation Starlight, in Taiwan.[110] Not surprisingly, it has played a central role in the Cross-Straits Dialogue between Beijing and Taipei: both the initial 1993 meeting establishing the dialogue and the November 2015 summit dialogue between Xi Jinping and Ma Ying-jeou that forged top-leader ties were held in Singapore.[111]

Singapore likewise engages intensively with the Vietnamese and Philippine militaries, both of which have extremely delicate relations with China. Since the late 1980s, at least, Singapore has also enjoyed active relations with Myanmar, including its military—two decades before the United States moved to normalize relations. Indeed, Singapore was the first country to supply arms and ammunition to Burma's military leaders when they came to power in 1988, although that backing took place before the massacres of 1990.[112]

Singapore's ethnic diversity naturally colors its diplomacy on security questions. Yet the tiny city-state has effectively converted a potential vulnerability into a diplomatic strength that other nations can reference with profit. Many of Singapore's top political leaders, together with nearly three-quarters of its population, are ethnically Chinese, which generates a natural affinity with Greater China, and a corresponding fear elsewhere in the Southeast Asian region of precisely that affinity. Singapore works to allay those regional anxieties, however, and to broaden its range of potential partners, by making the 10-member ASEAN regional forum a central focus of its formal diplomacy. It pointedly refrained from recognizing the People's Republic of China, for example, until 1990, after the last of its ASEAN partners, Indonesia, had done so first. Singapore also frequently appoints foreign ministers from its Indian and Malay minority ethnic communities, currently numbering together roughly a quarter of the local population.

Singapore's security strategy in the diplomatic realm appears to have three central components. First of all, as just suggested, it strives to be nonthreatening to other regional powers, building their confidence through such tactical tools as the "ASEAN-first" policy, which has clearly prevailed at least since the Vietnamese invasion of Cambodia in 1978.[113] An additional aspect of this trust-building approach has been the traditional appointment of an Indian- or Malay-origin foreign minister, despite the overwhelming local Chinese ethnic majority.

A second pillar of Singapore's security diplomacy has been conscious alignment with the broad security interests of key global powers, beginning with the United States. Apart from the bilateral political-military measures already mentioned, this approach has involved support for active U.S. involvement in the ASEAN post-ministerial talks and the ASEAN Regional Forum, as well as for U.S.-inspired free trade initiatives such as the Trans-Pacific Partnership. Singapore also pushed very strongly (and successfully) for the conclusion of a U.S.-Singapore bilateral free trade agreement in 2003—the first such agreement with the United States in East Asia and the third that the United States concluded globally, after those with Israel and Jordan. Singapore has consistently recognized the interrelationship between strong security ties and intimate, free trade-oriented economic relations.

A third element of Singapore's security diplomacy that other players could emulate with profit is Singapore's appreciation and use of the many multiple chessboards that are emerging in international affairs. As a diminutive city-state, it has the unusual option of operating either as a city or as a nation, allowing it to finesse the complex politics of East Asia to an unusual degree through a multilevel strategy. Singapore can, for example, deal in a routine municipal capacity with Taipei, the provincial government of Taiwan, or any one of numerous local governments in mainland China, or in India. Yet it can also engage with national leaders in Beijing and New Delhi through state-to-state relations. In addition, Singapore actively develops functional ties of importance to its national development by cultivating NGOs such as the World Water Council, through conferences like its Singapore International Water Week, held traditionally in June.[114]

Networks: Singapore's Appreciation of the "Washington Dimension"

More than any other nation in the Pacific, save possibly South Korea, Singapore has also appreciated the importance of proactive local public affairs efforts in Washington, D.C., as an integral element of an effective global security strategy. It has recognized clearly, to a greater degree than much larger nations such as Japan, Indonesia, and at times China, that the "penumbra of power" in Washington—the informal world of think tanks, mass media, and syndicated commentators—has become a key battlefield in the struggle for global strategic influence.[115] In dealing with the dynamic, multidimensional Washington sociopolitical environment that is now emerging, Singapore has pioneered some important tactics that arguably make it the most influential Asian nation in Washington—tactics that other nations could potentially employ with profit.

Singapore's key tactics—conspicuously—do *not* include much classical lobbying. Indeed, unlike Japan, Korea, China, and Taiwan, Singapore's formal diplomatic representatives do not employ significant numbers of professional lobbyists. In fact, its embassy rarely employs any lobbyists at all, except on very specific, short-term issues.

Unlike most other nations with major influence in Washington, Singapore also lacks a large embassy in the U.S. capital. Indeed, it has only 20 diplomats formally posted there in an embassy one-tenth the size of China's, right across the street. Singapore does, however, make full use of its small diplomatic corps, pointedly appointing an ambassador of extraordinarily high credentials and keeping that increasingly knowledgeable envoy on station for many years. Its current ambassador, Ashok Kumar Mirpuri, for example, is a graduate of the Harvard Business School Advanced Management Program, and his predecessor, Chan Heng Chee, was a distinguished university professor. Ambassador Chan was posted in Washington for 16 years, developed an extremely broad range of contacts, and served on a variety of influential advisory boards, including those of the Council of Foreign Relations and the International Institute for Strategic Studies. Like former UN ambassador Tommy Koh, Ambassador Chan has become an ambassador at large following her return to Singapore in 2012, allowing her to continue invoking her formidable global network in the interests of Singapore's diplomacy.[116]

Although Singapore's embassy is small, it has used that diminutive scale to advantage. Its officers are "outward oriented," spending the bulk of their time covering Capitol Hill and meeting with media and think-tank contacts, rather than with internal administration. This small scale also allows it to respond quickly to relevant developments, an invaluable asset in the age of short news cycles and the Internet. The Singapore Embassy leverages its resources through joint programming with major think tanks, such as the Brookings Institution and the Center for Strategic and International Studies (CSIS), which are playing an increasingly influential role in informal Washington agenda setting. Singapore places substantial emphasis in Washington on cultivating policy networks that can provide both informal intelligence on emerging local political-economic developments and also feedback on past actions that Singapore is taking or considering. To this end, the ambassador hosts frequent informal dinners for a mixture of current and former U.S. officials, as well as opinion leaders. The embassy also hosts larger receptions, ranging from Chinese New Year receptions to jazz festivals, as well as cultural and charity events, to broaden and maintain networks.[117]

Singapore likewise works actively to develop and sustain its trans-Pacific networks, by organizing frequent visits of its national leaders to Washington. Prime Minister Lee Hsien Loong frequently visits Washington as do key ministers. Despite Singapore's small population and diminutive geo-economic scale, its leaders typically enjoy strong entrée into top Washington policy circles owing to its perceived status as a loyal U.S. ally, despite the lack of formal alliance relationships.

Conclusion

Visionary yet highly pragmatic leadership has no doubt contributed significantly to Singapore's remarkable economic and diplomatic successes over the past half century. That leadership, however, has operated within a broader sociopolitical context of one-party and technocratic dominance that has made flexible, market-oriented neoliberal policies possible and has generally enhanced their effectiveness. This chapter has situated Singapore's government and public policies in broader comparative context, identifying Singapore as a smart state and exploring how the smart state's minimalist but enabling policies actually operate in Singapore itself.

Singapore, as noted at the outset, devotes a substantially smaller part of its GDP to the public sector than is common in other industrial democracies, and government officials make up a smaller share of the national workforce than is common elsewhere, while incurring only limited costs to the state itself. Broad coverage is provided to the citizenry, but co-payment ratios are high. In Singapore the self-help principle—through compulsory savings and subscription to compulsory catastrophic insurance programs—is also important, with the supplementary provision of minimalist safety nets. These distinguish the Singapore welfare system from pure laissez-faire.

Singapore's smart state pursues minimalist, enabling governance with respect to economic development as well as to social welfare. Its government is divided into relatively small public organizations, many of which are statutory boards congenial to private business. These bodies—autonomous agencies of government established by acts of parliament that are overseen by government ministries—are a distinct Singaporean organizational form that insulates sensitive policies from political intervention and allows them to operate in a purposive but market-oriented fashion. The Economic Development Board, in its efforts to attract foreign investment, as well as the Housing and Development Board, in its work at improving the local housing stock, are two complementary vehicles of this type. They allow Singapore to pursue and politically sustain minimalist, enabling government amid the powerful domestic and international pressures that confront its exposed political economy in a turbulent world. The EDB and the HDB are complemented by a multitude of government-linked enterprises—market-oriented yet infused with public purpose—that also serve as conduits in Singapore's emergence as a global policy laboratory, described more fully in chapter 5.

Within the international sphere, Singapore again pursues a smart policy mix. It is minimalist in the sense of maintaining a relatively compact diplomatic corps and professional military, considering its ambitious global orientation and serious national-security vulnerabilities, which are related to its small size and exceptionally strategic location. At the same time, Singapore's close security relations with major nations, beginning with the United States, as well as its pragmatic multidirectional diplomacy, ensure its national security with limited expenditure in absolute financial terms, as well as limited foreign commitments and entanglements.

One of the formidable assets of Singapore's tiny city-state in the 21st century is its simultaneous configuration as both state and city. Singapore is thus able to participate in an authoritative way on multiple chessboards of international affairs. Given that the populous giants of the developing world, such as China and India, are in the throes of transition from rural to urban even now, this dual status as nation state and city gives Singapore's smart-city policies in the transportation, energy, and environmental areas transcendent importance of their own, as will be clear in the chapters to come.

Singapore as Smart City
BUILDING A LIVABLE, SUSTAINABLE URBAN COMMUNITY

A blighted urban jungle of concrete destroys the human spirit.

—LEE KUAN YEW (1995)

Globalization is making it easier than ever before to compare best-practice responses to common social problems across the world, and to collaborate in devising solutions. Singapore's responses to universal human challenges certainly deserve serious consideration, not only because of its record of socioeconomic success as a state but also due to its parallel achievements as a city. Singapore's distinctive example provides especially valuable insights in coping with the historic, ongoing urban transformation now being fueled by revolutionary developments in the field of information and communication technology (ICT).

The foregoing pages have recorded Singapore's solid overall record of socioeconomic success as a state, in comparison with both developing and advanced industrial nations. They have also explored the national policies that have helped achieve that success. In this chapter the parallel achievements of Singapore as a city are considered, together with the insights that Singapore's distinctive example provides in coping with the historic, ongoing urban transformation, fueled by revolutionary ICT developments, of the 20th and 21st centuries.

In 1950 cities were home to 30 percent of the world's population, or about 746 million people. By 2014 that number had grown by nearly 483 percent, to over 3.6 billion.[1] And according to United Nations projections, by 2050 it will likely grow to well over 6 billion, or two-thirds of the global total, with over 82 percent of that figure living in developing nations.[2] In Asia alone, more than 122,000 people drift into cities *every day,* primarily in India, China, and Southeast Asia, looking for a better life and opportunity to work.[3]

Urbanization first became a pervasive socioeconomic trend in Europe during the eighteenth and nineteenth centuries, before spreading to the Americas. Today Europe is 73 percent urbanized, North America 82 percent, and Latin America and the Caribbean 80 percent.[4] Asia at 48 percent urban and Africa at 40 percent have yet to fully conform to this global trend. Three of the world's four largest nations in population terms—China, India, and Indonesia—continue to harbor huge rural populations that will most likely migrate to the cities over the next few decades. All these giants lie in close proximity to Singapore. Singapore's achievements as a smart city are thus highly relevant to these neighbors, as well as to the rest of the rapidly urbanizing world. Indeed, Singapore is a veritable "urban policy laboratory" and "urban policy hub" for the entire world, especially its developing nations.

The challenge of urban transformation is occurring in a diverse range of urban settings (figure 5-1). The most explosive growth in recent years has occurred in sprawling megacities of over 10 million people, such as Shanghai, Mumbai, Jakarta, and Manila, whose number nearly tripled between 1990 and 2014, from 10 million to 28 million. Their problems of transportation, sanitation, and even in some cases social stability remain massive and often unsolved. Going forward, the megacities will be joined by slightly smaller cities of 5 million to 10 million (figure 5-1), the size of Singapore, whose ranks will grow even faster and also pose serious social, economic, and even political challenges.

This massive urban migration, still in its relative infancy, has already produced some grotesque, sprawling, and close to uninhabitable urban centers. Metropolitan Jakarta, for example, now has 28 million people, many of them lacking access to running water or stable electricity supply; Metro Manila is another sprawling megalopolis of 15 million to 20 million. Both cities are in virtual transportation gridlock, as local environmental problems, among the world's most serious, continue to deepen.[5] Similar urban problems are proliferating in India, which now has half of the 20 most polluted major cities in the world.[6]

The transportation and environmental challenges already encountered by megacities like Bangkok, Jakarta, and Manila make clear that the classical Western model of urban life characterized by an industrial system and a car

Figure 5-1. *Rising Number of Urban Centers*

Population in millions

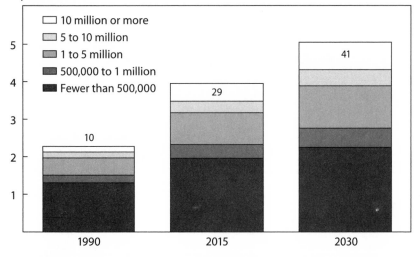

Sources: United Nations, *World Urbanization Prospects: The 2014 Revision*, tables 17b and 17d (http://esa. un.org/unpd/wup/).
Note: Numbers at top or above bars represent the number of megacities—those with populations of ten million or more.

culture does not fit the emerging realities of the developing world, even if citizens of Asian, African, or Latin American countries should desire it. There is a pressing need for an alternate paradigm. And the case of Singapore, with its combination of dense population and livable eco-city configuration, facilitated by intensive use of interactive ICT technology, deserves serious consideration as a plausible and much-needed alternative paradigm.

The dominant, unavoidable challenge of life in Singapore is, as in high-density environments elsewhere, diminutive physical size. As mentioned in an earlier chapter, Singapore has more than 6 million people squeezed into an area of just over 700 square kilometers, less than four times the size of Washington, D.C. Since Singapore is an island—and simultaneously a nation whose boundaries are coincident with its island shores—it must work within that unavoidable and unalterable constraint. And its high population density serves as a powerful catalyst for tech-savvy, smart-city development, based on an Internet of Things concept, with government harnessing information and communication technologies to promote economic renewal, social cohesion, improved city administration, and efficient infrastructure management.

The Holistic Nature of Singapore's Smart Urban Policy

One of the most distinctive aspects of Singapore urban planning is its *holistic* character—the way in which individual sector-specific policies, such as those targeting transportation, land use, housing, and the environment, are woven into a systematically integrated overall approach.[7] Singapore urban planning also has a pronounced social-engineering dimension—which evinces "developmental" character similar to that of Northeast Asian industrial policies.[8] Singapore urban policy has sought to transform local society along three dimensions: (1) from an immigrant petty-trader society into a high-technology, cosmopolitan nation; (2) from a plural society of distinct ethnic communities into a more unified, harmonious collectivity; and (3) from a wasteful energy consumer and polluter into a tasteful, vibrant eco-city that can be a model of sustainable development for the broader world. In the process, it has recorded achievement in all eight categories of the Asian Green City Index, published by the Economist Intelligence Unit, which consistently puts Singapore at the head of the Asia-Pacific region.[9]

The Singapore government's systematic effort over the past three decades to transform the city-state into an "intelligent island," wired with the latest interactive ICT technology, illustrates this holistic approach at work.[10] The National Computerization Plan began this process in the early 1980s (1980–85), by computerizing the civil service and expanding Singapore's IT manpower pool fivefold. The National IT Plan (1986–91) deployed specialized computer networks for the trading, legal, and health care communities.[11]

In 1992 the National Computer Board intensified the formal effort to build a smart Singapore by releasing *A Vision of an Intelligent Island: The IT 2000 Report*.[12] This seminal projection declared that Singapore would devote 15 years to systematically building state-of-the art computing, optical-fiber transmission, and cybernetic-feedback systems capable of integrating homes, workplaces, and public institutions. Singapore would thus become one of the first countries in the world to possess a truly advanced nationwide information infrastructure.

The ambitious IT 2000 report was succeeded, upon its successful implementation, by *Intelligent Nation 2015*, a 10-year master plan for using info-comm technologies that was announced in May 2005.[13] Like its predecessor, *Intelligent Nation 2015* was holistic in character, seeking to use IT both to enhance the competitiveness of key economic sectors and to build a well-connected society. The 2015 report placed special emphasis on globalizing

Singapore—enhancing access to the world's intellectual resources and leveraging Singapore's role as a global laboratory through the export of its ideas, products, and services to the global marketplace.[14]

In its systematic efforts to create a so-called intelligent island, Singapore's government has spent billions to create advanced infrastructure and has specified related standards for new public housing, in which over 80 percent of Singaporeans now live. These standards stipulate that every new home must have built-in connections to the national high-speed broadband integrated-services digital network. New residences are also to be connected to a smart grid capable of monitoring and regulating energy consumption.[15] And they are to have convenient facilities for recycling waste.[16]

By 2014 Singapore had already provided home computer access to 86 percent of all homes, and household broadband access to 87 percent.[17] In keeping with the broad-access concept implicit in "minimalist government," Singapore also operates a Digital Inclusion Fund. This fund helps provide low-income households with Internet access, supplies funds for IT purposes to voluntary welfare organizations, and helps students from low-income households buy personal computers at subsidized prices.[18]

The Land-Use Challenge

There is no scarcer commodity in Singapore than land, and national priorities for its allocation and use play a prospectively decisive role in shaping the nation's future, as Lee Kuan Yew recognized over half a century ago. Singapore, after all, has a population density of nearly 8,000 people per square mile—more than 20 times that of Japan, 15 times that of Korea, and 230 times that of the United States.[19] That density is also higher than in such other global cities as New York, London, Tokyo, and even Hong Kong (figure 5-2). Stimulated also by economic growth and the attractiveness of living in Singapore, density has provoked explosive land-price increases across the city-state.[20] The government feels strongly that land use is central to maximizing Singapore's commercial potential, while simultaneously satisfying the housing, transportation, recreational, and other needs of its people.[21]

One of Singapore's well-developed national institutions for managing land allocation and land use is the Urban Redevelopment Authority (URA), which is the designated national planning authority of Singapore. Together with the Housing and Development Board, it oversees Singapore's urban infrastructure.

Figure 5-2. *Singapore's Extraordinarily High Population Density*

Population per square kilometer

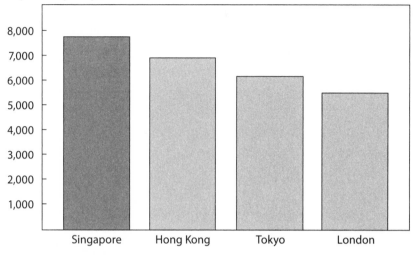

Sources: For Singapore and Hong Kong (2014), see World Bank, *World Development Indicators* (2014). For Tokyo (2015), see www.metro.tokyo.jp/ENGLISH/ABOUT/HISTORY/history03.htm. For London (2015), see www.bbc.com/news/uk-england-london-31056626.

Meanwhile, the Land Transport Authority (LTA) estimates future road and rail transportation patterns, plans infrastructure, and licenses vehicles as well as transit services. In addition, the Public Transport Council approves and regulates bus and train fares, in an effort to manage traffic flows, and the Energy Market Authority ensures a reliable, secure, and efficient energy supply. At the ministerial level, the Ministry of Environment also plays a key role in controlling pollution, while the Ministry of National Development handles housing, and the Ministry of Transport deals with mass-transit issues.

Singapore's Holistic Planning Process

The careful way in which land-use and transportation planning are integrated is another illustration of the holistic character of Singapore urban policies, synergistic with the latest interactive ICT technology. These policies allow for dense urban developments that are functional, self-sufficient, and aesthetically pleasing, yet do not feel overcrowded.[22] This combination lifts the spirits of residents, builds a vibrant sense of community, and reduces commuting time, thereby raising productivity.

Living and working environments are integrated through a planning process featuring two important and distinct elements: the Concept Plan and the Master Plan.

The Concept Plan

The Concept Plan presents a general and long-term guide to strategic land-use and transportation development over a 40- to 50-year time frame. In accordance with the holistic bias of Singapore public policies, this document strives to ensure that there is sufficient land to meet anticipated population and economic growth, with both workplace and housing configured to simultaneously provide a pleasant living environment and efficient overall energy use. It is implemented through government land sales, with the government's development-control group evaluating and granting approval for individual projects consistent with planning strategies and guidelines.

The Concept Plan is formulated by the Urban Redevelopment Authority and is reviewed every 10 years, with input from other government agencies as well as public feedback. This system makes it possible to monitor new socioeconomic developments for consistency with the Concept Plan, and to flag any need for adjustment to the plan itself. The latest Concept Plan review was carried out in 2011.[23]

The Concept Plan attempts to incorporate and to systematically integrate a broad range of government objectives. A high priority of Concept Plan 2001, for example, is to foster an inclusive society with a "unique character and sense of history."[24] This proposal addresses the city-state's continuing challenge of managing diversity and has led to the "adaptive reuse of old buildings" as well as the creation of "heritage towns." It has also validated land allocation for museums in prominent locations that give positive treatment to Singapore's multiple ethnic traditions and that highlight the blending of those traditions into an increasingly cohesive national identity.[25]

Another priority of the Concept Plans is the creation of integrated growth centers, known as new towns, such as Jurong and Paya Lebar, which are largely self-sufficient in terms of local commercial, educational, health, social, and recreational facilities. New towns are not such a novel phenomenon—they have actually been a central aspect of Singapore urban policy since the late 1960s (figure 5-3). Their principal functional role, however, has changed, from supporting industrial development to more comprehensively promoting socioeconomic decentralization, often in postindustrial contexts. The Jurong Town Corporation, founded in 1968 to support Singapore's first industrial

Figure 5-3. *Singapore's Key New Towns—Jurong and Paya Lebar*

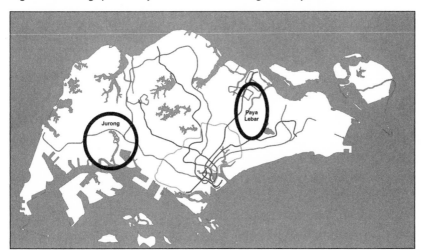

Source: Urban Redevelopment Authority, *Master Plan 2014* (www.ura.gov.sg/maps/).

estate, was the first model case, but has been followed by projects like Paya Lebar and Tampines, that were more focused on social than industrial infrastructure. Singapore is now the only country in the world having more than 80 percent of its inhabitants living in an urban environment systematically planned from scratch, which is locally reinterpreted to match the constraints of high-rise, high-density public housing.[26]

Growth centers like the new towns simultaneously promote multiple policy goals, including economic efficiency, in holistic fashion. They not only spread jobs across the island and increase access to green space but also provide a wider choice of locations to meet future economic needs. Through integrative housing policies, they can also encourage stable ethnic relations. However, these new-town growth poles also necessitate enhanced energy-efficient public transport, and the Concept Plan works out these linkages among housing, transport, and energy use in general terms.

The Master Plan

The URA's Concept Plan has a more concrete and operational counterpart: the Master Plan. It is the statutory land-use projection that translates the broad, long-term strategies of the Concept Plan into detailed operational measures over a 10- to 15-year time frame. The Master Plan provides the basis for day-to-day land-use regulation by prescribing the zoning, maximum development intensity (that is, the ratio of built-up area to site area), and building-height limits for individual parcels of land. The plan also spells out conservation areas and nature reserves, to limit adverse environmental implications.[27] The URA updates the Master Plan every 5 years, utilizing the same open consultative approach that it employs for the Concept Plan reviews. The current Master Plan was implemented in 2014.[28]

The URA's principal tool for implementing the Master Plan is the development control system, organized around permits that enable the government to keep tight control over the development of all land in Singapore. The prior permission of the URA is required for an extremely wide range of land-use decisions, including change in the use of buildings or land, the construction of new buildings, the subdivision of buildings or land, major additions or alterations to existing buildings, and all work done within an established conservation area. In evaluating applications for permits, the URA seeks to ensure that contemplated transformations are consistent with the planning parameters set out in the Master Plan.[29]

In its 2030 Work, Live, and Play Program, unveiled in 2014, the Ministry of National Development envisions "Smart Work Centers" that will help to finesse Singapore's serious land-use challenges discussed above, by proposing "flexible" forms of work that allow employees to contribute from virtually anywhere with almost anyone, and at different times.[30] In accordance with this approach, Singapore plans to establish alternate working spaces, with professional office-like facilities, near residential areas. This provides professional collaborative spaces closer to home, thus helping to simultaneously ease energy, environment, and transport problems in holistic fashion.

Singapore's Unique Transportation Management System

Whatever flexible working programs it may adopt, Singapore will remain a crowded island, with extremely high population densities. Hence both the Concept and Master Plans for land use consistently emphasize decentralization, to enhance the prospects for livable yet economically efficient environments. The proposed ideal is multiple moderately sized and self-sufficient residential communities, clustered at some distance from a central business district. Yet it is difficult to reconcile that multipolar concept with Singapore's inherent high densities, given the energy and environmental challenges that go along with being a crowded urban center. Historically, rising affluence has brought a rapid rise in the number of cars traveling its roads as high as

12 percent a year between 1975 and 1990.[31] That level was neither economically efficient nor environmentally sustainable.

In response, Singapore has impressively inhibited automobile use. It has done so partly through urban planning that optimizes facilities for pedestrians and bicycle traffic, especially around local housing and commercial complexes.[32] Singapore has also endeavored to minimize traffic by creating clear incentives, such as the Electronic Road Pricing (ERP) system, for car owners not to drive unnecessarily.

Through far-sighted traffic-management policies making extensive use of transponders and other advanced ICT technology, as well as demand-based pricing, Singapore has, in short, been able to avoid transportation gridlock, in sharp contrast to most urban centers of both advanced industrial nations and the developing world.[33] For one thing, it has successfully promoted increased public transport use during peak hours—from 59 percent in 2008 to 63 percent in 2012.[34] It has also kept auto transport moving smoothly. Average car speed on arterial (main) roads during peak hours has recently been calculated at 27 kilometers per hour (kph), or 17 miles an hour—much higher than in London (16 kph) and Tokyo (11 kph).[35] The cost of transportation to commuters is also lower than in almost all other major urban centers: 8.9 percent of GDP per commuter, versus 15 percent in New York City, 14 percent in Paris, and 11 percent in Beijing.[36]

Secrets of Transportation Policy Success

This successful transportation recipe has two key ingredients. One is a convenient and increasingly well-connected public transportation network that provides alternatives to private vehicles.[37] The other is an effective set of demand-management measures that regulate traffic flow and thus keep road congestion in check.[38] Transportation policy thus features both an infrastructure and an operational dimension. As in other of its policy spheres, Singapore integrates the two in holistic fashion, capitalizing on the latest ICT technology.

Singapore's diversified public transport system consists of a heavy rail network (mass rapid transit, or MRT) and a light rail system (light rapid transit, or LRT), as well as public buses and taxis. More than half of daily commuter trips are made on public transport, with over half of that share by bus and another third by MRT.[39] Buses are thus a key part of the system as a whole, especially in outlying parts of the island, with virtually all of the buses being air-conditioned.[40] Public policy encourages efficiency and innovation in how routes are managed through competition among bus operators under the Government Contracting Model system. Operators must compete periodically for the right to provide a package of bus services designed by the LTA. This system is being gradually introduced as current bus service operating licenses expire.[41]

Singapore's government has put exceptionally high investments into mass transit. The first MRT lines, for example, for which construction began in May 1982, cost over S$5 billion.[42] Yet despite these high capital costs, Singapore's government has kept commuting prices low.[43] Both MRT and LRT are extremely inexpensive in comparison with train services in most other parts of the world and relative to local income. Individual transportation costs are lower in Singapore than in most major urban centers: only 9 percent of GDP per capita, versus 15 percent in New York City, 15 percent in London, and 13 percent in Shanghai.[44] Government pricing policies have thus encouraged Singaporeans to take the subway or the bus as their preferred mode of transportation, rather than socially and environmentally disruptive alternatives. Smart cards ("Ez-link"), similar to those used in Tokyo or Washington, D.C., have also encouraged mass transit by making it more convenient.

While Singapore has systematically provided its inhabitants with public alternatives to individual private transport, its most innovative policies have been on the demand side. It has systematically discouraged car ownership, as well as vehicle usage at peak times of day, while also penalizing travel through predictably crowded parts of the island during periods of highest prospective use. Singapore's transportation-policy approaches have been developed in consultation with some of the top transportation specialists in the world, including authorities at the World Bank and Harvard University, although their recommendations have not always been adopted.[45] Singapore's mass-transit approaches are now being widely emulated internationally.[46] China, in particular, is considering Singapore's transportation policy seriously in such areas as electronic road pricing (ERP).[47]

Key Transportation Management Concepts

Singapore's distinctive method of dealing with demand focuses on inhibiting both private car ownership and driving. Car ownership is controlled through a quota system, and car usage is managed through a three-part system of surcharges for driving into the city center, or on highways and key roads when congested. The three central concepts can be explained as follows:

Vehicle Quota System (VQS). This arrangement helps to regulate Singapore's private vehicle population. Between 1990 and 2009, Singapore capped vehicle growth at an annual rate of 3 percent and has since reduced that ceiling still further. Prospective car owners are required to bid for a Certificate of Entitlement (COE) under the VQS, valid for 10 years, and also to pay an annual road tax based on their engine capacity. Once the COE expires, the holder must apply for renewal at the prevailing COE price, which discourages ownership of less efficient and more pollution-prone older cars.[48] In addition to the open-market value of a vehicle, owners must pay a registration fee (S$140), an additional registration fee equal to the market value of the vehicle, an excise duty reaching 20 percent of original market value, and a 7 percent goods and services tax.[49] With all these taxes and fees included, a BMW 320i sedan, for example, would cost around US$140,000 in Singapore, or more than three times its U.S. sticker price. And a major part of this prospective cost is the US$55,000 that the buyer must pay for a COE.[50]

Area Licensing Scheme (ALS). This is one of two major mechanisms Singapore employs to control vehicle-usage patterns, and thus to reduce traffic congestion at peak intervals. First formulated in 1973, and applied to the Central Business District in 1975, ALS was the first system in the world to charge cars for driving into congested urban areas. It divides Singapore into various districts with traffic-control restrictions based on expected levels of congestion. In its original formulation, ALS was a manual road-pricing system, requiring substantial manpower for enforcement. Since it proved quite inconvenient and inflexible in adjusting road prices so as to constrain excessive demand, the system was eventually replaced by electronic road pricing.[51]

Electronic Road Pricing (ERP) System. Introduced in September 1998, this mechanism for controlling vehicle flows is built on the basic concept of ALS and electronically collects taxes when private-car drivers enter a congestion-prone area. ERP integrates new technology incorporating transponders, which has greatly eased the problem of enforcement while also opening the way to a much more sophisticated and flexible tariff system. The ERP system now allows for differentiated charges, depending on vehicle type, time of day, and zone through which a vehicle is traveling. [52] Between 2012 and 2014, this system was refined, through the introduction of park-and-ride as well as off-peak pricing arrangements, so as to cut in half the previous vehicle growth rate.[53]

The ERP system's basic tool is the transponder ("in-vehicle unit"), which is inserted in almost the entire vehicle population of Singapore.[54] Gantries

Figure 5-4. *Singapore's Electronic Road-Pricing System*

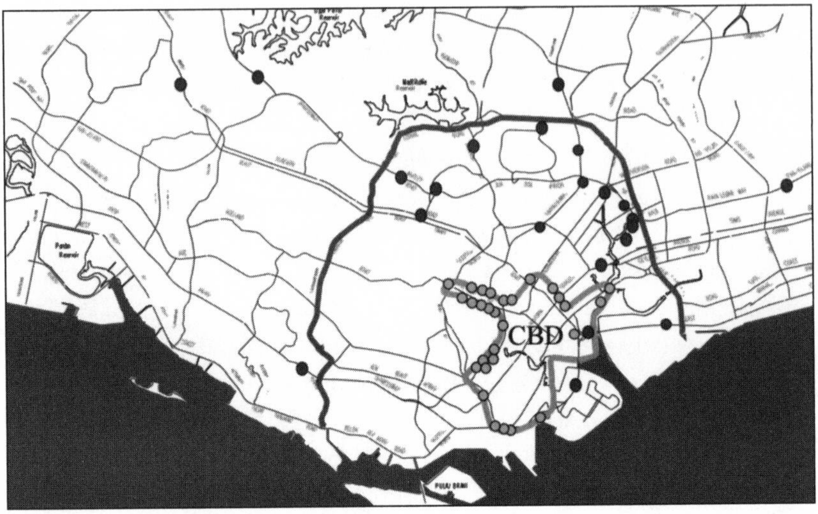

Source: Singapore Land Transport Authority.
Note: Circles represent the locations of the ERP gantries. The outer circle is the Outer Ring Road. Area within the inner circle is the Restricted Zone (RZ). CBD denotes Central Business District.

have been erected across Singapore at 29 entry points to its most congested parts, known as restricted zones, where those gantries monitor all traffic passing into each zone. When any except an emergency vehicle passes into the zone between the peak hours of 7:30 A.M. and 9:30 A.M. on weekdays,[55] the transponder automatically calculates ERP charges, which are deducted from the stored value on a smartcard slotted into the transponder. This process is repeated when vehicles enter expressways or other main roads that are experiencing congestion. Each transaction is consummated by using a dedicated short-range radio frequency connecting the ERP overhead gantry equipment and the transponder (see figure 5-4 for the geographical configuration of the ERP system).

Vehicles that violate the monitoring and payment system by not having their transponders in working order have photographs of their rear license plates automatically taken, as a basis for enforcement and issuance of a summons. ERP charges vary for different half-hour periods throughout the day, ranging from S$2.50 for a car moving into the restricted zone during rush hour to only 50 cents during quieter periods. Motorcycles, delivery vehicles, taxis, and buses all have different types of responders, leading to different payments. A motorcycle, for example, pays only half of what a car pays.

ERP charges are reviewed every three months and are tied to the prevailing speeds being experienced during a particular half hour, so as to minimize traffic congestion.

The Environmental Dimension

Singapore's land-use planning naturally has a clear environmental aspect—indeed, that is a defining feature differentiating it from most other Asian planning efforts. For well over two decades—since 1992—a Green Plan, periodically revised, has identified nature sites and enforced a government pledge that 5 percent of the city-state's total land area will be reserved for nature conservation.[56] This environmental thrust is a central element of Prime Minister Lee Hsien Loong's policy platform, in recognition of the need to "work hard to preserve our green spaces" in the face of a growing population and "more built-up city."[57]

Singapore has long been known as the Garden City, and government has worked for over four decades to maintain that reputation, beginning with the extensive planting of plants and shrubs.[58] The 2002 arrangement, for example, expanded recreational space,[59] followed in 2008 by an island-wide Leisure Plan, which sought to enlarge the park-connector network, a series of interconnected green areas along walking and cycling thoroughfares, while expanding more conventional green areas as well.[60] The 2012 plan established a National Biodiversity Reference Center[61] and a Community-in-Bloom gardening program that has inspired the establishment of over 600 gardening groups.[62]

Singapore's most recent environmentally related plan, which simultaneously addresses multiple policy targets, includes school carnivals with environmental themes and workshops for transforming waste materials into crafts.[63] The plan is a National Parks Board initiative at a pleasant 101-hectare waterfront site, designed to enhance both environmental and historical appreciation. Through a combination of museum exhibits, such as the Discovery Center on Singapore history, and cultural performances, "edutainment" offers learning experiences about Singapore's history in an enjoyable natural context.[64] At the same time, it enriches the lives of both residents and tourists while impressing them with the value of Singapore's diversity, even as it contributes to economic development.[65] The Singapore River development project, which draws tourists inland from the emblematic Ma Lion statue along Singapore's coastline into the heart of a new restaurant district along the river, through cruises with a historical theme, is another prominent "edutainment" effort.

Attracting the World

Both the Concept Plan and the Master Plan stress that culture as well as respect for the environment should be key priorities in Singapore's future, and that both enrich the lives of Singaporeans and make their city-state more attractive to the broader world. One major undertaking given priority in the Master Plan is the Esplanade Theatres on the Bay complex, the largest international performing arts center in Singapore and patterned after Lincoln Center in New York City.[66] At a total development cost of S$600 million, the theaters complex includes a 1,600-seat concert hall, a 2,000-seat theater, a 250-seat recital studio, a 220-seat theatre studio, a rehearsal studio, outdoor performance spaces, and the Esplanade Mall. This complex, its central buildings configured in an ambiguous shape variously conceptualized as a microphone or as Singapore's beloved durian fruit, was opened on October 12, 2002.[67]

Singapore's land-use planning, sensitive as it is to both culture and environment, has naturally made ample room for tourism of an unusually edifying variety. A key element has been edutainment projects like the National Museum and the Singapore River cruises, as well as Esplanade Theatres on the Bay, and especially Gardens by the Bay. At the innovative Gardens, opened in 2011 on reclaimed land, visitors roam through 250 acres of themed vertical gardens and conservatories, designed to show the virtues of sustainable natural ecosystems.[68]

The attractions include several 100-foot concrete "super-trees" resembling oversized stone palm trees, each dripping with ferns, orchids, and bromeliads. Although they serve as the backdrop to a nightly laser show, the super-trees actually incorporate various green-energy initiatives. Seven of them feature photovoltaic cells. Others are air exhausts from the Energy Center and Cooled Conservatories, thus filling a systemic ecological function. A remarkable variety of self-contained biospheres within the Gardens by the Bay also help visitors to understand the impact that temperature and water availability have on plant life, and the concrete and immediate threat that global warming thus poses to human existence.

Capitalizing on Singapore's far-sighted water-management policies, a marina for water sports has been constructed next to one of Singapore's 19 water-supply reservoirs. A few years ago Singapore modified its existing public road configuration, adding racing pits and other support structures, to create an urban F-1 course. In September 2008, the construction complete, it began hosting the only race on the global F-1 circuit in Southeast Asia, after a 35-year lapse. Running at night, this became the first nighttime F-1 race in world history, stretching from 6 to 9 P.M.[69] It has also become the first street circuit in Asia of the F-1 series, thus emulating Monaco's own classic F-1 street race.

Building on the exotic theme, articulated even by Lee Kuan Yew, of Singapore becoming the "Monaco of Asia," Singapore's normally staid planners allocated space (largely above the skyline) for Southeast Asia's most elaborate casino, which opened in 2010.[70] In order to generate revenue from tourism, while limiting the corruption of local morals, Singapore's planners have thoughtfully introduced a stiff S$100 admission fee for locals that does not apply to foreigners, who can present a passport to secure exemption. Obviously, the government is not averse to encouraging foreigners to engage in gambling that generates needed foreign exchange, even as it works to discourage Singaporeans from corrupting themselves by doing the same thing. Once again, Singapore's planners are thinking synergistically and holistically about how to maximize national interest, by using central location to become a regional and global hub across a broadening variety of socioeconomic sectors.

Stewarding Scarce Resources

Asia's transcendent political-economic reality is simple: population pressure on resources is intensifying, as rising national affluence gradually gives more individual purchasing power to local citizens. This pressure forces ever higher the price of real estate, food, water, energy, and ultimately quality consumer goods. In a small, exposed economy like Singapore, raw materials are naturally in short supply, with their procurement subject to major financial and political constraints. Hence neutralizing resource vulnerabilities is a national project of major significance.

Singapore has three resource vulnerabilities so substantial that they constitute a major challenge to national security: food, water, and energy. Those vulnerabilities, as throughout much of the developing world, are rooted in a simple but perverse Malthusian equation: the pressure of rising population on finite food supplies. With nearly half of the world's population clustered within less than 3,000 miles of its island shores, this challenge—and Singapore's response—is both intensely immediate for Singapore itself and highly relevant for the huge, teeming mass of developing Asia that surrounds it.

Food Supply

Food security is an endemic problem in the developing world, especially in South and Southeast Asia, regions very close to Singapore. India's malnourished population approaches 225 million—a number nearly equal to the population of Indonesia, the world's fourth most populous country.[71] The populations of nearby Bangladesh, Laos, Cambodia, and Sri Lanka are close to 40 percent malnourished.[72] And these populations are growing rapidly, even as rising affluence among the local upper classes, and in neighboring countries such as China, intensifies pressure on existing food stocks, especially of feed grains. Singapore lies in the midst of this deprivation, imports well over 90 percent of its food,[73] and is naturally vulnerable to the drastic fluctuations in supply and prices that are endemic in such a food-short region.

The food-supply problems of the developing world are especially severe in urban centers, where over 80 percent of the world's urban population will reside by the year 2050—a total of over 5 billion people.[74] At present, over 80 percent of the land suitable for raising crops worldwide is already in use, according to the Food and Agriculture Organization, with about three-quarters of the remainder historically laid waste by poor management practices.[75] The world clearly needs new techniques of food production to avoid widespread future starvation.

Singapore is the third most densely populated nation on earth, with over 5 million people crammed onto a landmass of just over 700 square kilometers. It grows only 7 percent of its own food locally.[76] Nevertheless, Singapore is working to enhance its own food security through some innovative experiments undertaken by public-private partnerships and the use of advanced technology for urban food production. These efforts could well provide clues, in the "laboratory to the world tradition," as to how both developing and advanced industrial nations might efficiently address their urban food-supply problems in future years.

One important Singapore innovation is the vertical farm. At least two futuristic demonstrations of this concept have been initiated, with government support. One project will be the 26-story EDITT Tower, with EDITT standing for "Ecological Design in the Tropics." Over half of the tower's surface area is to be covered by organic vegetation, with solar panels generating up to 40 percent of the building's energy demands.[77]

A second key demonstration project, actually completed and opened in 2012, is the world's first low-carbon, water-driven, rotating vertical farm, Sky

Green, which grows tropical vegetables in an urban environment. This farm consists of a series of aluminum towers, some of them up to 9 meters high, each containing 38 tiers equipped with troughs for the vegetables. It employs a high-rise vertical farming system to achieve significantly higher yields per unit area of land with minimal land, water, and energy resources.[78]

The water used to power the rotating towers is recycled within the system and eventually used to water the vegetables. Each tower consumes only 60 watts of power daily—roughly the same amount as a single light bulb. The multilayered vegetable tower rotates very slowly, taking about eight hours to complete a full circle. As the plants travel to the top, they absorb ample sunlight; as they descend, they are watered from a hydraulic system that also drives rotation of the tower. Even in its infancy this system produced urban-grown vegetables that cost just 20 cents more per kilogram than comparable imported varieties.[79]

A further Singapore innovation has been rooftop gardens. These have increased rapidly since the urban expansion of the 1990s, aided by government regulations. These require buildings to integrate green space into their designs, so as to help reduce energy consumption, since greenery cools buildings by absorbing sunlight.[80] The government also encourages urban farming start-ups.

In keeping with the concept of "Singapore as a laboratory for the world," foreign firms have been testing and refining their innovative ideas about urban farming in Singapore, with the intention of diffusing the fruits of their research worldwide. Japanese firms have been in the very forefront of technologically advanced farming under space constraints, and they have begun operationalizing their work in Singapore.[81] Panasonic, for example, began trial operation of a vegetable factory in Singapore in July 2014, using its cutting-edge technologies relating to light and temperature control in order to produce burdock and other fresh root vegetables for local school meals and boxed-lunch businesses.[82] To support the urban farming concept, the national park farm program also offers free gardening workshops for visitors and tourists and is also pioneering research and demonstration projects relating to rooftop and vertical vegetable gardens.

Water Supply

Water, like food, is an indispensable dimension of human security, and a resource that is coming under increasing pressure worldwide owing to the dual impact of population increase and economic growth. Singapore confronts the challenge of water supply creatively and holistically at home and then diffuses its insights abroad. Domestically, it secures water supply from diverse sources, through innovative technology such as recycling, catchment, and high-tech retreatment. Internationally, Singapore actively exports its acclaimed expertise; the government has clearly considered the water industry a strategic growth sector, at least since 2006, and enthusiastically supports private-sector efforts through funds for research initiatives.

As with food, the challenge of water supply is especially intense in Asia beyond Singapore's shores. The problem is threefold: access to safe, potable water is lacking, especially in less developed nations such as Laos and Cambodia, as well as poorer urban areas elsewhere; water supply is being seriously depleted both in arid regions and in heavily populated areas, especially in nations such as Pakistan; and water quality is becoming a dire concern worldwide, particularly among the teeming populations in the tropical nations surrounding Singapore.[83] Worldwide, more people die as a result of polluted water than are killed by all forms of violence combined, including wars. Indeed, 1.8 million children five years of age and younger die from water-related diseases annually, or 1 every 20 seconds.[84]

Singapore has made important breakthroughs in the reprocessing of the most polluted water resources, including sewage. It is also working on the all-important water-depletion issue, which has a serious impact on the ability of heavily populated nations to produce food inasmuch as 70 percent of global water consumption goes to agriculture.[85]

Singapore's approach to the water issue provides valuable lessons for others, beginning with the conservation efforts it has pioneered in the urban farming area. In addition, it discourages wasteful or excessive use of water with a two-level tariff for both homes and businesses. Singapore has also forged innovative policies for expanding supply, especially through recycling and water catchment. At Changi International Airport, for example, rainwater runoff is collected from various locations for reuse: runways, associated turfed areas, and roofs of buildings; it is collected from rooftops throughout Singapore.[86]

Many of these creative policy measures owe much to the statutory-board structure through which they are articulated. That structure insulates policy from political pressures, since the boards are only indirectly accountable to the public and to politics, through their supervisory ministries. By providing competitive salaries to their employees, the boards are also sure to attract the ablest employees.

The Public Utilities Board (PUB), which has played a key role in Singapore's innovative water-security policies, was founded in May 1963 with broad original responsibilities for water, electricity, and gas. It thereafter divested electricity and gas, to focus on its most important mandate: to ensure an efficient, adequate, and sustainable water supply in Singapore. Its basic approach was to be a "price-minus strategy" of providing high-quality service while keeping costs low.[87] Since the early 2000s, following the breakdown of water-supply negotiations with Malaysia, which previously had supplied the bulk of Singapore's water, the PUB also gained more urgent and strategic responsibility for realizing water-resource independence.

The PUB has pursued water-resource independence through a "four-tap strategy" stressing local catchment, recycling, desalinization, and the systematic minimization of imports. Through these diverse measures, it manages both the supply and the demand side of the water equation. On the demand side, the PUB has stressed economical water use as well as the need to introduce a water-conservation tax, while softening the impact by invoking a user-friendly character named Water Wally to appear in campaigns encouraging Singapore residents to conserve water wherever possible.[88] The PUB has worked to encourage the public to take joint ownership of the water-resource issue through its Active, Beautiful, Clean Program, which won the 2013 Global Water Award.[89] In the course of pursuing its four-tap strategy and related public-relations efforts, the PUB has also overseen some striking innovations, particularly the introduction in 2003 of NEWater recycled from used water for both human and industrial use.[90] This can now meet up to 30 percent of the nation's current water needs.[91]

To facilitate its new strategic role as a supplier and processor of water resources vital to human livelihood, PUB responsibilities were expanded in 2001 to include sanitation, formerly under Environmental Ministry auspices. Under PUB direction, Singapore's highly focused water policies have gotten progressively greater international acclaim, including several international awards.[92] Singapore has capitalized on and amplified this acclaim by annually hosting Singapore International Water Week. It has also moved to consolidate its position in the water industry by strengthening its local research base. Backed by substantial public funding, the National University of Singapore and Nanyang Technological University were recently ranked as the world's top two academic institutions in water research.[93] Singapore's holistic water policies facilitate both foreign investment in Singapore and emergence of a competitive water-resource services export industry. That growing sector strategically and intelligently targets close to 200 cities of at least 1 million people in the developing world that are expected to need purer water and better sanitation over the coming generation. Once again, Singapore emerges as a global laboratory in the water-policy sector.

Even Singapore's efficient public authorities cannot readily carry their country's distinctive innovations to the broader world without input from the private sector, key support coming from Hyflux, a firm headed by a former nominated member of parliament, Olivia Lam. With strong government backing, Hyflux has opened two large desalination plants that since 2013 have produced a quarter of Singapore's drinking water.[94] Hyflux is also deploying its distinctive approaches to desalination, water recycling, and wastewater treatment worldwide, with operations in China, Algeria, and most recently Latin America.[95] Its Algerian project is the largest membrane-based seawater desalination plant in the world.[96]

Energy Supply

Almost like water and food, energy is also vital to human existence across the civilized world, since it provides heat, while fueling both manufacturing and transportation. And as in the case of those other vital resources, demand for energy is rising rapidly, propelled by economic growth and the emergence of high-consumption societies. With the doubling of the world's population between 1970 and 2015, for example, the number of automobiles in use globally increased fivefold.[97] And as with food and water, energy demand is also rising especially rapidly among Singapore's neighbors. Between 2004 and 2009 energy demand in China jumped 40 percent, which constitutes 63 percent of the total increase worldwide. In India it rose by 20 percent, which represents over half of the remainder.[98]

To make matters worse, the overwhelming share of incremental energy demand in the Asian giants is being met by coal. This is seriously compounding world environmental problems, particularly global warming. China is now by far the largest generator of carbon dioxide emissions on earth, accounting for 26 percent of the world's total emissions—far ahead of the United States, in second place, with 15 percent.[99] China's massive contribution to global warming is primarily due to its heavy—and expanding—use of coal.

How does Singapore's experience—its expertise and responses—speak to these deepening energy problems, especially in the developing world? In what ways does it serve as an energy laboratory for other cities, especially in the developing world?

Like the major nations of Asia, and of many European states as well, Singapore is deficient in energy, and a major energy importer—13th largest on earth.[100] Although its location on the Strait of Malacca, almost equidistant between the Persian Gulf and the major economic centers of Northeast Asia, has enabled it to become a major oil refiner, marine bunkering center, and oil transshipment port, those traits are rooted in geography, and only marginally applicable elsewhere. Yet Singapore's emerging role in liquefied natural gas (LNG) is quite distinctive, counterintuitive, and relevant to the emerging energy security and environmental challenges that confront the Asian giants as well. It is in the use and distribution of LNG that Singapore seems most clearly to be a policy laboratory for the world.

In 2013 Singapore consumed an estimated 60,359 TJ (terajoules) of natural gas—an increase of almost 52 percent since 2009.[101] Most of this gas is consumed in the electric-power sector, which was over 95 percent dependent on gas in 2015, up from 61 percent in 2003.[102] This is the most energy-efficient, cost-effective, and environmentally friendly option for Singapore, which has no nuclear power and is not geographically well suited to develop alternatives such as solar, wind, and geothermal power.

Traditionally Singapore has used piped gas from neighboring Malaysia and Indonesia, both of which have ample supplies. Continued piped-gas imports from the two countries are infeasible for Singapore over the long term, however, for a number of reasons: Malaysian and Indonesian domestic demand is rising; Singapore has experienced supply disruptions, originating in its neighbors, which it fears could affect its reputation as an efficient business base; and Singapore's own natural gas demand is rising, especially in the power sector.[103] Adding liquefied natural gas to its energy mix is thus a key element in strengthening Singapore's energy-security strategy.

In keeping with its far-sighted, long-term oriented approach, Singapore first set aside land for a gas terminal in September 1999.[104] In August 2006—seven years later—the government announced that it planned to import gas and to build its first receiving terminal to meet future energy needs, while diversifying its sources of natural gas. In March 2013 Singapore's first natural gas terminal became operational on Jurong Island. In February 2014 Prime Minister Lee Hsien Loong formally opened the terminal and announced that feasibility studies were under way regarding a second receiving terminal, which the Energy Market Authority estimates could be operational by about 2025 or 2030.[105]

Capitalizing on its sophisticated financial and commodity-trading infrastructure, Singapore is also working actively to become Asia's trading hub for LNG. Japan and Korea are much larger importers of gas, taking about half of total imports between them. Singapore plans, however, to capitalize on its geographical location, halfway to the Persian Gulf and close to Australia (another major gas exporter), and on the likelihood that China will emerge as an even larger gas customer than Japan and Korea.

Singapore's timing characteristically appears excellent, what with the changes emerging in the traditional structure of long-term gas contracts related to rising production capacity outside the Persian Gulf—in new American shale gas, Russian gas, and Australian Northwest Shelf production—and to the growth of new consumers in China and India. The geopolitical linkages between supply and demand that Russia and others have pursued make the expansion of natural gas markets even more attractive to consumers.

Non-OECD Asia is expected to nearly double its share of total world natural gas consumption, from 13 percent in 2012 to 25 percent in 2040, with China and India leading consumption.[106] From 2005 to 2014, global LNG trade increased by an average of 6 percent per annum, double the growth rate of pipeline gas trade; and Southeast Asian countries such as Indonesia became major energy importers.[107] All of these trends—both economic and geopolitical—should be favorable to the emergence of an Asian natural gas market. The major question is where it would be located.

Shanghai established a domestic spot-trading platform for natural gas in July 2012, followed by the Shanghai Petroleum and Natural Gas Exchange in July 2015.[108] With its characteristic long-term orientation, Singapore began preparing many years before that and is also developing a sophisticated ecosystem to support LNG trading, including a secondary gas trading market, which could have important transnational functions, especially within Southeast Asia. Lacking any significant players before the 2008–09 global financial crisis, Singapore now has about 30 companies with LNG gas trading or marketing desks. Several major global players, including oil majors Shell and Gazprom, as well as major financial institutions like Citibank, have set up teams in Singapore to capitalize on the surge in shipments of gas to China and India. Several of these companies have expanded their LNG desks with activities ranging from trading and marketing to origination, operations, and risk management.

On the regulatory front, Singapore's government has introduced a 5 percent concessionary corporate tax rate for LNG trading income, to help promote the development of an LNG trading hub in Singapore. This has encouraged a number of major LNG industry players to consider using Singapore's LNG terminal capacity for the storage and reloading of liquefied natural gas, both before and since terminal operations began in 2013.[109] The Singapore government's strategic combination of tax abatements and infrastructure provision, in the form of LNG terminals, is having a decisive impact on prospects for Singapore's emerging role as Asia's preeminent liquefied natural gas market, thus simultaneously enhancing both the tiny nation-state's global competitiveness and its comprehensive national security.

On the demand-management side, Singapore's Intelligent Energy System is also a veritable laboratory for energy solutions.[110] This system provides timely information to optimize and reduce energy consumption and thereby helps to manage energy needs. Smart technical adjustments, through improved estimation and control of the supply-demand equation, can help to reduce both the average price of electricity and its volatility.[111]

Conclusion

Singapore is not only a smart state adept at providing high levels of national welfare and security at minimal cost to its citizens, but also a smart city that is creating a livable urban environment featuring quality housing, home ownership, easy and efficient transport from place to place, and impressive innovations in resource management and environmental protection. Its policies address the needs of citizens at both the local and national level in notably prescient fashion, capitalizing on the latest ICT technology, including the Internet of Things.

Singapore's singular emphasis on urban development and its impressive innovations in transport, resource management, and environmental protection are clearly supported and leveraged by its unique character as a city-state with clear resource and environmental constraints of its own. These qualities and its handling of the resulting challenges make Singapore well suited to become a de facto global laboratory for pioneering approaches to urban problems. Because it is small, unambiguously urban, and holistically organized,

Singapore is able to focus on these issues more intensely and efficiently than most nation-states. Unlike larger countries such as China and Japan, it has no rural sector or complex regional interests to impede innovative urban policies. Furthermore, its institutions feature unusual coordination mechanisms, such as the EDB, and a lack of stovepiping, which makes for a broad, integrated approach to policy that is synergistic with the rapid advance of the Digital Revolution.

A historic transition from rural to urban living is now occurring across the most populous nations of the developing world—including Singapore's huge neighbors, China, India, and Indonesia. Hundreds of millions of people are leaving farms and villages for cities. Singapore's urban innovations, capitalizing on the latest technology, clearly have broad relevance beyond its shores, as the following chapters suggest.

Singapore as Smart Global Hub
CATALYST FOR IDEAS AND ACTION

If we want to be a First World oasis, we must produce
First World conditions ... then you are in the game.

LEE KUAN YEW (2011)

The preceding pages have examined a wide range of Singapore public policies, which in turn address an unusually broad range of momentous global problems. At the national level, it is clear that Singapore's smart state has pragmatic but unorthodox answers to the challenges of social welfare and economic development that both enable citizens in dealing with their personal challenges and at the same time minimize governmental costs. At the subnational level, Singapore's smart city develops and adopts approaches to transportation, housing, energy efficiency, and environmental protection, capitalizing on the Digital Revolution and Internet of Things, that provide exceptional living conditions for local citizenry.

Many of Singapore's policy approaches are, to be sure, highly creative, and relevant to the resolution of pressing global problems, including sustainable urban development and the crisis of the welfare state. They are the result, this chapter suggests, of an intense, transnational interaction among intellectual innovators overseas, often in major universities and research institutes of the advanced industrial world; multinational corporations; business and political clients in the developing world; financiers; Singaporean entrepreneurs; and government officials. In this complex yet fertile interaction, Singapore strives self-consciously to serve as a global hub, sponsoring and profiting from worldwide interactions for which it serves as platform and promoter, and thus propelling itself to advanced economic standing, avoiding the middle-income trap.

Singapore's role as a global hub has four dimensions:

—Creating *infrastructure* for global interactions: first-rate airports, communications facilities, legal services, financing, and energy supply, for example.

—Attracting *foreign investment* and foreign intellectual inflow.

—Creating and testing unorthodox yet practical ideas, capitalizing heavily on the information and communications technology revolution, as a sort of *global laboratory.*

—*Disseminating*—indeed, exporting—products and services to the broader world.[1]

Through a dynamic process of inbound flows of capital and ideas, creative synthesis within Singapore, and ultimate export to aid in the resolution of global problems, Singapore as a global hub is playing an increasingly important international role—especially in matters of urban development, where it has special comparative advantage as both city and state.

Creating Infrastructure for Global Interaction

One of Singapore's greatest potential strengths, and arguably a possible vulnerability as well, is its location. The Lion City lies astride the world's most important sea route at a critical chokepoint, within a seven-hour flying- time radius of half the population of the globe. As a smart state, Singapore naturally works to convert this geographical vulnerability into a commercial strength, by transforming itself into a transportation and logistics hub. The first requisite for that conversion is clearly infrastructure.

Singapore's seaport is the largest transshipment port in the world.[2] And since 1986 it has almost continuously been one of the two busiest container ports on earth. Singapore is the focal point for about 200 shipping lines with links to more than 600 ports in over 120 countries. The port has the ability to handle more than 2,000 containers per vessel, with a turnaround time of less than 12 hours, and it operates around the clock.[3]

Changi International Airport is likewise a high-volume, state-of-the-art facility, consistently ranked in recent years as the best or second-best airport on earth.[4] It is served by over 4,500 flights, connecting to 280 cities in 60 countries and handling close to 2 million tons of air cargo annually.[5] Together with Singapore port, Changi has made Singapore the world's busiest transshipment hub, handling about one-seventh of the entire world's container transshipment throughput.

Thanks first and foremost to its strategic location and state-of-the-art physical infrastructure, Singapore has become a formidable global logistics center, ranked recently by the World Bank as the number one logistics hub in Asia.[6] It now houses 20 of the top 25 third-party logistics companies in the world's regional or global headquarters.[7] It is also the world's largest transshipment port, as just mentioned. There are over 7,000 logistics companies in Singapore, employing over 180,000 people, or more than 9 percent of Singapore's workforce.[8] They handle everything from aircraft spare parts to petrochemicals and "cool cargo," including live seafood, meat, flowers, and pharmaceuticals.[9]

Even in the emerging era of e-commerce, Singapore appears to be holding its own as a global hub, owing to the far-sighted innovations that one would expect of a smart state. Its main postal service is currently spending US$145 million on a new e-commerce logistics center, in anticipation of a Southeast Asian e-commerce boom. The center became fully operational during 2016, with the ability to handle 100,000 packages daily.[10] The Alibaba Group, China's e-commerce giant, has already bought a minority stake in SingPost, as part of a tie-up to create an international e-commerce logistics business.[11]

It is not simply strategic location and well-designed physical infrastructure that sustain Singapore as such a formidable logistical hub. Finance, communications, and legal infrastructure, leveraged by advanced, smart infocom technology, are also crucial.[12] So is the government regulatory framework, including customs clearance. Innovations such as TradeNet 4.0, an electronic national single window that provides a one-stop platform for trade permits from 35 controlling agencies, harnesses advanced infocommunications technology, to help make import, export, and transshipment of goods the most efficient in the world.[13] That technology is thus used as a key productivity tool in the logistics sector. Analogous sector-specific IoT applications in health care, tourism, and legal services are also enhancing efficiency in those areas.[14]

A Promising Hub for Energy Trading

Infrastructure is far more than roads, bridges, and airports—that is eminently clear in the emergence of Singapore, a city-state devoid of oil and gas reserves, as a powerful global energy trading center. Singapore is located directly astride the energy sea-lanes from the Persian Gulf to Asia, through which nearly 15 million barrels of oil—approximately three-fourths of the Gulf's total exports—flow every day.[15] Over the past half century it has become the most important oil-refining center in the world, after Houston and Rotterdam. And aided by rapid growth in China and Southeast Asia, the energy flows outbound from Hormuz, eastward to the Strait of Malacca, are likely to steadily increase, for at least another two decades.[16]

Given the growing stream of transregional Asian energy flows, Singapore's central role in the global energy sector—upstream, downstream, and in mediating trade flows—is a natural one. That role has been traditional in oil and petrochemicals but is expanding into natural gas as well, especially in the liquefied natural gas sector. As liquidity rises in global gas markets, with the advent of large-scale U.S. shale gas production and the onset of American gas exports, the traditional prevalence of oil-linked long-term contracts shows prospects of eroding. Spot and futures gas markets are accordingly growing in prospective importance. And Singapore, with its deep-water harbor, thriving financial center, rule of law, new multi-user open-access natural gas terminals with reexport capability, and market-oriented regulators, has the potential to play a major role in the future.[17]

An Emerging International Financial Hub

In an important synergy with its trading and logistic capabilities, both critical dimensions of quality infrastructure, Singapore is also the leading insurance marketplace in Asia, with a transparent legal framework that bolsters its capabilities as a hub for trade finance.[18] Global macroeconomic and geopolitical trends likewise enhance its potential as a center for wealth management activities. The surplus nations of Asia, led by China and Japan, today hold more than half of global foreign-exchange reserves.[19] Singapore itself has over US$248 billion in such holdings, ranking as 10th largest holder in the world.[20] A substantial part of the remainder is held in the Middle East, with which Singapore has strong traditional ties.[21]

Although most of the emerging surplus nations lack sophisticated capital markets or the capacity to manage international funds on a global basis, Singapore is more experienced, with a more advanced financial infrastructure, including state-of-the-art Asia dollar and commodity futures markets. For many Asian, Russian, and Middle Eastern investors, it is also more attractive geopolitically and in regulatory terms than traditional Western centers such as New York, London, or even Switzerland. Operationally, Singapore has major advantages over Tokyo, because its business hours overlap with Europe, which Tokyo's do not. Although Switzerland in 2013 remained the world's top center for managing international funds, Singapore was right behind and appeared on the verge of surpassing Switzerland as a global tax crackdown and tighter regulation weakened the Swiss relative appeal to investors.[22]

Singapore has played a significant global financial role ever since the late 1960s, when the Monetary Authority of Singapore reduced local banking taxes in 1968 to compete better with Hong Kong and thus gave rise to the Asia dollar market.[23] In 1984 the Singapore International Monetary Exchange (SIMEX) was created, patterned after the Chicago Mercantile Exchange, as Asia's first financial futures market.[24] SIMEX moved rapidly into global partnerships with the Chicago Merc, opening the door to round-the-clock options trading worldwide.[25] By April 2014 average foreign-exchange volume in Singapore had reached more than $370 billion daily,[26] nearly half of North America's entire foreign exchange trading volume ($811 billion),[27] and significantly more than that of Japan,[28] which has a much larger economy than Singapore.

Attracting Global Capital and Know-how

Capital formation is unquestionably one of the most daunting and most universal challenges that any nation—advanced industrial or still developing—faces in the 21st century. Through a variety of means—including both private action and government fiat—Singapore has done a fine job of encouraging its citizens to save and has also ensured a high rate of domestic investment. Yet for a small nation with large ambitions, these measures are not enough. Attracting foreign investment plays a critical role as well.

Despite the pronounced volatility of Southeast Asia, Singapore has been highly successful in securing large-scale foreign financial commitment to its future. Direct foreign investment, which was relatively static for the first three decades after independence, has been on a steady long-term upward trajectory since the early 1990s (figure 6-1). Furthermore, it has soared since 2011 despite sharp setbacks after 9/11 and, to an even greater degree, following the Lehman shock of 2008–09. An increasing component has come from the emerging Asian giants, China and India.

Today Singapore has one of the highest inbound foreign direct investment penetrations in the world, with the net inflow reaching 22 percent of GDP in 2014, compared with 2.6 percent in China and 0.4 percent in Japan.[29] Singapore is currently host to over 7,000 foreign multinational corporations, more than half of which use the city-state as their regional and in some cases global headquarters.[30] General Motors, for example, oversees key segments of this giant firm's business in Asia-Pacific, Africa, the Middle East, and part of

Figure 6-1. *Net Direct Foreign Investment Flows into Singapore, 1970–2014*

Current US$ million (balance of payments)

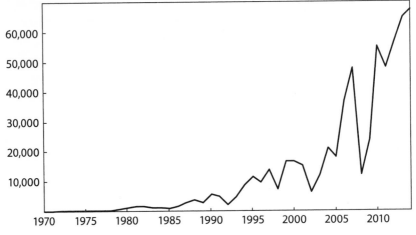

Source: World Bank, *World Development Indicators* (1970–2014) (http://data.worldbank.org/indicator/
BX.KLT.DINV.CD.WD).

Europe from Singapore, with a staff of over 120 employees.[31] In 2012 Procter
and Gamble moved the global headquarters for its beauty and baby-care business, including its biggest brand, Pampers, from the United States to Singapore[32] and in March 2014 opened a S$250 million Singapore innovation
center at Biopolis.[33] Kellogg also moved its Asia-Pacific headquarters from
Sydney to Singapore in 2013.[34]

Needless to say, the rising foreign corporate interest in Singapore has a
great deal to do with its business-friendly tax and trade policies. Singapore has
no capital-gains tax and caps corporate tax at a flat rate of 17 percent, along
with personal tax rates at 20 percent, also providing liberal abatements.[35] The
city-state has 21 free trade agreements with 32 economies and offers attractive
incentives for multinationals to relocate headquarters operations to Singapore.[36]

As was indicated in chapter 4, one key institutional pillar of Singapore's
distinctive package for inbound foreign investment has long been the Economic Development Board, founded in 1961, less than two years after Lee
Kuan Yew first took power. With a staff of fewer than 600 employees, the
EDB runs 21 offices in key global cities and flexibly negotiates with both
major established multinationals and promising start-ups in an effort to bring
them to Singapore, or to enhance their local presence there. It places a special
emphasis on drawing in regional or global headquarters units.

In order to encourage foreign investment, the EDB established the Cluster Development Fund and Co-investment Program, which co-invests with foreign multinational corporations and local enterprises in joint ventures and strategic projects.[37] This program has been especially active in the electronics area, since an EDB investment mission in the late 1960s led to an influx of U.S. multinationals engaged in semiconductor assemblies for export. The EDB also partners extensively with multinationals through co-investments in key industrial products, and in industrial training. The latter has included joint training centers to produce skilled craftsmen in tool and die making, precision machinery, computer numerical control machinery, computer-aided design and manufacturing, and advanced metrology.

Since the early 1990s, foreign investment in Singapore has begun to rise discontinuously, accelerating with particular vigor since around 2002 (see figure 6-1). Changes in the global geopolitical environment, particularly the end of the cold war, which afforded Singapore-based ventures new access to Vietnam, China, Russia, and other parts of the former East Bloc, were likely one factor that led to Singapore's unprecedented emphasis on rapidly growing high-technology, precision-equipment, and service sectors in particular. First-class infrastructure, including some of the world's best airports, ports, and communications facilities, were another big embedded plus, dating from earlier days of Singapore's modernization.

The first of the new policy arrangements of the 1990s for facilitating investment was the SIJORI Growth Triangle Partnership, proposed by First Deputy Prime Minister Goh Chok Tong in 1989 and consummated under his prime ministership in 1994.[38] This arrangement standardized and liberalized economic relations between Singapore and the adjacent Johore area of Malaysia, as well as the nearby Riau Archipelago of Indonesia, to allow flexible relocation of labor-intensive activities to those adjacent areas, with lower land and labor costs than in Singapore itself. This liberalized trading relationship, synergistic with high value added production in Singapore, was a stimulus to foreign direct investment in Singapore itself.

Creating and Testing Ideas: Singapore as Intellectual Crossroads and Laboratory

As a nation according ever greater priority to the sciences, Singapore has since the Asian financial crisis of 1997–98 systematically worked to transform itself into a center for applied, yet technologically and organizationally sophisticated research, development, and systems applications. It has, in short, sought to become a "knowledge economy" that harnesses the power of computers, telematics, and heuristic communities of researchers and officials to boost growth and economic value added.[39] Strong emphasis has thus been placed on upgrading universities and training facilities—for example, through the creation of the National Science and Technology Board (1991); A*STAR (2001); the Research, Innovation, and Enterprise Council (2006); and the National Research Council (2006). Singapore has also inaugurated research excellence programs to support strategic partnerships between major global science research institutions such as the Massachusetts Institute of Technology and Cambridge University, as well as key local players, such as the National University of Singapore.

Through these partnerships, Singapore's smart state is working to further enhance the local environment for technologically sophisticated foreign direct investment. In its typical holistic approach, it seeks to exploit linkages among various priority areas. Sectors that the National Research Foundation has emphasized and into which foreign direct investment has flowed with particular vigor include biomedical sciences, environmental and water-purification technologies, and clean energy, as well as interactive and digital media. Since 1991 total annual research and development expenditures under the five-year National Technology Plan increased nearly tenfold, from S$2 billion (1991–95) to S$19 billion (2016–20).[40]

Like Japan and Korea before it, yet in a more globalized way, Singapore has worked systematically not only to generate ideas of technical significance but also to test and to commercialize them—becoming a "living laboratory" or "test bed" focused on operationalizing real-world applications in such fields as energy efficiency, transportation, health, and sanitation. Many of its projects are holistic and interdisciplinary in nature—developing an urban planning and sustainable development niche with huge applicability in the populous surrounding nations, as their citizens move from the countryside to rapidly growing cities.[41]

Singapore's new emphasis on test-bed activities is reflected in the Biopolis and Fusionopolis science complexes at Buona Vista, in the southwestern part of Singapore Island, near National University. The government has already invested S$1,100 million in phase one of these research parks,[42] in an effort to integrate them spatially, together with a Mediapolis complex (figure 6-2), so as to promote interdisciplinary research.[43] The Biopolis configuration, involving government, academic, and corporate researchers—roughly

Figure 6-2. *Singapore's Integrated Research One-North Hub*

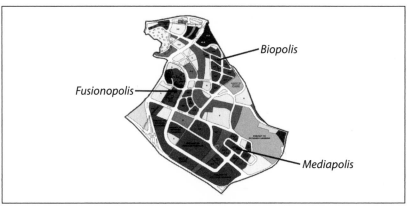

Source: Economic Development Board, *Biopolis, Fusionopolis, Mediapolis* (www.edb.gov.sg/content/
edb/en/why-singapore/ready-to-invest/setting-up/business-location/one-north.html).

half being foreign—focuses on biomedical research, especially diagnostics, and was completed in 2006. It has attracted a broad range of multinational firms, including Novartis, Danone, Abbott Labs, Procter and Gamble, and Chugai Pharmaceuticals.[44] In 2010 the Roche-Singapore Center for Translational Medicine was established to undertake research on diagnostics and pharmaceuticals,[45] and in late 2014 a new Diagnostics Development Hub was also launched there to encourage partnerships to invest in making Singapore a global leader in biomedical research and development.[46]

Fusionopolis is a parallel science park, located near Biopolis to facilitate interdisciplinary research, that specializes in infocomm technology, mass media, physical sciences, and engineering. Laboratories at Fusionopolis focus particularly on high performance computing, data storage, and microelectronics. The research park was completed in October 2008.[47] Although its research concerns center on the physical sciences, they also include the interface with medicine, including medical equipment and bioelectronics. Both Biopolis and Fusionopolis thus probe technical questions that will be increasingly fundamental in human terms to an Asia now on the verge of rapid aging.

Perhaps the most substantial development in the research field was the establishment in 2007 of the Campus for Research Excellence and Technological Enterprise (CREATE) program, for building transnational research partnerships with major universities abroad.[48] The first such enterprise—and arguably the most ambitious to date—was the Singapore-MIT Alliance for Research and Technology (SMART), which also represented MIT's first cooperative research venture overseas. The alliance has established interdisciplinary research groups in five technical areas (biosystems, environmental modeling, infectious diseases, future urban mobility, and low-energy electronic systems) where the two sides anticipate holistic technical breakthroughs of commercial and social importance.[49] Headed by senior MIT faculty members, research projects engage over 900 MIT and Singaporean participants, including faculty, postdoctoral fellows, and graduate students.

Since the alliance program was launched in 2007, Singapore has concluded 10 research partnerships with major foreign universities and polytechnic institutes. These include 2 from the United States (University of California at Berkeley and MIT), 2 from China (Peking and Shanghai Jiao Tong universities), and 3 from Israel (Hebrew and Ben-Gurion universities, as well as Technion-Israel Institute of Technology). The other 3 partners are from Britain (Cambridge), Germany (Technical University of Munich), and Switzerland (ETH, in Zurich).[50] Visiting researchers from these institutions are housed and provided laboratories at the CREATE campus in Singapore, which has received a budget allocation of S$19 billion for the 2016–20 period.[51]

In 2013 Singapore established a research facility in the nutritional field as well: the Clinical Nutrition Research Center, which is a joint initiative of the Singapore Institute for Clinical Sciences, A*STAR, and the National University Health System. The center specializes in basic and translational human nutrition research involving studies across the life cycle. Topics range from the impact of micro- and macronutrient intake on human physiology, especially in Asia, to the role of food structure in human nutrition.[52]

As a result of Singapore's strong commitment to research and development—such as a S$16 billion research and development budget (2011–15) to improve performance in science, technology, and innovation—the smart state's universities are steadily rising in regional and global academic standings.[53] For 2015–16, the National University of Singapore ranked 26th, rising from 34th in 2010–11 in the *Times Higher Education World University Rankings*, making it the highest-ranking Asian institution.[54] Meanwhile, Nanyang Technological University ranked 55th, rising from 174th for the same period, climbing 119 places, and excelled in a different evaluation by Times Higher Education that specifically looked at universities under 50 years of age, ranking 2nd in the world by that measure.[55] Singapore also hosts over 70,000 foreign students annually, although the government has begun to cap spaces for international students recently, in order to preserve more positions for local applicants.[56]

Singapore's efforts to create institutions and consortia that enhance its role as a smart global hub are leveraged by extensive conference programs. At the local level, the Urban Sustainability R&D Congress, for example, provides a platform bringing government agencies, research institutes, and private firms together to discuss urban sustainability solutions on which Singapore might focus.[57] To promote their homeland as a living laboratory, this congress was first held in 2011, as "Urban Solutions Living Lab."[58] Singapore government officials invite foreign companies at these sessions to partner with local actors on a diverse range of R&D activities leveraging Singapore's excellent public infrastructure, for test-bedding activities.

At the international level, Singapore holds a wide range of global conferences to build networks, to amass knowledge, and to showcase local achievements in its priority sectors. Three recent examples are Singapore International Water Week, Clean Enviro-Summit Singapore, and the World Cities Summit—all held in conjunction in Singapore in June 2014. The oldest of these, Singapore International Water Week, has been held in Singapore continuously since 2008 and drew more than 20,000 attendees from 133 countries in 2014.[59] The biennial World Cities Summit drew delegates from 208 cities in 64 countries to Singapore in the same year.[60] It awards a Lee Kuan Yew World City Prize that honors cities and their key leaders for achievement in fostering liveable, vibrant, and sustainable urban communities around the world.[61] The 2012 recipient of the Lee Kuan Yew Prize was New York City and its mayor Michael Bloomberg.[62] By honoring Bloomberg, a major U.S. political figure and founder of Bloomberg L.P., Singapore gained both publicity and increased attendance at its related technical conferences as well. The 2014 World City Prize winner was Suzhou, in China's Jiangsu Province, drawing substantial attention across Asia as well.[63]

Another notable conference, convened annually for a global audience since 2008, is Singapore International Energy Week. This is a week-long global platform for energy professionals, policymakers, and commentators.[64] In 2014 it attracted over 10,000 participants from 60 countries, furthering two key strategic objectives of Singapore's smart state: becoming a living laboratory and also a leading global energy hub.[65]

Exporting Solutions

In assessing the Singapore model's broader relevance, it is vital to remember that the model applies to two spheres of governance: the municipal and the national. Singapore is at once a city (with less than half the population of New York) and a nation-state (one of the 193 members of the United Nations), and it operates effectively in both spheres.

Singapore's Smart Institutions for Teaching the World

Singapore's key institutions for spreading its gospel of efficiency engage selectively with a broad range of international actors, including both nations and cities, as well as NGOs and multilateral bodies like the International Monetary Fund, World Bank, and United Nations Development Program. Singapore relies on a variety of entities to support its outreach endeavors. Some have links with government, such as the Singapore Cooperation Program (SCP); the Singapore Cooperation Enterprise (SCE); SCE's International Partnerships Team, which spearheads partnerships with intergovernmental organizations (IGOs) like the World Bank Group; and a wide variety of training programs. These programs offer bilateral training between Singapore and various developing countries (generally on a government-to-government basis), and some are third-country training programs operated with NGOs and multilateral institutions as well as national governments. Singapore thus deals at all levels with a broad range of international actors, thereby enhancing its tactical flexibility in addressing global problems.

Founded in 1992, the Singapore Cooperation Program (SCP) is a conventional overseas development assistance (ODA) program under the Ministry of Foreign Affairs that focuses on bilateral government-to-government training programs, which often also involve other international agencies.[66] It was supplemented in 2006 by the Singapore Cooperation Enterprise (SCE), a quasi-public entity that has since become one of Singapore's most important coordinators of requests to learn from the tiny yet dynamic global laboratory.[67] The SCE was a joint initiative of the Ministry of Trade and Industry and the Ministry of Foreign Affairs designed to respond effectively to, and to capitalize on, the avalanche of foreign requests to tap Singapore's development experience. SCE is commercially oriented and fee-based.[68]

Cooperation between Singapore and developing nations typically begins with SCP-managed Bilateral Technical Assistance Programs (BTAP).[69] These overseas development programs share Singapore's expertise in public governance, transportation, education, health care, urban planning, and information technology through training initiatives, and many develop into projects handled by SCE on a commercial basis. Many deal with such practical subjects as workforce development and public-sector capacity building.

Since August 31, 2012, SCE has been an integral part of International Enterprise Singapore (IES), the government agency that spearheads the overseas growth of Singapore-based companies and promotes Singapore's international trade.[70] Through the collaboration of SCP and SCE, the government has integrated its commercial attempts to promote Singapore-based firms with its more altruistic efforts to diffuse the practical philosophy of Singaporean success. The combination is unusually effective, and thus a model for the broader world, for two reasons: it mobilizes market incentives to ensure that resources are efficiently directed toward projects of genuine mutual interest and viability, and it mobilizes market incentives to ensure rapid implementation.

In the few years since its inception, SCE has worked in over 30 countries around the world, to complete more than 150 projects applying Singaporean expertise to global problems.[71] The methods have often begun with SCP-sponsored study visits to Singapore and training projects there, followed by Singaporean consulting work and implementation overseas. Commercially oriented SCE projects have been undertaken on every continent except Australia, with a special emphasis on Asia.

SCE deals with all manner of overseas organizations, on a broad range of projects. Some insight can be gained into the functional breadth and global scope of its activities through the SCE's "Our Reach" website, which provides country- and city-specific examples listing some of its past work. Following is a small sample of these endeavors:

—Indonesia: consultancy services for the preparation of water-treatment plant in Bandar Lampung for public-private partnership transaction.

—Maldives: capacity-building program for the Maldives Customs Service in the area of intellectual property rights, plant-disease regulations, and technical barriers to trade.

—Vietnam: training programs and study visits on urban planning for the Hanoi Ministry of Construction and the Ho Chi Minh City People's Committee.

—China/Jiangsu: training programs and study visits in areas of industrial-park management, environmental protection, and logistics management.

—Abu Dhabi: advisory services on public-sector human resource management and development for the Abu Dhabi Department of Civil Service, study visit for the Tourism Development and Investment Authority on topics relating to land registration, study visits on workforce development, as well as offender rehabilitation for relevant government agencies.

—Brazil: master-planning advisory services for the State of Minas Gerais.

—Oman: strategic financial advisory services for the Capital Market Authority of the Sultanate of Oman (CMA).

—Russia: study visits for senior Russian officials in areas such as tourism, investment promotion, and high technology.

—Saudi Arabia: General Investment Authority in urban planning, Student Leadership Development Program for King Abdulaziz University.

—Nigeria: training programs in urban planning and building code control for the Lagos State Ministry of Physical Planning and Urban Development.

The SCE has an International Partnership Team explicitly dedicated to spearheading interaction with IGOs and their developing-country members, so as to provide a convenient, consolidated window for access to Singapore expertise.[72] These collaborative IGOs include the Asian Development Bank, the Commonwealth Secretariat, the United Nations Development Program, and the World Bank Group. The partnership team also works closely with local philanthropic organizations in Singapore such as the Temasek Foundation to organize co-financing solutions that augment advisory services and customized training programs, so as to support knowledge transfer and capacity development for the governments of developing countries being aided.

Among the most distinctive and productive ways in which Singapore disseminates its ideas is through its so-called Third World Country Training Programs (TWCPs), sponsored primarily by SCP, as already mentioned. Several of these ODA initiatives are partnered with individual countries, mainly in the industrialized world, notably Australia, Canada, France, Germany, Japan, South Korea, Luxembourg, New Zealand, Norway, Thailand, and the Vatican. Singapore also teams up with a broad variety of IGOs and NGOs, including the Asian Development Bank, the Colombo Plan, the Commonwealth Secretariat, UN Economic and Social Commission for Asia and the Pacific, the International Atomic Energy Agency, the International Civil Aviation Organization, UNICEF, and UNDP.[73]

Exporting Goods and Services Back to the Broader World

Although investment from abroad—both capital and technology—is crucial in building the sinews of competitiveness, exports of goods and services are the bottom line. At that game, as in attracting inbound investment, Singapore has been succeeding dramatically. Ever since the late 1970s—around the time of the second oil shock—Singapore's exports have been steadily rising, and today they total around US$600 billion annually (figure 6-3).

Figure 6-3. *Singapore's Rising Exports of Goods and Services, 1972–2014*

Current US$ million (balance of payments)

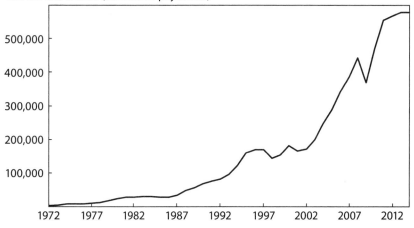

Source: World Bank, *World Development Indicators* (1972–2014) (http://data.worldbank.org/indicator/
BX.GSR.GNFS.CD).

Singapore's highly dynamic export profile is closely related to the similarly dynamic pattern of foreign investment. Not surprisingly, the role of top-ranking global multinational firms actually investing in Singapore is overwhelmingly important in Singapore's export portfolio as well. Its many regional and bilateral free trade agreements provide a policy backdrop that encourages exports, as will trans-Pacific trade liberalization also.[74]

Exports of goods (75 percent of total exports in 2014)[75] have historically centered on the production of hydrocarbon-related products, capitalizing on Singapore's position as the third-largest oil-refining center in the world after Rotterdam and Houston.[76] Today refined oil products constitute roughly a quarter of Singapore's goods exports, with chemical products providing an additional 13 percent.[77] Interestingly, however, Singapore has diversified substantially away from its entrepôt role as a raw-material processor; today machinery and equipment, most of it high-tech products such as medical equipment and aircraft components, make up nearly twice the share of goods exports that refined oil products do. Significantly, over two-thirds of Singapore's machinery exports are "re-exports," meaning goods fabricated elsewhere, with proprietary overall high-tech elements added in Singapore itself.[78]

Land, of course, is a significant constraint on manufacturing in crowded Singapore, but the island finesses this problem in two ways: by reclaiming land from the sea for industrial sites and by decentralizing economic activity away from central areas. Singapore's most prominent industrial zone, the Jurong Industrial Estate, for example, was built on reclaimed land at the far west of the island, with workers' housing attached, and connected with the urban center of Singapore by well-planned expressways and light rail.[79]

Services, which account for 25 percent of Singapore's total exports, are an even more dynamic element of Singapore's export picture than high-tech manufactures, particularly over the past decade. The largest portion—close to half—is in transport (33.8 percent) and travel (12 percent), capitalizing on Singapore's strategic location as well as the fine port and airport facilities that have emerged as a consequence. The next largest shares—and the fastest growing of late—are in financial (14.5 percent) and related business services.[80] Flowing from its deeply ingrained holistic conception of political-economic affairs, Singapore has developed a formidable capacity in facilities management—of everything from ports and airports to hotels—that is bringing it increasing returns worldwide. It is no accident that the Sochi, Russia International Airport,[81] the Gwadar Port in Pakistan,[82] and the Burj Al Arab Jumeirah five-star hotel in the United Arab Emirates, are all currently, or have recently been, in part managed by Singaporeans and represent one powerful variant of Singapore service exports.[83]

Singapore and E-Government Abroad

A basic pillar of minimalist government in Singapore, as discussed in chapter 4, is the use of computer technology to maximize efficiency and transparency while economizing on labor costs. E-government builds on the formidable reality that, owing to far-sighted government infrastructural policies of the past two decades, 90 percent of Singaporean homes now have broadband. Thanks to e-government systems like Singapore Personal Access (SingPass), Singaporeans need only one password to access hundreds of online services provided by over 60 government agencies. Indeed, they can do everything from borrowing books from the National Library to filing their taxes and applying for passports online, making queues in government offices virtually unnecessary, except to pick up processed official documents.[84] Singapore has been widely recognized in the e-government area, from the United Nations as well as from academia, and is actively spreading its insights around the world.[85]

Among the most forceful vehicles for global dissemination is Crimson Logic, a government-linked Singapore enterprise that now engages projects in over 30 countries.[86] Crimson Logic provides end-to-end e-government solutions, drawing on Singapore's own domestic experience, and is marketing actively around the world on such matters as trade facilitation, judiciary, tax, health care, and information technology security. In 2013, for example, it introduced an integrated electronic customs management system in Oman; in 2013 its work in Trinidad and Tobago—half a world away—also won the United Nations Public Service award for "Promoting a Whole of Government Approach in the Information Age." In May 2014 it launched the Kenya Electronic Single-Window System, its first major project in Kenya, and its 18th live trade-facilitation project worldwide. In July 2015 Crimson Logic partnered with the Rwanda Development Board to jointly launch the Rwanda Technology Association Program.[87]

Singapore's Model and the Cities of the World

Three centuries ago, as the Industrial Revolution gained force in the Western world, humankind began embarking on a great transformation—from feudal, largely rural society to a much more urban and socially integrated variant.[88] Although largely completed in the affluent industrial nations, that transformation is still continuing in the developing world; 52.5 percent of Asia's massive population, for example, still remains rural.[89] By 2050 urbanization and natural population increase will add 2.4 billion people to the cities of the world—more than 650 million in India and China alone—putting enormous strains on transportation, energy supply, and sanitation.[90]

Singapore's experience thus speaks clearly to the cities of the world, especially those that must transform or re-create themselves to meet the immense new demands imposed by urbanization. Dealing with these issues is at one level a technical question, where policy dialogues linking Singapore with municipal counterparts elsewhere is central. Because of the importance of smooth adjustment to looming urban problems for broader social peace, however—transport, energy supply, sanitation, and environmental quality, to name a few—national governments also necessarily take an interest in Singapore's model, encouraging both their cities and their social-affairs ministries to engage with it. This imperative is especially strong in large developing nations with complex and massive urban transformations under way domestically, such as China, India, and Indonesia.

Singapore's Urban Management System and the Broader World

As mentioned earlier in this volume, Singapore's diminutive scale as a political unit creates not only considerable economic and social challenges but also some unique opportunities. Many of these opportunities lie in the area of urban planning, especially in promoting Singapore's unique approaches to urban issues on the international stage in a more dynamic and versatile way than either nations or cities can normally do.

Singapore's dual character as a city and a nation aids it in responding quickly and creatively to emerging urban challenges, because national and local governments are, after all, closely aligned there and can readily support one another. The national government is acutely conscious of urban problems—in contrast to the situation in many nations with politically dominant rural sectors, such as Japan. This facilitates rapid policy response, in tandem with readily available budgets and relatively simple policy implementation owing to the city-state's compact scale.

Singapore's unique dual character proves useful in the international dimensions of urban policy as well. Singapore can participate in United Nations urban programs as a nation-state. It can also involve itself flexibly in the C-40 network of global mayors. It can likewise engage with national leaders in Beijing, as Lee Kuan Yew did so smoothly in organizing the city-level Suzhou urban special economic zone project during the early 1990s.[91]

Singapore's diminutive size as a nation has aided it particularly in dealing with the People's Republic of China. Less geopolitically challenging to China than a larger nation, Singapore is able to bring its neo-Confucian cultural sensitivities and organizational strengths to come flexibly into play without geopolitical constraints. At the same time, it can deal easily with cities and provinces across China, including Taiwan. Indeed, it has interacted with local authorities across the developing world in the guise of a peer community that has found technologically and organizationally unique answers to common problems. Between 2014 and 2040, the number of cities the size of Singapore is expected to grow by nearly 50 percent, with such cities housing over 400 million people by the end of that period.[92] Singapore will have unique technical capabilities to aid in the building of those cities.

A particularly striking feature of Singapore's dual character is its ability to deal flexibly with ambiguous international situations. Singapore's PSA International, for example, administered the politically ambiguous, strategically important Gwadar port in Pakistan, located less than 400 miles from the Strait of Hormuz and built in cooperation with China. The PSA also undertook projects in Vietnam during the early 1990s, just as the U.S. embargo was ending. And it has dealt flexibly with Taiwan, especially at the city-to-city or city-to-province level.

The multifaceted Singapore urban-planning model is, of course, more relevant to some countries than to others. Its holistic, integrated, and somewhat technocratic approach presumes the existence of a stable political environment and a cohesive bureaucracy, which is not the case in much of Africa, Latin America, and the Middle East. The model appears much more relevant to the cities of China, Vietnam, and to a lesser extent India than to locales further afield. Major cities in those large nations, such as Shanghai and Mumbai, are also developing their own expertise in public transportation, land-use management, and urban planning. This potential competition makes Singapore's standing as an urban-planning model for others uncertain, unless it continues to ceaselessly innovate, as Prime Minister Lee Hsien Loong, among others, has continually stressed.[93] In Singapore the perpetual revolution in land use and urban planning thus continues, driven by continuing apprehensions about the future.[94] To all indications, that ongoing transformation in urban policy is proceeding constructively, although the future is always uncertain.[95]

In its commitment to ongoing innovation in urban matters, Singapore appreciates the importance of global best-practice search mechanisms, as well as systematic transnational cooperation. In this sense, it is well suited to become a diminutive laboratory for the broader world, as illustrated by its future-oriented urban transport programs. The most far-reaching endeavor of this kind, the Singapore-MIT Alliance for Research and Technology, was founded in 2007, to explore future urban mobility systems, their sustainability, and implications for societal well-being.[96] Once developed, the new concepts will be prime prospects for application throughout the rapidly growing urban centers of Southeast Asia, China, and India, which lie in close proximity to Singapore and are experiencing serious and deepening energy, transport, land-use, and environmental challenges.

Urban Learning from Singapore in China

Without doubt the most globally consequential flow of Singapore expertise is currently, and for over three decades has been, toward China. Strong relationships of trust were established between Lee Kuan Yew and Deng Xiaoping during Deng's October 1978 visit to Singapore, on the very eve of the Four Modernizations.[97] And those ties have only deepened and strengthened in the succeeding years. They have involved top Chinese leaders such as Wen Jiabao and recently Xi Jinping in a major way, and they have provided the basis for Singapore's deep working-level support over the years for China's epic transformation.

The long-term logic of Sino-Singaporean cooperation is clear, even beyond the strong network of leadership ties. China's historic transformation from rural to urban society is a massive, complex, and politically delicate transformation that could easily destabilize China, and no doubt broader patterns of international affairs, if it is not undertaken sensitively and efficiently. Singapore, for its part, has distinctive technical expertise, creativity, and ability to mobilize intellectual resources worldwide that strongly complement China's massive urban challenges and could hold the key to smoothly resolving them. To strengthen the rationale for such cooperation still further, Singapore is culturally congenial with China, while presenting little geopolitical threat.

Currently the Singapore Cooperation Enterprise (SCE) operates 24 projects in China, many of which have a counterpart in Chinese local government.[98] The majority of these projects involve study visits to Singapore by local officials from throughout China, frequently also including training programs for such bureaucrats in Singapore. Several projects also involve actual undertakings on the ground in China, in areas such as urban development, greenery, environmental protection, energy conservation, public housing, and transport. Many likewise involve industrial-park management.

One variety of cooperation that illustrates the pervasiveness of Singapore's expertise at the grass roots in China is microcredit. Fullerton Financial Holdings, a subsidiary of Singapore's asset-management fund Temasek, has partnered since 2009 with the Bank of China to set up village banks in rural areas that enable small businesses and lower-income families to pursue business opportunities that better their lives.[99] It now operates over 50 village banks in 10 provinces, serving more than 300,000 customers, financing modern greenhouses, microloans to help retirees start up small businesses, and other such activities. Fullerton is also offering financial solutions based on Singapore expertise to the rural poor in both India and Indonesia.[100]

Complementing these diversified study and technical assistance programs are major demonstration projects on the ground in China (figure 6-4). Four, in particular, are in advanced stages of development and thus provide considerable insight into how Singapore actually transfers expertise from its domestic urban policy laboratory to China. These projects are substantively important not only in supporting China's economic development but also in addressing the energy and environmental challenges that are casting a deepening shadow over China's urban future.

China-Singapore Suzhou Industrial Park. Founded in 1994, this is the largest cooperation project between China and the Singapore government, as

Figure 6-4. *The Evolving Pattern of Singapore Cooperation Projects in China*

Internet of Things
Chongqing Connectivity
Initiative
Starting year: 2015
Under planning

*Knowledge-based
economy oriented*
Guangzhou Knowledge City
Total area: 123 km²
Starting year: 2010

*Eco-urban
development*
Tianjin Eco City
Total area: 31.23 km²
Starting year: 2008

Manufacturing oriented
Suzhou Industrial Park
Total area: 80 km²
Starting year: 1994

Source: Created by author.

well as the oldest one.[101] Located physically near Jinji Lake, to the east of Suzhou's old city, the park covers 80 square kilometers, with a planned residential population of 1.2 million. Although initiated by Singaporeans, it also incorporates investment by a variety of Fortune 500 multinationals such as Samsung, UPS, and Motorola.

The Suzhou Industrial Park is configured to encourage innovation and entrepreneurship, while attracting high-tech industries. Software-focused information technology, as well as biotechnology, is the sector-specific concern. The park's major shareholders include a Chinese consortium, which holds 52 percent of the project, and a Singaporean consortium holding 28 percent, with the balance in the hands of various multinational firms.

Sino-Singapore Tianjin Eco-City. This project was first proposed by Singapore senior minister Goh Chok Tong to Chinese prime minister Wen Jiabao in April 2007 and finalized with Goh's successor, Lee Hsien Loong, seven months later.[102] The second major Sino-Singapore cooperation project following Suzhou, the Tianjin venture is intended to pool the expertise and experience of Singapore and China in urban planning and sustainable development. The objective is to create, over a 10- to 15-year implementation period, a socially harmonious, environmentally friendly, and resource-efficient city for a population of 350,000 people. In this respect, the project is intended to serve as a practical model for sustainable development elsewhere in China. Unlike the Suzhou Industrial Park, this Tianjin project is operated on a commercial basis, by the private sector. This organizational profile helps to ensure that it is a practical, commercially viable project that can be replicated elsewhere in China. Suzhou, Guangzhou, and several cities in Sichuan Province have already begun to emulate it.

Sino-Singapore Guangzhou Knowledge City (SSGKC) Project. This project originated in a September 2008 meeting between Guangdong party secretary Wang Yang and Singapore prime minister Lee Hsien Loong.[103] The project broke ground in June 2010, and a joint-venture agreement was signed five months later. By late 2011 major European firms such as ABB, Philips, and Siemens had been brought on board through memos of understanding. Groundbreaking of the Ascendas OneHub GKC, the Knowledge City's first integrated business park, took place in March 2012, with Nanyang Technological University of Singapore and the University of Warwick in the United Kingdom becoming involved in November 2012 and March 2014, respectively.

Following on from the cooperation established under the Suzhou and Tianjin ventures, this rapidly evolving project in southern China aims to create a sustainable city that is attractive to individuals as well as knowledge-intensive industries. It thus serves as a model and a catalyst for Guangdong's economic advance up the value chain from labor-intensive export industry. The project prioritizes six pillar industries: next-generation information and communications technology, biotechnology and pharmaceuticals, clean technology, next-generation materials, culture and creative industries, and science and education services. Like Singapore itself, the Guangzhou project is also developing what both describe as its Headquarters Economy capabilities.[104]

The Guangzhou Knowledge City is located on a site covering 123 square kilometers, about 35 kilometers from Guangdong's provincial capital, and is expected to ultimately house a population of 500,000.[105] Like the Tianjin project, it is commercially based and organized by a 50–50 joint venture company, the Sino-Singapore Guangzhou Knowledge City Investment and Development Company, Ltd. On the Singapore side, the major partner is an affiliate of the powerful Temasek Holdings, and on the Chinese side an affiliate of the Guangzhou Development District.[106]

The Chongqing Connectivity Initiative (CCI). This ambitious new Sino-Singaporean project arises from the Chongqing Municipal Government's September 2012 cooperation agreement with China Mobile to jointly build an Internet of Things industrial base in Chongqing.[107] This was followed in 2014 by plans for the development of 10 strategic emerging industries related to IoT. The project was then launched in November 2015, when Xi Jinping first visited Singapore as president of China.[108]

Chongqing is an especially auspicious location for Sino-Singaporean cooperation for three reasons. Most significant from a logistical perspective, it lies at the confluence of two important rivers, one being the Yangtze, in a heavily populated area in the heart of China, where water, air, and land routes—and their efficient interconnections—play a vital role. With its focus on efficient logistics, the project also has great bearing on the explosive growth of southwestern China—much higher than the national average—and would complement the rapidly developing international transportation linkages across the Eurasian continent.[109] Because Chongqing is one of four municipalities under the direct administration of the Chinese central government, the project will also facilitate the transfer of lessons learned there across China as a whole.

The Chongqing Connectivity Initiative focuses on promoting modern connectivity and services—precisely the core of Singapore's own technologically driven expertise—in order to address the strategic need of a water, rail, and land-transport connecting point located in the heart of both China and Eurasia, as Chongqing happens to be. The initiative has identified four areas of priority: finance, telecommunications, aviation, and logistics.[110] Its first joint implementation committee meeting took place on January 8, 2016; three days later, 11 deals were signed with Singapore business with a total investment value of over US$6.5 billion.[111]

Collaboration between Chongqing and Singapore since late 2015 has concentrated on two of the priority areas: logistics and finance. A project to reduce the logistics cost of the Chongqing-Xinjiang-Europe railway by 60 percent, relative to airfreight, began in April 2016 with a plan for 50 logistically facilitated cargo trips during 2016, to be increased to 100 in 2017.[112] Meanwhile, a finance agreement reached by China and Singapore would increase capital-market connectivity by extending to Chongqing Municipality the same cross-border renminbi initiatives that currently exist with respect to the Sino-Singapore joint projects in Suzhou and Tianjin.[113] These projects are only the beginning of a far-sighted initiative deploying the info-technology skills of Singapore's smart city-state to accelerate both Chinese economic growth and the emergence of a new Eurasian continentalism.

Korean Emulation of Singapore

Like China, South Korea has been paying close attention to Singapore's successes of late, across a broad range of policy spheres. As a developed economy, with a strong industrial base of its own already, Korea has been primarily interested in Singapore's innovations and successes in services, including even casinos, and in infrastructure development, especially ports and airports. However, it has also watched with interest Singapore's development of industrial parks and "knowledge cities" in China, where Korea may hope to compete in supporting China's economic development. Many Koreans also find Singapore's "balanced diplomacy"—the ability to stay on good terms with both the United States and China simultaneously—to be of interest.[114]

The clearest case so far of Korea emulating Singapore is in the development of a high value added port industry so as to energize national economic progress. Having the largest transshipment port in the world, with 85 percent of its total cargo volume in that category, Singapore is clearly recognized in Korea as the best benchmarking target for Busan Port, Korea's largest. To that end, Busan Port Authority in October 2013 established a Singapore research group, known as Singhouse, to examine just how the Port of Singapore operates, and how those lessons can inform Busan's own efforts to become a world-class port-logistics city.[115]

The Korean government is also closely following Singaporean local-level cooperation projects in China, in an effort to develop effective Sino-Korean business models and lines of strategic direction. In 2012, for example, the government-owned Korea Land and Housing Corporation did a detailed study of five cooperative city-level industrial projects in China. Three of them (the three described in the preceding section) were Singaporean, suggesting Singapore's prominent role in supporting industrial development within China.[116]

Singapore's Cross-Regional Cachet

Global surveys, such as those of the World Bank and the World Economic Forum, rank Singapore very highly on their various measures. But to what degree do actual foreign decisionmakers far from Singaporean shores, and with different cultural proclivities, actually reference and emulate its practices in the real world?

India

Singapore's bilateral policy experience with India has not been as extensive as it has with China, although the Singaporean model is gaining increasing traction there. A number of projects in India thus far are enterprises with IGOs like the Asian Development Bank, in further partnership with the powerful Temasek Foundation, which supports training programs based on the Singapore model.[117] Singapore has, for example, as a lead partner helped to build the $250 million International Technology Park Bangalore, together with the Karnataka Industrial Areas Development Board.[118] It has also undertaken a major project on urban management with the government of Kerala, engaged in sewage wastewater planning and public-private partnership capabilities with the Delhi Jal Board, and has explored wastewater recycling options for the Bangalore Water Supply and Sewage Board, to name a few examples.[119]

India's Ministry for Urban Development has also been actively exploring the relevance for Indian cities of Singapore's model of long-term, 30- to 50-year development planning. Indian cities typically use shorter, 10- to 20-year time horizons. The ministry has also stressed the relevance of Singapore's strategic urban-planning model for the emergence of new cities, and the systematic development of suburban areas around such urban configurations.[120] Most recently, Singapore has been planning the development of Amaravathi, the new capital of Andhra Pradesh.[121]

In December 2014 International Enterprise Singapore signed a memorandum of understanding for master-planning Amaravathi and its surrounding region, based on smart-city holistic concepts that simultaneously promote sustainability in the economic, environmental, and social dimensions. The master plan includes provisions for water and road networks, bus rapid transit capable of being upgraded to a mass-transit network, and also for the institutional capacity for training government officials.[122]

The advent in 2014 of the Modi administration in India enhanced prospects for diffusing Singapore urban-planning expertise to South Asia. Modi's ambitious plan to create 100 smart cities, beginning with Amaravathi, obviously created major new cooperation prospects, building on Singapore's state-of-the-art expertise in information management, land-use planning, transportation policy, skills development, and housing.[123] Port management and infrastructure development were other areas in which the Singapore model held considerable relevance for India, as diplomats and technocrats in both countries recognized.[124]

Singapore's relevance for India pertains not only to the challenge of urbanization. Paradoxically, Singapore also provides paradigms for rural development, as noted earlier. One important reference point in this regard is microcredit, where Fullerton Financial Holdings, a subsidiary of the Singapore sovereign wealth fund Temasek, has over 400 branches to dispense small-scale loans in the Indian countryside.

Russia and Its "Near Abroad"

A bit further afield, Singapore has been increasingly active in spreading its apolitical management and systems-engineering expertise within the former Soviet Union. Jurong International, for example, is developing and managing a special economic zone at Pskov, in the vicinity of St. Petersburg.[125] Recall, too, that Changi Airports International helped build and provide management expertise for Sochi International Airport, opened just before the 2014 Sochi Olympics. And since 2013 Singapore IE, a statutory board under the Ministry of Trade, has been coordinating architectural design, urban mobility transport, and smart-city solutions for a special economic zone (SEZ) in Innopolis, one of Russia's newest techno-parks, in the Tatarstan-Volga region of Russia.

Singapore government-linked firms are also active in Kazakhstan, which has recently established 10 SEZs. Jurong Consultants, a unit of state-owned JTC, has been engaged since 2013 in devising a strategic plan for SEZ development. Jurong will also ultimately coordinate the management of these Kazakh SEZs and simultaneously work to attract investors.[126]

Central Africa

Even more striking answers to the question of Singapore's global relevance can be found in Rwanda, in the heart of Africa, more than 5,000 miles from Singapore. Rwanda has had virtually no previous cultural or political-economic contact with Singapore, yet has most enthusiastically adopted the Singapore model.

Two decades ago, Rwanda was wracked by one of the bloodiest civil wars in recent world history. During 1994 over 800,000 people were killed in what can only be described as a three-month rampage of genocidal massacre, exterminating one-tenth of the entire national population. The bloody conflict was finally ended by Paul Kagame, a guerilla leader who seized power amid the chaos. He has led Rwanda, formally or informally, ever since, serving as president since 2000.[127]

Rwanda, with a population of over 12 million people in a country the size of Maryland, is one of the most densely populated nations in Africa.[128] It is also among the world's poorest, ranking 154 out of 170 countries, with a per capita GDP of only US$690.[129] To compound its difficulties, Rwanda is landlocked, with no major domestic raw-material endowments to speak of.

Paul Kagame has long been famously ambitious for his country, and hyper-active in seeking solutions around the world to his country's clearly pressing developmental challenges. Early in his tenure, Kagame enlisted the support of Bill Clinton and Tony Blair, leaders of their respective nations at the time of the ghastly genocide, and hence apparently felt special responsibility for supporting Rwanda's revival.[130] Despite his formidable overseas backing, Kag-ame initially lacked a concrete and persuasive model to guide the economic development that he so fervently desired for his tragically wounded country.

An obsessive policy wonk with a reflective bent, Kagame visited Singapore in 2007 to study how the city-state had transformed itself from a regional trading post into a global business capital.[131] He was especially intrigued with how the Lion City had found a pathway to rapid growth without extensive natural resources. In its lack of a raw-material base, Kagame saw strong par-allels to his native land. While in Singapore, Kagame visited the Economic Policy Board and was impressed with its "one-stop shopping" approach to attracting international investors and to orchestrating economic development more generally.

Returning to Rwanda, Kagame became an outspoken advocate of the Sin-gapore model of economic development. As he noted at a recent business gathering in Kigali, his nation's capital, "What God gave to Singapore is what has been given to all of us. . . . We are not seeking to become Singapore, but we can be like Singapore."[132] Apart from demonstrating a pronounced enthusiasm for Singapore's general approach, he has emulated several specific Singaporean institutions and strategic priorities.

Most striking institutionally has been Kagame's adoption of Singapore's Economic Development Board concept. In 2008, the year after the study trip to Singapore that left such a strong impression, he established the Rwanda Development Board, a single "go-to" agency for local development, whose organizational structure and modus operandi closely parallel its Singapor-ean antecedent.[133] Rwanda's EDB receives hands-on advisory support from its Singaporean counterpart, as well as the World Bank and the private office of former British prime minister Tony Blair. Like the Singaporean EDB in its early days, when it had been strongly supported by Lee Kwan Yew, Rwanda's own Development Board builds astutely on the formal global network of its national leader.[134] Kagame's Presidential Advisory Council, working closely with the Development Board, meets once annually in Kigali and once in New York City and includes an impressive range of international personalities, ranging from Harvard Business School strategist Michael Porter to the evangelist Rick Warren.[135]

Kagame has also adopted the strategic focus of Singapore on service industries, as epitomized in his Vision 2020 program, developed explicitly with Singaporean input. Furthermore, Kagame has emulated Singapore's tactics of using advanced telecommunications and global financial tools—smart capabilities—to neutralize the "tyranny of distance" and to link a geographically remote nation to the core of the advanced industrial world. To this end, Rwanda has laid over 2,300 kilometers of fiber-optic cable domestically, encouraged the acquisition of cell phones, and promoted the expansion of online services, such as one allowing rural farmers to check crop prices on their cell phones. Around ten percent of the Rwandan population is now connected to the Internet.[136]

Creating an information society capable of becoming a regional communications hub requires, of course, a strong focus on technical education. Kagame's Rwanda has also drawn that lesson from the Singaporeans. At the president's instigation, Rwanda has introduced a "one-laptop, one-child" policy in rural schools and is intensively encouraging elementary and secondary students to become computer literate.[137]

At a more advanced level, Rwanda has persuaded Carnegie Mellon University to establish a master's program in technical services in Kigali—the first of its kind in Africa.[138] Intent on promoting tourism and international education, Kagame in 2009 prioritized English as the sole language of education in Rwanda, from the fourth grade of elementary school on.[139] Once again, this parallels the use of English as a means of transcending local ethnic differences that has been employed in Singapore.

Further evidence of Kagame's emulation of Singaporean principles comes in his approach to foreign investment, corruption, and the rule of law.[140] As in Singapore, Rwanda under Kagame is absolutely intolerant of corruption, which is remarkably limited for an African nation. To attract foreign investment, Kagame has streamlined authorization processes through "one-stop shopping" at the Rwanda Development Board and insisted that the rule of law prevail.

In response to these innovations, Rwanda has seen a surge of foreign investment, as well as inbound foreign lending. Together, these capital flows helped propel growth to 8 percent a year between 2004 and 2010.[141] Tourism has, since 2011, become the dominant foreign-exchange earner and helped to support rapid growth as well. Thousands of miles from Singapore itself, Rwanda's systematic emulation of the Singapore model over the past decade has thus brought increased economic prosperity to the heart of Africa, and growing credibility to the smart model that Singapore itself presents to the broader world.

Relevance throughout the Developing World

Singapore's model, a multifaceted policy laboratory, shows prospective relevance far in the developing world beyond Rwanda and Singapore's Asian neighbors. Its extraordinary successes in desalination are of direct interest in the Middle East and North Africa. Its waste-recycling and waste-treatment practices have resonance in both sub-Sarahan Africa and in Latin America. And its infrastructure construction and management expertise—for ports, airports, railroads, pipelines, and even hotels—has relevance everywhere in the world.

In Sum: A Global Laboratory?

For a post–cold war world in the throes of socioeconomic transition, the immediate, life-and-death challenges of development are daunting in every sector of society: transportation; energy, food, and water supply; and personal security, to name a few. On top of these, the twin challenges of making development sustainable from an environmental point of view while rendering it acceptable to the citizenry from a political point of view are likewise pressing, especially in the huge, teeming nations of the Eurasian continent, such as India and China. The ability of these giants to achieve stable transition is a matter of great consequence to the entire world.

Although a tiny city-state, with a population less than 1/200th that of China and only slightly larger as a share of India's population, Singapore has shrewdly transformed itself from a labor-intensive to a knowledge-intensive economy, in which research and development projects, innovative technology, and transnational interaction play a major role. Singapore has been remarkably innovative in dealing domestically with problems of great global consequence, particularly for the developing world, capitalizing on the Digital Revolution and the Internet of Things. Within the past decade, it has begun to systematically engage the world, and thereby to export its expertise in such areas as smart-city development, transportation, infrastructure, and e-government.

Singapore has engaged the world, in the first instance, through training programs—often provided on a concessionary basis to developing nations, as a form of foreign aid. Thereafter it has typically moved to advisory services on a commercial basis, often through government-linked companies with sophisticated info-com capacities, such as Crimson Logic and PSA International. Through its interactive development assistance to the nations of Asia, Africa, the Middle East, and Latin America, and beyond, sharing its manifold policy successes, smart Singapore is fueling the fires of innovation around the world and thus playing a critical role in easing the epic global socioeconomic transition from rural to urban that is now unfolding, while simultaneously making economic growth more sustainable for citizens throughout the world.

7
Conclusion
SINGAPORE'S POLICY LABORATORY
AND THE GLOBAL FUTURE

We take the future for granted only at our peril.

—LEE KUAN YEW (1955)

As a city that is also a nation, in a world where the challenges of governance are growing ever more complex, Singapore is at once an anomalous outlier and a potentially evocative paradigm. It is atypical, yet also a model whose highly distinctive policies could help resolve some of humankind's most acute and vexing social security challenges. Small though it is, Singapore appears destined to serve as a policy-design laboratory for some of the largest nations and the most gargantuan problems on earth.

Singapore bears particularly close examination because its sustainable state and urban policy model, leveraged by the Digital Revolution and the Internet of Things, provides such a fresh and apt perspective on governance in today's world. It shows how to tackle challenges of transnational importance in a world where markets are almost completely globalized, but governance is not. As Singapore is an economically advanced and technically sophisticated city-state, in the heart of the developing world, its example is not only timely but also broadly relevant. It provides insights for dealing with both G-7 welfare-state crises and also the epic rural-to-urban transition under way in the developing world, in an era of historic technological change.

In reviewing the intellectual journey of the preceding chapters, it is important to recall the key research questions with which it began. The general concern has been why Singapore, across the half century of its independence,

163

has proved so successful. More specifically, how—despite vulnerabilities and constraints—has this diminutive city-state managed to remain competitive in a rapidly changing global economy, while providing sustainable social protection and also building a livable urban environment? The answers to these puzzling questions lie in the nature of Singaporean governance—particularly in the island's distinctive institutions and policies.

In simple terms, Singapore has been successful because it has been smart in a dual sense: it has been pragmatic and also technologically empowered in the same way that a smart grid or a smart bomb is thought to be. Singapore policymaking has become smart—at the level of state, city, and global hub—because it has learned to perceive and respond effectively to both domestic and foreign challenges. Its state is smart because it is both minimalist and enabling; it is smart as a city also, owing to its integrated and holistic approach to urban problems, summoning innovative technology together with the wisdom and efficiency of its leaders to address them.

Some would also characterize the Singaporean smart state as amoral, or even immoral, especially in its treatment of guest workers and dissenters. The guest workers, in particular, form a major segment of Singaporean society—more than a third of the labor force—yet have lowly pay with few rights and privileges. The dissenters are much fewer but are inhibited in ways that are said to blunt their vital function of aiding social self-correction.

Singaporean smart-state architects would reply that they have had little choice in their mode of public configuration. Historically, their nation was born in a tough time in a tough neighborhood—amid the Vietnam War, enduring ethnic disorder, Britain's withdrawal from east of Suez, and two oil shocks in its first few years of statehood. Geo-economically, theirs is a nation devoid of both resources and manpower, in a region with a surplus of both. Only by selectively importing and employing under tight controls, in strategic yet transitory fashion, can they maintain autonomy while enhancing productivity. Singapore, the city-state's architects argue, has had no choice.

To answer the central research questions of how and why this distinctive sort of political economy has emerged and prospered in its volatile, competitive corner of the world, this book has explored subquestions that ultimately became chapters in their own right. Chapter 2 considered what prompted Singapore to strive so persistently to become smart, in the sense of being pragmatically responsive, and to retain that orientation even when other nations, such as Japan and many European states, began to lose their sensitivity to external challenge. Chapter 3 explored chronologically how smart capabilities emerged in Singapore and were strengthened, in both their human and technological dimensions, while leadership supported that capacity enhancement. Chapters 4 and 5 considered the operation of smart capabilities at the state and city level, respectively, in Singapore, while chapter 6 showed how Singapore has capitalized on globalization by nurturing transnational smart hubs on its own soil. These pages have shown, in short, how smart institutions emerged in Singapore, how they function, and what the implications are for the city-state's broader relations with the world.

Concrete Discoveries

Much about Singapore's governance applies concretely and practically to the broader world, especially to the 40 percent of humanity within 3,000 miles of its narrow confines that still has large segments struggling to emerge from poverty. Singapore has designed and implemented global best practices in a broad range of areas: traffic management, energy efficiency, water policy, public housing, microcredit, and ethnic relations, just to name a few. These innovative practices, many leveraged by information and communications technology, make substantial contributions in addressing some of the world's most pressing human-security challenges—global warming, energy overconsumption, and racial conflict among them. And Singapore's innovations make those contributions at a variety of levels, in transforming personal and municipal incentives while motivating entire nations to innovate as well.

One of the most important findings here must doubtless be the concrete details of smart institutional design in Singapore at both the national and local levels, which amount to global best practice across a vast range of components. Following are just a few specific examples that public policy schools and governments worldwide, especially in the developing world, could study with profit:

—*The Housing and Development Board,* which provides quality, low-cost housing for over 80 percent of Singapore's population, at minimal direct cost to government.

—*The Central Provident Fund,* which ensures that citizens have post-retirement savings, while also mobilizing capital for national investment.

—*The Economic Development Board,* which effectively attracts foreign investment, integrating the related efforts of other agencies while monitoring markets in search of new strategic opportunities for local Singaporean business.

—*The Temasek Holdings National Investment Company,* which enhances national wealth and economic stability through global operations, supporting local firms while simultaneously minimizing moral hazard through its market-oriented approach to core holdings.

At a broader level, some distinctive general characteristics of "smart" Singapore public policy have international relevance:

Holistic approaches to policy. For reasons dating back to camaraderie among the Old Guard of the nation's founders, and including innovative personnel policies, Singapore policymakers routinely consider the interactive effects of various policies and think of national policy in a more unified fashion than is common in most nations. This way of thinking, combined with a congenial, open institutional structure, gives Singapore unparalleled capacity to deal with the Digital Revolution and the emerging Internet of Things.

Inclusive, community-building ethnic policies. Harboring an unusually diverse population in a region with a history of ethnic strife, Singapore has forged, to a remarkable degree, a sense of common identity. It has also mobilized its diverse citizenry as a bridge to their powerful ancestral homelands, although the surge of guest workers and wealthy expatriates into Singapore over the past two decades is complicating that equation.

Shrewd small-state diplomacy. Singapore has ensured its national security in a turbulent region dominated traditionally by larger powers through pragmatic "leapfrog diplomacy"; aggressive "poisoned-shrimp" military deployments; virtual alliances that maintain credibility without permanent basing, while allowing flexible, multidimensional ties with outsiders; and active informal lobbying in key capitals around the world.

Responsive yet minimalist government. Singapore offers broad public health coverage, high-quality public housing, and insurance against catastrophic risk at significantly low cost to the general public, although the definition of "public" itself often omits a large guest-worker segment of the population.

Smart-city development. The government employs information and communications technology creatively, with increasing attention to the Internet of Things, creating efficient cybernetic mechanisms for minimizing the use of scarce resources, such as water and energy, while maximizing information flows.

Equally notable are Singapore's specific policies that are formidably effective in achieving their declared objectives:

Water policy. Although a tiny, crowded city-state of little more than 700 square kilometers, with less than 6 million inhabitants, Singapore is nearly self-sufficient in its water supply, owing to a distinctive, successful "Four Taps" policy emphasizing catchment, import efficiency, desalination, and recycling.

Housing and land-use policy. Singapore efficiently provides its citizens and permanent residents with quality, low-cost housing that enables them to build a financial nest egg, assuring them of a stake in society that in turn facilitates social stability.

Transport policy. The government ensures smooth, relatively rapid transit across a crowded island at minimal environmental cost through market-oriented pricing policies, leveraged by the latest interactive ICT technology.

Food supply. Although predominantly urban, Singapore manages to be largely self-sufficient in vegetables and fruits through urban farming while keeping overall food costs down through receptivity to imports.

International trade and investment. Singapore has emphatically embraced free trade and worked zealously to encourage multinational firms, particularly their headquarters units, to base themselves locally, with a special focus on services.

National security. This city-state retains relations of trust with both the U.S. and other large powers, contributing to regional security through joint exercises, information exchanges, and ad hoc provision of facilities, without an extensive foreign troop presence or formal alliance ties.

Diplomacy. Singapore maintains dynamic and intense relations with bodies at all levels of the international system, including nations, cities, and supranational as well as multilateral bodies, maximizing its unique advantages as a city-state. It also deftly finesses ideological and geopolitical conflict, simultaneously maintaining constructive relations with the People's Republic of China, Taiwan, Israel, the Arab world, and Russia, without losing the trust and regard of the United States. It also operates with unusual local political effect in Washington, D.C.

Transnational partnerships. To an unusual degree, Singapore appreciates the power and value of transnational intellectual exchanges and works to systematically nurture them by becoming a smart global hub. It fills this role by attracting foreign investment and by supporting, through the National Research Foundation, strategic partnerships that link Singapore's own institutions and world-class universities overseas, particularly in the sciences and engineering.

Global contribution. Although one of the smallest nation-state members of the international system, Singapore retains formidable influence beyond its shores without overseas military deployments or an extensive foreign-aid program. It maximizes "soft power" principally through the way it exports its own efficient, technologically enabled domestic practices, especially those relating to urban development. It often does so on a mutually agreeable commercial basis, through such mechanisms as training programs, turnkey construction projects, and consulting arrangements such as those of the successful e-government consulting firm Crimson Logic. Singapore also gains respect by serving as a catalyst in the realization of broadly accepted global goals such as the creation of global and regional free trade regimes.

Shadows? Of course, no nation is perfect—in domestic practices, social organization, or approach to international affairs. Like many globalized societies, including the United States, Singapore seems to be afflicted with deepening social and economic inequality, which has its greatest impact on transient residents. Rising real-estate prices—ironically reflecting the desirability of living there—compound inequality of assets. Singapore also has a low birth rate, is relying more and more on potentially restive foreign guest workers, and could be experiencing a gradual middle-class disaffection with the one-party dominance that has brought much prosperity and innovation in the past.

Self-correction mechanisms. Although Singapore's policies and their consequences do have some dysfunctional aspects, the city-state also has unusual, smart self-correction mechanisms, particularly a strong market reliance, rooted in its exposed character as a diminutive actor in a much larger global system. It also has unique institutions with unusual self-corrective features, such as its Economic Development Board, and—at least so far—a crisis-oriented and self-reflective leadership that has shown an ability to adjust course in response to new challenges. In harnessing the promise of the Digital Revolution, the deepening technological bias embodied in smart-nation, smart-state Singapore helps minimize the overcrowding and social unease that a more traditional manufacturing or resource-sector bias like that of its Asian neighbors might engender. Singapore's continued relevance as a global laboratory will depend fatefully on whether it can remain sensitive to global trends and still employ these self-reflective and self-correcting features.

Implications for Theory

This review of Singapore public policy affirms the potential global importance of "virtual states"—actors of limited scale with high concentrations of expertise—in international relations today. It suggests, however, that finer distinctions need to be made among those virtual states. Such entities can operate flexibly at multiple levels of international affairs—national, transnational, and subnational—often simultaneously. They can also respond rapidly to international developments—a valuable and, for them, indispensable trait in the volatile globalized world now emerging.

Domestic institutions, in particular, bear close inspection, because they can critically affect the stability and responsiveness of virtual states to strong external pressures. In Singapore's case, distinctive, cross-sectoral institutions like the Economic Development Board substantially augment responsiveness, as well as policy integration. Others, such as the Housing and Development Board, markedly enhance stability. The character of these institutions may well enable Singapore to respond to, and capitalize on, globalization more effectively than many other virtual states can, including some of those in the Middle East.

Singapore's successes in this regard raise questions about the empirical relevance and heuristic value in the 21st century of the developmental state model, highly fashionable a generation ago. Many nation-states, especially those in East Asia, continue to rely on "plan-rational," state-directed efforts, specifying priority sectors to transform their economies, as that older model prescribes. Bureaucratic actors may be at a disadvantage, however, both in understanding and in responding to the accelerating pace of global change, especially given the dangers of clientelism and routinization that beset them, even when they do enjoy some degree of embedded autonomy. By comparison, the smart-state paradigm offers a more realistic prescription for governance today in its emphasis on a state's ability to comprehend and respond pragmatically to outside forces, using technological supports where possible, but without an overambitious roadmap. Singapore provides a good example of a smart state in operation that is more relevant in today's volatile, uncertain global world than the confident developmental state models of yesteryear in the vein of Chalmers Johnson's MITI.

As outlined earlier in this book, a variety of bureaucratic pathologies, described by Stigler, Downs, Crozier, and others, can potentially distort nation-state behavior. Nevertheless, such maladies, not to mention the developmentalist paradigm, can be avoided while still according respect or even precedence to elite officials. Transparency, through e-government, together with the embedded bureaucratic distance from regulated institutions generated through the use of statutory boards can, for example, arrest clientelist tendencies of bureaucratic relations with private firms that George Stigler feared. This research thus suggests the limits to some classic theoretical critiques of bureaucratic management, with Singapore as an outlying case that illustrates ways to transcend state shortcomings.

In illustrating ways to transcend state shortcomings, Singapore's outlying case expands upon classic theoretical critiques of bureaucratic management, confirming the pitfalls of an uncritically positive view of bureaucratic capabilities—particularly in directing major changes in economic life. Elite bureaucratic players rarely have the wisdom and political capacity to lead a strategic transformation of economic structure, especially in an era of massive and deregulated transnational capital flows. Volatility and uncertainty in the globalizing world, coupled with the underlying lack of incentives for risk-taking in the traditional bureaucratic state, particularly with respect to transnational undertakings, make strategic, future-oriented bureaucratic management of economic affairs implausible today, if it ever was. More market input and calculated state support for entrepreneurship and transnational enterprise are clearly needed.

The Singapore case also validates the concept of the smart state—an entity that efficiently perceives and responds to external challenge (geographical, demographic, financial, political, technological) and to markets, using the latest advances in ICT technology, without presuming to direct the course of events in dirigiste fashion. Singapore became smart through political and organizational innovation that optimized prospects for harnessing the Digital Revolution.

Cities, like states, can also become smart, thereby solving problems efficiently and enhancing their role in international affairs. The constructive role of cities in world affairs is gaining attention in the face of grassroots problems that are in contrast to the political and ideological preoccupations of nation-states. Cities, many argue, can be uniquely effective both in advancing democracy and in addressing pressing global socioeconomic challenges that have a mundane grassroots dimension. Indeed, Singapore's example suggests that smart cities can play a pivotal and globally significant socioeconomic role—on such issues as the environment and transportation—although there need not be a correlation to grassroots democracy. Singapore's experience also shows the importance of the symbolic role that smart cities can play as manageable laboratories for policy innovation.

In concrete policy terms, a systematic understanding of best-practice cases and the smart mechanisms for disseminating them can be a useful guide for addressing global problems. As Micklethwait and others have recently emphasized, there is a growing consensus that the Western "entitlements" model of public policy is today facing enormous financial and political constraints, especially when applied to the problems of heavily populated developing nations. The Singapore model holds special potential for addressing such problems through its distinctive elements—institutions, uses of technology, leadership structures, and personnel arrangements—and the supportive leadership and personnel structures that turn aspirations into innovative reality. Concretely, Singapore's example suggests how to create not only livable cities (a challenge of particular importance in the populous, traditionally rural developing world) but also fiscally viable welfare states (highly relevant in economically advanced nations as well).

Issues for Future Research

There seems little question in retrospect that Singapore's response to the social, economic, and political challenges the city-state has confronted over the past half century has been remarkable. Cross-national surveys repeatedly rank it among the most effective national systems on earth. Most of these analyses present Singapore's impressive policy profile as a homogeneous unit, carried out under the general leadership of the late Lee Kuan Yew. Without depreciating Lee's historic and extraordinary contribution to the early phase of Singapore's development in any way, this research also highlights the innovative contribution in later years of Goh Chok Tong and Lee Hsien Loong. Their roles surely merit further research and commentary, as does Singapore's enlightened response to globalization and digitalization.

The very first pages of this book noted shadows on the remarkable story of Singapore's growth and transformation, including the challenges of migration and socioeconomic inequity. A flood of both guest workers and well-heeled foreigners into Singapore is putting pressure on sociopolitical stability and the viability of Singapore's middle class. How these trends, exacerbated by globalization, will affect Singapore's future is a subject of major importance.

Although the outstanding success of Singapore's smart-state, smart-city paradigm cannot be denied, especially in comparative perspective, what is not so clear is to what extent Singapore's experience is transferable to other parts of the world today, or how relevant its performance of the past will be to the global future. That subject clearly requires more careful research.

Diffusion processes will obviously be crucial in determining when and how the concrete practices embedded in the Singapore "smart-city, smart state" model will be transmitted to the broader world. One distinctive empirical finding of this work, with prospective theoretical significance for future research on international relations, is the concept of a smart global hub.

Socioeconomic communities like Singapore's "One-North," including Bio-polis, Fusionopolis, and Medianopolis, are important nodes for diffusion—both into and out of smart states and smart cities. The operation and global functional role of these emerging smart hubs deserve further study.

Chapter 6 noted that many nations, cities, and NGOs around the world are already trying to emulate Singapore's experience. Most of these efforts, how-ever, have begun in the very recent past—mainly over the past five years—so the verdict is still out on their success. More systematic analysis, particularly concerning the importance to success of unique Singaporean institutional features such as the EDB, HDB, CPF, and Temasek Holding, as well as Sin-gapore's hybrid smart-city–smart-state character, is needed to understand the degree to which the Singapore policy paradigm is transferable elsewhere.

There is also, of course, the normative question of desirability. Even if Sin-gapore's experience is transferable, is it really something that other nations or cities should seek to emulate? And at what level—national or simply munic-ipal? Singapore's policies do have a moralistic, neoliberal, and in some ways soft-authoritarian tone, despite their democratic form. They clearly have a powerful attraction, especially as subnational solutions, in China and other nations with similarly daunting challenges of governance. But how desirable would they be elsewhere?

The future relevance of Singapore as a laboratory to the world also relates profoundly to prospects for the global future itself. Should one envision, as a paradigm of sociopolitical organization, a future in which, as Benjamin Barber hypothesizes, "mayors rule the world"?[1] Or, alternatively, should it be a "new feudalism" model of decentralized decisionmaking and influence, as Tanaka Akihiko forecasts, in which small and medium-size national powers have greater maneuverability than in the past?[2] In terms of socioeconomic evolution, will it be dominated by growth and urban transition, especially within the developing world, which will cause housing, transport, and envi-ronmental problems to mount? If such trends are in prospect, as seems likely, the future relevance of Singapore's past and present to the global future will be a powerful one that cannot be ignored.

Implications for Future Policy

The future relevance of Singapore as a laboratory for the world of course depends upon prospects for Singapore's own ability to track and respond to global trends and also on the evolution of those trends themselves. Cautious confidence seems warranted on both counts. Singapore can be expected to continue being adaptive and globally oriented, even as the urban and environmental issues on which it has pioneered global best practice—particularly the construction and sustenance of smart cities—become increasingly important for the world as a whole.

Circumstances thus far strongly point to Singapore's potential as such a laboratory, especially in the realm of smart cities. Many countries would do well to recognize the city-state's achievements, particularly its neighbors—the teeming nations of East, Southeast, and South Asia, such as China, India, Indonesia, Vietnam, Myanmar, and Bangladesh. They are currently undergoing a historic urban transition that makes Singapore's successes at housing, transportation, energy efficiency, and environmental protection of special relevance. In the longer run, the same transition will likely accelerate in Africa and parts of Latin America, making Singapore's experience increasingly relevant there as well.

The epic urban transition of the global present and future is clearly a matter of central concern to multilateral development institutions such as the World Bank, the International Monetary Fund, the Asian Development Bank, and other regional financial institutions. They, too, need to know more, and in more detail, about Singapore's experience; their propensity to study Singapore and to interact with it is already increasing, virtually every day. The same imperative exists for national development agencies, such as the U.S. Agency for International Development, Japan International Cooperation Agency, and Korea International Cooperation Agency. As Japan is by a substantial margin the largest donor country in Asia, the potential for bilateral cooperation between its development agency and Singapore should be especially great. And the prospects for Singapore-Korean cooperation are also substantial.

Bilateral collaboration between China and Singapore has been dynamic within China but slow to expand to include third countries, for understandable historical reasons. Yet cooperation between the two in broader multilateral contexts could become highly dynamic in future years as well. This could be especially true should China-centric institutions such as infrastructure banks, which would likely do much to promote smart city development, become more prominent on the global scene. The advent of the Asian Infrastructure Investment Bank and the New Development Bank (formerly the BRICS Bank), both with their locus in China, will make a pattern of deepening Singapore-China cooperation in multilateral contexts increasingly likely.

If Singapore's expertise does indeed have powerful international relevance, especially to emerging trends in the developing world, multinational firms need to pay attention also. Such trends should bolster the rationale for partnerships with Singaporean firms and government entities, already strong. It should also strengthen the rationale for investment in Singapore, thus augmenting its role as a laboratory for the world. The potential synergies between enlightened multinational interest and Singapore's emerging global role would appear to be strong.

The rationale for deeper scholarly understanding of the Singapore model is also compelling, especially in public-policy schools. Singapore, after all, appears to represent global best practice, with its unusual responsiveness to the Digital Revolution and IoT, in many sectors of the political economy, including transportation, energy efficiency, electronic governance, and smart-city development. Harvard Business School and other such institutions have already done case studies on its overall economic development policies.[3] Yet more refined work is needed, benchmarking Singapore, on specific government bodies, para-public structures, sectoral policies, and institutional prerequisites for smart-state development in the Internet age.

Toward An Invigorated Global Policy Dialogue

As globalization proceeds with increasing momentum around the world, and as mutual interdependence rises, the importance of transnational policy dialogue increases as well. Although domestic institutions and macroeconomic circumstances will no doubt continue to vary substantially around the world, the very reality of growing interdependence and of pressure to conform to common global imperatives makes at least a consideration of best-practice solutions from elsewhere vital. Many of these solutions are complex and unappreciated domestically in key nations, making public-consciousness raising a further reason for invigorated global policy dialogues.

Singapore appears to have developed a formidable array of those best-practice solutions—relevant to industrial and developing nations alike. Its smart state has pioneered minimalist, enabling solutions, addressing the crisis of the welfare state as well as the challenges of economic development. Its smart city is coping, in microcosm, with housing, transportation, energy, health care, and environmental challenges through innovative, technology-driven approaches that likewise bear broader consideration, especially in the developing world.

Singapore, as a small city-state in a turbulent world, thus has deep stakes in a cooperative global system, with much to contribute to an intensified and truly global domestic-policy dialogue. The New Synthesis project on new frontiers in public administration—involving Canada, Brazil, the Netherlands, the United Kingdom, and Australia, as well as Singapore—has made an important recent start in this process, focusing on such important shared global problems as health care, global warming, and criminal justice.[4]

An expansion of such dialogue, from a holistic perspective that transcends the narrow regulatory concerns of specific agencies, or the parochial perspectives of individual nations, is very much in the global interest. Such dialogue will no doubt intensify Singapore's role as a constructive and multifaceted laboratory for a more integrated and interdependent world that is even now emerging, driven by the historic transformations of the Digital Revolution.

Appendix
CHRONOLOGY OF SINGAPORE'S EXPERIENCE

1923: Construction of Britain's principal naval base in East Asia begins at Singapore.

1942: Japanese occupy Singapore.

1945: After Japan surrenders in August, Britain assumes military administration of Straits Settlements.

1946: Dissolution of the Straits Settlements results in Singapore becoming a distinct crown colony of the United Kingdom.

1947: A dangerous shortage of rice leads to rationing, malnutrition, disease, violence, and black market activity.

1947: Beginning in May, strikes led by communists result in stoppages in public transportation, public services, and harbor operations.

1948: For the first time, Singapore holds limited elections on March 20, for six seats on Legislative Council.

1948: Britain declares state of emergency in Malaya and Singapore on June 18, after communists attack rubber estates and tin mines.

1954: Public Service Commission (PSC) comes into operation in January.

1955: Singapore's first legislative assembly established in April.

1955: Colonial government establishes Central Provident Fund in July.

1959: Lee Kuan Yew becomes first chief minister under self-government on June 5, following People's Action Party (PAP) election victory.

1959: Political Study Center formed in August to train civil servants.

1960: Prevention of Corruption Act passed in June.

1960: Housing and Development Board (HDB) established in February.

1960: Trade Union Act allows PAP-led government to deregister left-wing unions.

1961: Fire breaks out in residential precinct of Bukit Ho Swee on May 25. Four die, 85 are injured, 16,000 left homeless, and 2,800 homes destroyed.

1961: The PAP splits in July, with 13 pro-Communist PAP assemblymen breaking off to form Barisan Sosialis.

1961: Economic Development Board (EDB) established in August.

1963: On January 20, Indonesia announces *Konfrontasi* with armed incursions.

1963: Security operation, known as Operation Coldstore, results in the detainment of 113 antigovernment activists and key members of Barisan Sosialis in February.

1963: Public Utilities Board founded in May; on July 9, Federation of Malaysia Agreement signed among leaders of Malaya, Singapore, Sabah, and Sarawak.

1964: Ethnic riot between Malays and Chinese on Prophet Muhammad's birthday (July 21) results in 23 deaths.

1965: Singapore and Malaysia sign separation agreement on August 7, 1965; Singapore declares independence on August 9, 1965.

1965: Yusof bin Ishak becomes first president of Singapore in August, replacing Queen Elizabeth as titular head of state.

1965: Singapore joins United Nations in September.

1966: Recitation of the Singapore National Pledge, drafted by S. Rajaratnam, begins in August.

1966: Land Acquisition Act (October) gives state strong powers of eminent domain, later exercised in support of housing and transportation policies.

1967: Science Council of Singapore established.

1967: Singapore passes National Service Act in March, following Israeli legislation.

1967: Singapore becomes founding member of Association of Southeast Asian Nations (ASEAN) in August.

1968: Central Provident Fund coverage expanded to allow use of funds for home purchase, facilitating citizen stake in society.

1968: While prime minister, Lee Kuan Yew is a visiting fellow at the Harvard Institute of Politics in the fall.

1969: Seven days of ethnic riots leave 4 dead, 80 wounded.

1971: Benjamin Sheares becomes second president of Singapore in January.

1971: Majority of British military forces leave Singapore in October, after more than 150 years of sustained presence, apart from World War II.

1972: "Thirteenth month allowance" introduced in October for superior government service.

1974: Temasek Holdings founded in June to manage investments in government-linked companies (GLCs).

1975: Area Licensing Scheme (ALS) for traffic management introduced in June, for reducing traffic congestion at peak intervals.

1976: PAP wins all 69 parliamentary seats in general election in December.

1978: Deng Xiaoping visits Singapore on November 12 at Lee Kuan Yew's invitation.

1979: Speak Mandarin campaign introduced in September attempts to reduce number of Chinese dialects.

1979: "Wage correction policy" initiated, recommending high wage increases.

1980: PAP wins all 75 parliamentary seats in general election in December.

1981: Singapore operationalizes Civil Service Computerization Program, to promote e-government.

1981: Apple Computer—first company to manufacture PCs in Singapore.

1981: Singapore permanent UN representative, Ambassador Tommy Koh, assumes presidency of Third UN Conference on Law of the Sea in March.

1981: National Computer Board established in September, to promote computerization of the civil service, computer education and training, and development of computer services industry.

1981: C. V. Devan Nair becomes third president of Singapore in October.

1981: In October, Worker's Party breaks 16-year PAP electoral monopoly in Parliament.

1983: Singapore Trade Development Board (TDB) formed to develop Singapore as international trading hub, promoting local goods and services.

1984: Social Development Unit (SDU) established in January to promote marriage and increased social interaction among the educated.

1984: Gifted Education Program (GEP) implemented in Singapore in January.

1984: First silicon-wafer fabrication plant in Asia outside Japan opened.

1984: Singapore International Monetary Exchange (SIMEX) created in September, as Asia's first financial futures market.

1984: General election in December results in decline from 76 percent (1980) to 63 percent in PAP support level.

1985: Singapore experiences first policy-related recession in the second quarter of the year.

1985: Establishment of PAP Feedback Unit in March, under Ministry for Community Development.

1986: National Information Technology Plan issued.

1986: Public Sector Divestment Commission established in January.

1986: Newspaper and Printing Presses (Amendment) Bill introduced in parliament on May 5. Proposed bill allows government to restrict sale or distribution of foreign publications deemed politically sensitive and nonprofessional.

1986: PAP Youth Committee established, chaired by Lee Hsien Loong.

1986: First Town Councils established in September, devolving day-to-day management to residents.

1987: S$5 billion Mass Rapid Transit (MRT) becomes operational in November.

1987: Ministry of Education implements a national system of education as vernacular schools close.

1987: English officially designated first language of school instruction.

1988: Group Representation Constituency (GRC) scheme comes into effect on June 1, to ensure minority representation in parliament.

1988: Town Council Act passed in June.

1988: National Automation Master Plan launched in August to promote factory automation.

1989: Implemented in March, Ethnic Integration Policy (EIP) promotes racial integration.

1989: All urban planning functions come under single Urban Redevelopment Authority (URA) in September.

1989: Trade Net international electronic data-interchange system launched in October.

1989: First Singapore participation in UN peacekeeping in October.

1989: SIJORI Growth Triangle project first proposed (December), deepening economic links among Singapore; Johore, Malaysia; and Riau Islands of Indonesia.

1990: Transportation unit of Singapore's Public Works Department (PWD) institutes vehicle quota limit, known as Certificate of Entitlement (COE), in May.

1990: Singapore and People's Republic of China establish diplomatic relations in October, Singapore being the last ASEAN member to do so.

1990: United States and Singapore sign agreement in November allowing American military forces to access the facilities at Paya Lebar Airport and Sembawang Naval Port.

1990: After 31 years, Prime Minister Lee Kuan Yew steps down; Goh Chok Tong becomes new prime minister in November.

1990: Ministry of Information and the Arts established (November), following merger of Ministry of Community Development with Ministry of Communications and Information.

1991: Constitution revised in January to provide for direct election of president.

1991: Park Connector Network approved by Garden City Action Committee.

1991: National Science and Technology Board (NSTB) established in January; first five-year National Technology Plan issued.

1992: IT 2000 plan for information-industry development released.

1992: Singapore Cooperation Program (SCP) established under Ministry of Foreign Affairs to provide for development assistance.

1993: Asia-Pacific Economic Cooperation (APEC) Secretariat set up in Singapore in March.

1993: Ong Teng Cheong becomes first directly elected president in September.

1994: China-Singapore Suzhou Industrial Park founded in February.

1994: SIJORI formally established in December.

1995: Senior civil servant salaries benchmarked to six top private-sector professions.

1995: Public Service for the 21st Century Commission established in May to enhance quality of Singapore Civil Service (SCS).

1995: Parliament passes Maintenance of Parents Law in November, making children legally liable for financial support of indigent parents.

1996: Singapore hosts first World Trade Organization Ministerial Conference.

1997: "Thinking Schools, Learning Nation" initiative launched in June.

1997–98: Asian financial crisis begins in summer 1997 and continues through late 1998. Singapore dollar depreciates 16 percent, and Singapore stock index declines 54 percent.

1998: U.S. naval vessels to use local naval base from 2000 announced in January.

1999: S. R. Nathan becomes president without election in August, as only candidate found eligible to run.

1999: National Computer Board privatized.

1999: Techno-entrepreneurship 21 (T21) initiated under multi-agency effort.

1999: Infocomm Development Authority of Singapore established in December.

2000: Prime Minister Goh Chok Tong launches Speak Good English Movement (SGEM) in April.

2000: Biomedical Science Initiative launched in June, marking major drive to establish biomedical sciences as key pillar of Singapore economy.

2000: Singapore elected UN Security Council nonpermanent member in October.

2000: Singapore and New Zealand sign Singapore's first bilateral free trade agreement in November.

2001: Pipeline from Indonesia's Natuna field begins supplying natural gas in January.

2001: PAP wins 82 of 84 parliamentary seats in general election in November.

2001: Economic Review Commission created in December.

2002: Singapore and Japan sign Japan-Singapore Economic Agreement in January (becomes effective in November).

2002: National Science and Technology Board restructured as Agency for Science, Technology, and Research (A*STAR) in January, focusing on research and development capabilities.

2002: Trade Development Board renamed International Enterprise Singapore in April, with additional task of assisting Singapore-based companies' growth overseas.

2002: Singapore inaugurates Shangri La East Asian security dialogue in May.

2002: Economic Review Commission recommends Competition Law in May.

2002: "London Plus" strategy to exceed London's capabilities as international maritime center, as Singapore becomes international integrated logistics hub in November.

2003: SARS virus outbreak provokes 50 percent fall in Changi air traffic.

2003: Singapore establishes world's first bioengineering and nano-technology research institute.

2003: NEWater recycled-water plants opened in Bedok and Kranji in February.

2003: Airport Logistics Park Singapore opened on March 30.

2003: In May, Singapore signs free trade agreement with the United States, as first Asian nation to do so.

2003: Biopolis for biomedical sciences R&D begins construction at One North in June.

2003: Workforce Development Agency established in September.

2004: U.S.-Singapore free trade agreement becomes effective in January.

2004: Ban on chewing gum, first introduced in 1991, revised in March to allow sale of gum for health reasons. Gum available only through pharmacies.

2004: Educational Services Center established, to aid foreign students.

2004: Lee Hsien Loong sworn in as prime minister in August.

2005: Lee introduces five-day workweek on January 1.

2005: Government legalizes casino gambling in April; two casinos to be built.

2005: Intelligent Nation 2015 10-year informatics master plan announced in May.

2005: First municipal-scale seawater desalination plant opened at Tuas in September.

2005: Singapore and India enter into free trade agreement in August.

2005: Singapore Media Academy established in November.

2006: Lee announces Progress Package—cash distribution of budget sur-pluses to citizens—in February.

2006: In May, ruling PAP wins general elections, with 82 of 84 seats and 66.6 percent of vote.

2006: National Research Foundation (NRF) established.

2006: Research, Innovation, and Enterprise Council created.

2006: *Intelligent Nation 2015* 10-year master plan unveiled.

2006: Singapore Cooperation Enterprise (SCE) formed by Ministry of Trade and Industry and Ministry of Foreign Affairs.

2007: Research Centers of Excellence (RCE) program initiated.

2008: Singapore-MIT Alliance for Research and Technology (SMART) Center established in January.

2008: Earth Observatory of Singapore and Cancer Research Center of Excellence established.

2008: NRF establishes National Framework of Innovation and Enterprise (NFIE) program to commercialize technologies from R&D labs through formation of start-up companies in March.

2008: Singapore International Water Week launched in June.

2008: Singapore falls into recession because of global financial crisis.

2008: Fusionopolis, focusing on the arts, business, and technology, opens at One North in October.

2008: China and Singapore sign free trade agreement in October.

2009: Lease Buyback Scheme (LBS) of reverse mortgages inaugurated to help elderly unlock housing equity.

2009: Construction begins on Campus for Research Excellence and Technological Enterprise (CREATE) facilities in Singapore in July.

2009: Energy Market Authority launches Intelligent Energy System pilot smart-grid test program.

2010: Denmark, New Zealand, and Singapore tied as world's least corrupt nations, according to Transparency International.

2010: CREATE Centers on Electro-mobility in Cities and on Inflammatory Diseases in Asia established in June.

2010: Sino-Singapore Guangzhou Knowledge City project inaugurated in June.

2010: World Bank declares Singapore best country for running a business.

2010: Berkeley Educational Alliance for Research in Singapore announced in October; Ben Gurion, Hebrew University, and Nanyang Technological University also align.

2010: Chinese vice president Xi Jinping visits Singapore, breaking ground on S$44 million Chinese Cultural Center, in November.

2011: Changes in law permit Internet election advertisement.

2011: PAP wins majority of seats in general election in May with 81 of 87 seats and 60.1 percent of the vote.

2011: Singapore Center on Environmental Life Sciences and Engineering established in April, exploiting new technology in engineering and natural sciences.

2011: President S. R. Nathan steps down and Tony Tan elected president in August.

2011: CREATE project with Shanghai Jiao Tong University to establish Research Center on Environmental Sustainability Solutions for Megacities launched in December.

2012: Government-appointed committee recommends major pay cuts for ministers, including prime minister and president.

2012: Berkeley Education Alliance for Research in Singapore (BEARS) forms in January.

2012: CREATE collaboration in March with Cambridge University on carbon reduction in chemical technology.

2012: Prime Minister Lee Hsien Loong establishes Facebook page in April.

2012: Singapore and European Union conclude free trade agreement negotiations in October.

2012: Ministry of Communications and Information established in November, to succeed Ministry of Information, Communications, and the Arts.

2012: Chinese bus drivers strike, protesting pay discrimination in November.

2013: Inaugural Global Young Scientists Summit in Singapore in January.

2013: Demonstrators protest increasing population of foreign workers in February.

2013: Cambridge Centre for Advanced Research in Energy Efficiency opens in April.

2013: Singapore's first liquefied natural gas (LNG) terminal becomes commercially operational on Jurong Island.

2013: Innovation Cluster Program announced by Prime Minister Lee Hsien Loong.

2013: Riots in Little India involving 400 foreign workers (18 injured, 27 arrested), after Indian migrant worker is knocked down by bus in December.

2014: First three "Smart Work Centres" envisioned in Ministry of National Development's 2030 Work, Live, and Play are officially opened.

2014: PM Lee Hsien Loong launches Smart Nation Initiative in November.

2014: NRF unveils Virtual Singapore in December, a dynamic 3D city model and collaborative data platform bringing government, citizens, industry, and research institutions together to solve problems.

2015: Lee Kuan Yew passes away at the Singapore General Hospital in March.

2015: Singapore celebrates 50th anniversary of independence in August.

2015: PAP wins general election in September, taking 83 of 89 seats in 29 constituencies with 69.9 percent of the vote.

2015: Singapore joins two-year pilot project to develop global smart sustainable cities index.

2015: McKinsey establishes Digital Campus in Singapore.

2015: Chinese president Xi Jinping pays state visit to Singapore in November to commemorate 25 years of bilateral Sino-Singapore diplomatic relations.

2015: Sino-Singaporean Chongqing Connectivity Initiative launched in November by Presidents Lee and Xi, to explore Internet of Things.

2015: Chinese president Xi and Taiwanese president Ma hold first Cross-Straits summit in November at Singapore's Shangri La Hotel.

Notes

Chapter 1

The epigraph is a Tang Dynasty inscription, hanging in calligraphic form on the wall of Prime Minister Lee Hsien Loong's office at the Istana in Singapore.

1. See United Nations Department of Economic and Social Affairs Population Division, "File 2: Percentage of Population at Mid-Year Residing in Urban Areas by Major Area, Region and Country, 1950–2050," *World Urbanization Prospects: The 2014 Revision* (June 2014).

2. See, for example, Evelyn Huber and John D. Stephens, *Development and Crisis of the Welfare State: Parties and Policies in Global Markets* (University of Chicago Press, 2001); Stephan Haggard and Robert R. Kaufman, *Democracy and Welfare States: Latin America, East Asia, and Eastern Europe* (Princeton University Press, 2008); and John Micklethwait and Adrian Wooldridge, *The Fourth Revolution: The Global Race to Reinvent the State* (New York: Penguin Press, 2014).

3. See Raymond Vernon, *Sovereignty at Bay: The Multinational Spread of U.S. Enterprises* (New York: Basic Books, 1971), pp. v, 36; Daniel Yergin and Joseph Stanislaw, *The Commanding Heights: The Battle for the World Economy* (New York: Simon & Schuster, 1998); and Robert O. Keohane and Joseph S. Nye, *Power and Interdependence: World Politics in Transition* (Boston: Little, Brown, 1977).

4. See, for example, Rajan Menon, *The End of Alliance* (Oxford University Press, 2007).

5. On the deepening challenges confronting the Western welfare state and developing world skepticism of its relevance, see Micklethwait and Wooldridge, *The Fourth Revolution*, pp. 105–68.

6. On the concept of the virtual state, see Richard Rosecrance, *The Rise of the Virtual State: Wealth and Power in the Coming Century* (New York: Basic Books, 1999). In differentiating "virtual" and classic nation states, Rosecrance stresses political-military and geographic dimensions, rather than the cognitive and operational capabilities tapped through the "smart state" concept.

7. Micklethwait and Wooldridge, *The Fourth Revolution*, pp. 267–68.

8. Benjamin Barber, *If Mayors Ruled the World: Dysfunctional Nations, Rising Cities* (Yale University Press, 2013).

9. See United Nations Department of Economic and Social Affairs Population Division, "File 17b: Number of Cities Classified by Size Class of Urban Settlement, Major

Area, Region and Country, 1950–2030," "File 17d: Population in Cities Classified by Size Class of Urban Settlement, Major Area, Region and Country, 1950–2030," and "File 5: Total Population at Mid-Year by Major Area, Region and Country, 1950–2050," *World Urbanization Prospects: The 2014 Revision* (June 2014).

10. Ezra F. Vogel, *Japan as Number One: Lessons for America* (Harvard University Press, 1979).

11. For Singapore's rankings over the years, see World Bank, *Doing Business* (www. doingbusiness.org/).

12. The "Basic Requirements Index" covers four factors: institutions, infrastructure, macroeconomic environment, and health/primary education. Singapore was bested by Switzerland, home of the World Economic Forum, owing to its relatively weak performance in "innovation and sophistication factors," where it placed only 11th, compared with Switzerland at 1st. See World Economic Forum, *The Global Competitiveness Report 2015–2016*, pp. 320–21.

13. Ibid.

14. Starting a business in Singapore requires only three procedures, takes just 2.5 days, and costs only 0.6 percent of the average annual income of the founder. See World Bank, "Economy Profile: Singapore," *Doing Business 2016: Singapore*.

15. On the Global Competitive Index 2015–16, Singapore ranked first in the "efficiency of legal frameworks in settling disputes" category. See World Economic Forum, *The Global Competitiveness Report 2015–2016*. Similarly, Singapore ranked first in "economic globalization" for 2013 on the KOF Index of Globalization (March 4, 2016, version).

16. Singapore declined from number 5 in 2013 to number 7 in 2014, and then to number 8 in 2015 on Transparency International's global corruption perception index. Transparency International, *Corruption Perception Index 2015*.

17. See Jack Neff, "From Cincy to Singapore: Why P&G, Others Are Moving Key HQs," *Advertising Age*, June 11, 2012; and Colum Murphy, "GM to Move International Headquarters to Singapore from Shanghai," *Wall Street Journal*, November 13, 2013.

18. Alys Francis, "Digital Globalization: How MNCs Must Reinvent to Tap Asia's Growth Story," *Future Ready Singapore*, June 26, 2016.

19. Singapore Ministry of Manpower, "Living in Singapore: Key Information for Expatriates Living or Relocating to Singapore," last updated May 7, 2015.

20. World Economic Forum, *The Financial Development Report 2012*, p. 250.

21. World Bank, "GDP at Market Prices" (current US$), *World Development Indicators* (2014).

22. World Bank, "GDP per Capita" (current US$), *World Development Indicators* (2014).

23. Focus Economics, "Singapore Economic Outlook," June 21, 2016 (www.focus-economics.com/).

24. Figures for fourth quarter 2015 (external debt) and December 2015 (foreign-exchange reserves). On foreign-exchange reserves, see International Monetary Fund, "Data Template on International Reserves" (www.imf.org/external/np/sta/ir); on gross external debt position, see World Bank, "Quarterly External Debt Statistics" (data.world bank.org/data-catalog/quarterly-external-debt-statistics…).

25. The Genome Institute of Singapore (GIS), rather than Temasek, is technically Singapore's sovereign wealth fund. Temasek, however, is owned by the Ministry of Finance and is commonly referred to as a sovereign wealth fund (SWF) by foreigners. Temasek

received a perfect score of 10 for the quality of its operations from the Sovereign Wealth Fund Institute, together with seven other funds. See Sovereign Wealth Fund Institute, *Linaburg-Maduell Transparency Index,* First Quarter, 2016.

26. According to the Heritage Foundation's *2016 Index of Economic Freedom,* Singapore is the second freest economy in the world, in large measure because of its low tax rate (www.heritage.org/index/ranking). For more details on Singapore's taxation regime, see Inland Revenue Authority of Singapore, www.iras.gov.sg/irashome/default.aspx.

27. Top rates for personal income taxes are rising in 2017 to 22 percent. PriceWaterhouseCoopers, "Singapore: Individual- Taxes on Personal Income," *Tax summaries,* last updated December 17, 2015.

28. The United States, by comparison, ranked only 39th from the lowest with respect to unemployment rates in 2014. See World Bank, "Unemployment, Total (% of Total Labor Force) (National Estimate)," *World Development Indicators* (2014). Data were only available for 85 countries and regions.

29. This rating was by expatriates living in Asia. See Singapore Ministry of Health, "Overview of Our Healthcare System," 2003 (www.moh.gov.sg/content/moh_web/moh_corp_mobile/home/our_healthcare_system/overviewhealthcaresystem.html).

30. World Health Organization (WHO), *The World Health Report 2000—Health Systems: Improving Performance* (2000), p. 200.

31. WHO, *World Health Statistics 2010,* p. 55.

32. Singapore offers the world's fourth best health care infrastructure and enjoys the world's seventh highest overall life expectancy. Data drawn from World Competitiveness Yearbook 2010 cited in Singapore Economic Development Board, "Healthcare-World Class Healthcare Hub" (www.edb.gov.sg/content/edb/en/industries/industries/health care.html.)

33. Indeed, compared with 65 economies in 2012, Singapore ranked second in mathematics, third in reading, and third in science. Organization for Economic Cooperation and Development (OECD), "PISA 2012 Results in Focus" (www.oecd.org/pisa/keyfindings/pisa-2012-results-overview.pdf).

34. NUS ranked 26th globally, ahead of Beijing University (42nd) and the University of Tokyo (43rd). See Times Higher Education's "World University Rankings 2015–2016" (www.timeshighereducation.com).

35. Nanyang and NUS ranked 29th and 32nd, respectively, in this area in 2016. See "Global MBA Rankings 2016," *Financial Times* (http://rankings.ft.com/businessschool rankings/global-mba-ranking-2016); "Executive MBA Rankings 2015," *Financial Times* (http://rankings.ft.com/businessschoolrankings/emba-ranking-2015).

36. Times Higher Education, "150 under 50 Rankings 2016" (www.timeshigher education.com).

37. World Bank, "Internet Users (per 100 people)," *World Development Indicators* (2014).

38. World Economic Forum, *The Global Information and Technology Report 2015,* p. 9.

39. More than a quarter of Singaporeans shop online at least once a week. See "Singaporeans Are Southeast Asia's Top Online Shoppers: Visa Survey" (www.visa.com).

40. Changi Airport recently won the Skytrax award as the world's best airport for 2016. See www.changiairport.com/our-business/awards.

41. On "Best Seaport in Asia," see "Singapore Named Best Seaport in Asia for 28th Time," Channel NewsAsia, June 15, 2016; on rankings in terms of tonnage, see World Shipping Council (www.worldshipping.org).

42. For details, see Singapore Airlines, www.singaporeair.com.

43. Anshuman Daga and Kevin Lim, "Singapore Casinos Trump Macau with Tourism Aces," Reuters, September 23, 2013.

44. World Economic Forum, *The Travel & Tourism Competitiveness Report 2015*, p. 5.

45. Melissa Yeo, "10 Famous Celebrities You Won't Believe Emigrated to Singapore," *Must Share News*, January 16, 2015.

46. Liz Neisloss, "Why Is Facebook Co-founder Now in Singapore?," CNN, May 17, 2012; and David Yin, "Singapore Needs Immigrants, Says Jim Rogers," *Forbes*, June 6, 2013.

47. In 2015 Singapore had a total population of 5.5 million, of which nearly 3.4 million were citizens and 2.1 million were foreigners, including around 530,000 permanent residents and 1.6 million nonresidents. See Department of Statistics–Singapore, *Population in Brief 2015,* September 2015, p. 4.

48. Brenda Yeoh and Weiqiang Lin, "Rapid Growth in Singapore's Immigrant Population Brings Policy Challenges" (Migration Policy Institute, April 3, 2012); and Department of Statistics–Singapore, *Population in Brief 2015*, p. 6.

49. Singapore was followed in Asia by four Japanese cities, all tied for 32nd globally: Tokyo, Kobe, Yokohama, and Osaka. See Mercer's "2016 Quality of Living Worldwide City Rankings" (London, 2016).

50. World Bank, "Population Density (People per Sq Km of Land Area)," *World Development Indicators* (2015).

51. Anita Pugliese and Julie Ray, "Air Quality Rated Better than Water Quality Worldwide," *Gallup World*, May 14, 2012 (www.gallup.com/poll/154646/air-quality-rated-better-water-quality-worldwide.aspx).

52. Institute for Management Development (IMD), *IMD World Competitiveness Yearbook 2013* (Lausanne, Switzerland: IMD World Competitiveness Center, 2013).

53. Foreign domestic workers, for example, are excluded from the Employment Act and many key labor protections, such as limits on daily working hours. See Human Rights Watch, "World Report 2015: Singapore" (www.hrw.org).

54. World Bank, "Fertility Rate, Total (Births per Woman)," *World Development Indicators* (2014).

55. The Political and Economic Risk Consultancy ranked Singapore as having the least corrupt bureaucracy in Asia in 2016. See "Annual Review of Corruption in Asia, 2016" (www.asiarisk.com).

56. World Economic Forum, *Global Competitiveness Report 2015–2016*.

57. Transparency International, *Corruption Perception Index 2015*. Singapore was ranked number 8 in 2015.

58. In 1999–2000 Singapore was rated "partly free" by Freedom House, with a freedom rating of 5.0, a civil liberties rating of 5.0, and a political rights rating of 5.0, on a 1–7 scale, with 1 as best. By 2016 its rating in each category had improved to only 4.0. See Freedom House, *Freedom in the World—Singapore* (2016) (www.freedomhouse.org).

59. On Singapore's freedom-of-the-press ranking, see Freedom House, *Freedom of the Press 2015* (http://freedomhouse.org).

60. Amnesty International, "Singapore: Drop 'Strike'-Related Charges against Chinese Migrant Bus Drivers," February 7, 2013; and Human Rights Watch, "World Report 2015: Singapore" (www.hrw.org).

61. Department of Statistics–Singapore, *Yearbook of Statistics Singapore*, various editions.

62. Yeoh and Lin, "Rapid Growth in Singapore's Immigrant Population Brings Policy Challenges." The employers of guest workers are, however, typically required to insure their workers against major calamities, since the workers are not eligible for most local social services.

63. See, for example, Jake Maxwell, "Singapore Election to Test Immigration," *Wall Street Journal*, September 3, 2011.

64. Economist Intelligence Unit, *Worldwide Cost of Living Survey*, March 10, 2016.

65. For the Gini coefficient time series, see, for example, Department of Statistics–Singapore, *Key Household Income Trend*, for 2008, 2010, and 2013. The most recent version of the series was revised "to incorporate improved coverage of Government taxes and transfers," although the exact meaning of that expression remains unclear.

66. U.S. Department of State, *Foreign Relations of the United States, 1964–1968,* vol. 26, "Indonesia; Malaysia-Singapore; Philippines" (Washington: U.S. Government Printing Office, 2000).

67. "Why China's President Didn't Visit Singapore," *The Independent* (London), October 12, 2013.

68. Chinese Culture Forum, *Chronicle of PRC 1978* (http://chineseculture.about.com/library/china/history/blsyear1978.htm).

69. Ezra F. Vogel, *Deng Xiaoping and the Transformation of China* (Harvard University Press, 2011), pp. 287–91. Deng also met with Lee in 1980, 1985, and 1988.

70. Clarissa Oon, "The Dragon and the Little Red Dot: 20th Anniversary of China-Singapore Diplomatic Ties," *The Straits Times*, October 2, 2010.

71. Vogel, *Deng Xiaoping and the Transformation of China*, p. 291.

72. Ibid., p. 673.

73. Singapore Ministry of Foreign Affairs, "MFA Press Statement: Official Visit of His Excellency Xi Jinping, Vice President of the People's Republic of China to Singapore, November 14–16, 2010," and "MFA Press Statement: State Visit to Singapore by His Excellency Xi Jinping, President of the People's Republic of China, November 6–7, 2015" (both at www.mfa.gov.sg).

74. "Singapore and Russia Sign MOU to Increase Economic Cooperation," *Business Wire India*, June 26, 2014.

75. Changi Airports International (www.cai.sg/portfolio.htm). PSA International, a Singapore government–linked company wholly owned by Temasek, manages at least 28 ports, mainly container facilities, in 15 countries on four continents. See PSA International (www.globalpsa.com). An affiliate, PSA Marine, provides pilotage and towage services within the ports that PSA International manages.

76. Edwin Musoni, "President Kagame Calls for Increased Efforts to Development," *The New Times* (Rwanda), January 14, 2013.

Chapter 2

1. See, for example, Lindsay Davis, ed., *The Wit and Wisdom of Lee Kuan Yew* (Singapore: Editions Didier Millet Pte., 2013); Alex Josey, *Lee Kuan Yew: The Critical Years, 1971–1978* (Singapore: Times Books International, 1980); Alex Josey, *Lee Kuan Yew: The Crucial Years* (Singapore: Times Books International, 1980); and Peng Er Lam and Kevin Y. L. Tan, *Lee's Lieutenants: Singapore's Old Guard* (St. Leonards: Allen and Unwin, 1999).

2. For organizational structure, see John S. T. Quah, *Public Administration Singapore-Style* (Bingley: Emerald Group, 2010). For social coalitions and civil society, see Kent E. Calder and Roy Hofheinz Jr., *The Eastasia Edge* (New York: Basic Books, 1982), pp. 68–83.

3. Milton Friedman, while more concerned with Hong Kong, did speak of Singapore in his *Free to Choose* PBS series, noting that "economic freedom is a very important part of total freedom." On his comments, see Jim Zarroli, "How Singapore Became One of the Richest Places on Earth," National Public Radio, March 29, 2015.

4. Michael D. Barr and Zlatko Skrbis, *Constructing Singapore: Elitism, Ethnicity, and the Nation-Building Project* (Copenhagen: NIAS Press, 2008).

5. On the IoT, see Hakima Chaouchi, *The Internet of Things* (London: Wiley-ISTE, 2010); and Philip Howard, *Pax Technica: Will the Internet of Things Lock Us Up or Set Us Free?* (Yale University Press, 2015).

6. According to Michael Leifer, *Singapore's Foreign Policy: Coping with Vulnerability* (London: Routledge, 2000), p. 14, Venice is an appropriate geohistorical comparison for two main reasons: (a) Venice was simultaneously a great maritime trading center and a locus of major business enterprise; and (b) just as Venice served as the dynamic center of Europe during the Renaissance, Singapore has potential as a city of the future within Southeast Asia today.

7. In 2015 the total number of non-citizens living in Singapore was around 2.1 million. Of this community roughly 1.4 million were guest workers, 527,000 were permanent residents, and others were dependents. See Department of Statistics–Singapore, "Latest Data" (www.singstat.gov.sg).

8. Ibid.

9. World Bank, *World Development Indicators* (2014). Figures are for intertemporal comparisons calculated in terms of constant 2011 purchasing power parity.

10. See Cecilia Tortajada and Kimberly Pobre, "The Singapore-Malaysia Water Relationship: An Analysis of Media Perspectives," *Hydrological Sciences Journal* 56, no. 4 (2011): 611–13.

11. Prime Minister's Office Singapore, National Population and Talent Division, "Our Population Our Future: Issues Paper July, 2012," p. 31 (www.nptd.gov.sg).

12. Total employment grew by 32,300, while foreign employment grew by 22,600 (excluding foreign domestic workers). See Manpower Research and Statistics Department, "Labour Market 2015" (Singapore Ministry of Manpower: March 2016), pp. vii, 9 (www.mom.gov.sg).

13. Department of Statistics–Singapore, "Population Trends 2015," *Key Demographic Indicators, 1970–2015* (www.singstat.gov.sg).

14. Prime Minister's Office Singapore, "Speech by Prime Minister Lee Hsien Loong at the Singapore Manufacturers' Federation 80th Anniversary Dinner, September 2012."

15. Ministry of Trade and Industry—Singapore, "Challenge for Our Human Capital in the New Economy," *Economic Review Committee Report* (December 1, 2010), p. 14.

16. U.S. Energy Information Administration (EIA), "World Oil Transit Chokepoints" (www.eia.gov/todayinenergy/).

17. In 2014 there were 79,344 transits through the Strait of Malacca. See Marcus Hand, "Malacca Strait Traffic Hits an All-time High in 2014," *Seatrade Maritime News,* February 27, 2015.

18. In 2013 around 15.2 million barrels of oil a day flowed through the Strait of Malacca, compared with 56.5 million barrels a day in global maritime oil trade. See U.S. Energy Information Administration, "World Oil Transit Chokepoints." In addition, 525 million metric tons of commerce worth around $390 billion pass through the Strait of Malacca. See Joshua Ho, "The Security of Sea Lanes in Southeast Asia," *Asian Survey 46* (July–August 2006). On the challenge of terrorism, see Jeanette Tan, "S'pore Still a Target for Terrorism: PM Lee," *Yahoo Newsroom*, March 26, 2013.

19. World Bank, *World Development Indicators* (2015).

20. International Monetary Fund, "Official Reserve Assets and Other Foreign Currency Assets (Approximate Market Value)," *Data Template on International Reserves and Foreign Currency Liquidity (IRFCL)* (December 2015).

21. Singapore merchandise trade was 221.1 percent of GDP in 2015. World Bank, *World Development Indicators* (2015).

22. Ibid.

23. Between the Lehman crisis and September 2010, for example, the Singapore dollar appreciated more than 20 percent against its U.S. counterpart. Monetary Authority of Singapore, "Recent Development in the Singapore Economy," *Macroeconomic Review* (October 2010) (www.mas.gov.sg/monetary-policy-and-economics/monetary-policy/macroeconomic-review.aspx).

24. "Worldwide Cost of Living Survey," *The Economist*, March 10, 2016. Data from September 2015.

25. Saeed Azhar and Michael Flaherty, "Exclusive: Singapore's Temasek: Evolution, Not Revolution," Reuters, March 27, 2012.

26. Costa Paris and P. R. Venkat, "Singapore's GIC Suffers $41.6 Billion Loss," *Wall Street Journal*, September 30, 2009.

27. Internet Telecommunications Union, "The World in 2015," *ICT Facts and Figures 2015* (www.itu.int/en/ITU-C/Statistics/Documents/facts/ICTFFactsFigures2015.pdf).

28. See, for example, Leonard Binder and others, *Crises and Sequences in Political Development* (Princeton University Press, 1971); Raymond Grew, ed., *Crises of Political Development in Europe and the United States* (Princeton University Press, 1978); John W. Kingdon, *Agendas, Alternatives, and Public Policies* (Boston: Little, Brown, 1984); and Kent E. Calder, *Crisis and Compensation: Public Policy and Political Stability in Japan* (Princeton University Press, 1988).

Chapter 3

1. On the concept of "critical juncture" and the importance of such fateful intervals for policy evolution, see Kent E. Calder, *Crisis and Compensation* (Princeton University Press, 1988), pp. 39–42; Kent E. Calder and Min Ye, *The Making of Northeast Asia* (Stanford University Press, 2010), pp. 45–46; and Kent E. Calder, *The New Continentalism: Energy and Twenty-First Century Eurasian Geopolitics* (Yale University Press, 2012), pp. 53–54.

2. Max Weber, *Economy and Society: An Outline of Interpretive Sociology*, edited by Guenther Roth and Claus Wittich, translated by Ephraim Fischoff and others (University of California Press, 1978).

3. George Stigler, "The Theory of Regulation," *Bell Journal of Economics and Management Science* 3 (1971): 3–21.

4. Anthony Downs, *Inside Bureaucracy* (Boston: Little Brown, 1966).

5. Michel Crozier, *The Bureaucratic Phenomenon* (University of Chicago Press, 1964).

6. Samuel P. Huntington, *Political Order in Changing Societies* (Yale University Press, 1968).

7. Singapore unemployment, totaling 13.5 percent in 1959, was still 10 percent in 1965, and 4.5 percent even in 1973. See Lawrence B. Krause, *The Singapore Economy Reconsidered* (Singapore: Institute of Southeast Asian Studies, 1988), p. 5.

8. National Archives of Singapore, "Political Milestones," 2008 (www.nas.gov. sg/1stcab/PanelPDF/Section%20120-%20Political%20Milestones%201.pdf).

9. On the details and Lee's reaction, see Lee Kuan Yew, *The Singapore Story*, vol. 2 (Singapore: Singapore Press Holding, 1998), pp. 373–401.

10. Ashraf Ghani and Clare Lockhart, *Fixing Failed States: A Framework for Rebuilding a Fractured World* (Oxford University Press, 2008), p. 36.

11. Stephan Ortmann, *Politics and Change in Singapore and Hong Kong: Containing Contention* (New York: Routledge, 2010), p. 56.

12. Albert Lau, *A Moment of Anguish: Singapore in Malaysia and the Politics of Dis-Engagement* (Singapore: Times Academic Press, 1998); National Library Board, "PAP to Contest the 1964 Malaysian General Election," March 1, 1964.

13. Vijayan P. Munusamy, "Ethnic Relations in Malaysia: The Need for 'Constant Repair' in the Spirit of Muhibbah," in *Handbook of Ethnic Conflict: International Perspectives,* edited by Dan Landis and Rosita D. Albert (New York: Springer, 2012), p. 125.

14. Jamie Han, "Communal Riots of 1964," *Singapore Infopedia,* Singapore National Library Board.

15. Michael Barr argues, for example, that Goh Keng Swee, minister of finance at the time, approached Lee Kuan Yew in the early summer of 1965 with a proposal to negotiate with the Malaysian leaders for Singapore's secession, and that Lee had Goh negotiate in secret on this matter during July 1965. See Michael Barr, *Lee Kuan Yew: The Beliefs behind the Man* (Richmond: Curzon Press, 2000), pp. 79–80; as well as Sonny Yap, Richard Lim, and Leong Weng Kam, *Men in White: The Untold Story of Singapore's Ruling Political Party* (Singapore: Singapore Press Holdings, 2009), pp. 297–98.

16. May 16, 1966, when the first programmatic document of the Cultural Revolution was issued by China's Politburo, is said to be the formal onset of the Cultural Revolution, although related sociopolitical turbulence began the previous fall. See Guo Jian, Yongyi Song, and Yuan Zhou, *Historical Dictionary of the Chinese Cultural Revolution* (Lanham, Md.: Scarecrow Press, 2006), p. xliv. Also, Roderick MacFarquhar, *The Origins of the Cultural Revolution*, vol. 3: *The Coming of the Cataclysm* (Columbia University Press, 1977).

17. On the concept of "critical juncture" and the importance of such fateful intervals for policy evolution, see Calder, *Crisis and Compensation*, pp. 39–42; and Calder and Ye, *The Making of Northeast Asia*, pp. 45–46.

18. On Lee's philosophy, see his many classic autobiographical works, as well as Barr, *Lee Kuan Yew: The Beliefs behind the Man*; and Graham Allison and Robert D. Blackwill, with Ali Wyne, *Lee Kuan Yew: The Grand Master's Insights on China, the United States, and the World* (MIT Press, 2013).

19. Yap, Lim, and Kam, *Men in White*, pp. 358–62.

20. The Peranakans are people of mixed Chinese and Malay/Indonesian heritage whose ancestors were overseas Chinese who emigrated from China between the 15th and 19th centuries and became highly assimilated thereafter into Malay society.

21. "Singapore World's Busiest Port," *Manila Standard,* May 17, 1987, retrieved from Google News.

22. PSA International, "PSA Container Throughput for 2012," news release, January 11, 2013.

23. For timelines of Old Guard careers, see Lam Peng Er and Kevin Y. L. Tan, eds., *Lee's Lieutenants: Singapore's Old Guard* (Sydney: Allen and Unwin, 1999); and Jenny Tien, "Goh Keng Swee," "Toh Chin Chye," "Lim Kim San," and "S. Rajaratnam," *Singapore Infopedia*, Singapore National Library Board.

24. Ezra F. Vogel, "A Little Dragon Tamed," in *Management of Success: The Molding of Modern Singapore,* edited by Kernial Singh Sandhu and Paul Wheatley (Singapore: Institute of Southeast Asian Studies, 1989), p. 1035.

25. Ibid.

26. Jon S. T. Quah, *Public Administration Singapore-Style* (Singapore: Emerald Group, 2010), p. 5.

27. The People's Association of Singapore is a statutory board established on July 1, 1960, to promote, develop, and connect the people of Singapore together into a community that is racially harmonious, socially cohesive, and composed of active citizens. See People's Association, "About Us" (www.pa.gov.sg/about-us.html).

28. For details on ministerial configurations, see Singapore Government Directory (www.sgdi.gov.sg/).

29. "Statutory Boards," Singapore Government Directory, last updated April 8, 2016 (www.gov.sg/sgdi/statutory-boards).

30. Singapore does have five individuals designated to perform representational functions in various parts of the city-state, who are technically known as chairs of Community Development Councils (CDCs), but who might broadly be considered mayors. The CDC system was established in 1997 to address social welfare and other community issues most appropriately addressed at the local level. CDC chairs are selected from among members of parliament, thus conflating local and national governmental functions. On the CDCs and the mayoral functions of their chairs, see www.cdc.org.s/office-of-the-Mayor.

31. Prime Minister Lee Hsien Loong's National Day Rally, "A Home with Hope and Heart," August 2012 (www.pmo.gov.sg.)

32. On the rationale for statutory boards in Singapore, see Quah, *Public Administration*, pp. 46–48.

33. Department of Statistics–Singapore, *Yearbook of Statistics Singapore 2015* (www.singstat.gov.sg). The percentage is calculated using total labor-force data provided by the World Bank. The Singapore government and the World Bank published different numbers for the total labor force in 2014. Cross-national public sector comparisons are presented in chapter 4.

34. Ibid.

35. Prime Minister Lee Hsien Loong's salary was reduced, with his own assent, in 2012, in deference to local political sentiment. Yet he still enjoys an income of over S$2 million—one of the highest chief-executive salaries in the world, and over four times that of U.S. president Barack Obama. See Lucy Hornby, "Xi Jinping's Pay Far behind Global Peers Even after 62 Percent Rise," *Financial Times*, January 20, 2015; as well as Amanda Macias and Mike Nudelman, "Here Are the Salaries of 13 Major World Leaders," *Business Insider*, March 19, 2015.

36. Sukvinder-Singh Chapra, *Singapore's Civil Service* (Astana: Astana Economic Forum, 2013) (http://2013.astanaforum.org/en/events/russian); and "Parliament," *The*

Straits Times, February 15, 2006, p. H-4. Over 10 percent of ministerial appointments and 16 percent of statutory board employees are recipients of such elite scholarships. Department of Statistics–Singapore, *Yearbook of Statistics Singapore 2015*.

37. Ninety percent ownership refers to the percentage among resident households in HDB flats. Department of Statistics–Singapore, "Resident Households by Tenancy, Annual"; in 1959 only 9 percent of Singapore's population lived in public (SIT) flats, many of them rentals. Valerie Chew, "Public Housing in Singapore," *Singapore Infopedia*, Singapore National Library Board.

38. World Bank, "Singapore Local Economic Development: The Case of the Economic Development Board (EDB)" (siteresources.worldbank.org/INTLED/Resources/339650-1194284482831/4356163-1211318886634/SingaporeProfile.pdf), p. 2.

39. Economic Development Board (EDB), "Our Economic History: The Sixties" (www.edb.gov.sg/content/edb/en/why-singapore/about-singapore/our-history/1960s.html).

40. Henry Wai-chung Yeung, "Regional Development and the Competitive Dynamics of Global Production Networks: An East Asian Perspective," *Regional Studies* 43 (April 2009).

41. EDB, "Contact Us-Global Offices," last updated Jun 5, 2015.

42. The EDB typically selects potential candidates as they leave secondary school, funds them through university, and then bonds them to serve the EDB for a minimum period of five years (generally six years for English-speaking and five years for non-English-speaking individuals). Its scholarships are funded largely by multinationals that have benefited from investing in Singapore, and some EDB officials ultimately move to such multinationals after their bonded period with the EDB is complete. See www.edb.gov.sg.

43. On Heng Swee Keat, see www.pmo.gov.sg.

44. On Leo Yip, see www.pmo.gov.sg. Both Heng and Yip received Singapore Police Force (Overseas) Scholarships to study at Cambridge. Prime Minister Lee assisted Heng's entry into politics. As minister of education, Heng initiated Our Singapore Conversation, which has become the bedrock of the government's current policies relating to civil society. For details, see www.pmo.gov.sg.

45. Joseph Nye, "Smart Power: In Search of the Balance between Hard and Soft Power," *Democracy: A Journal of Ideas*, no. 2 (Fall 2006). This article is a review of Kurt M. Campbell and Michael O'Hanlon, *Hard Power: The New Politics of National Security* (New York: Basic Books, 2006).

46. Barr, *Lee Kuan Yew: The Beliefs behind the Man*, pp. 81–83.

47. See Lee Kuan Yew, *From Third World to First: The Singapore Story, 1965–2000* (New York: Harper Collins, 2000), p. 57.

48. On the "poisonous shrimp" approach, said to have prevailed into the 1980s as a central Singaporean defense stratagem, see Michael Leifer, *Singapore's Foreign Policy: Coping with Vulnerability* (London: Routledge, 2000), pp. 33–34; as well as Fang Fang and others, "Singapore's International Strategy Is Like a Poisonous Shrimp?," *The Straits Times*, October 4, 2013. Lee Kuan Yew himself is said to have used this analogy.

49. Lee, *From Third World to First*, pp. 14–15.

50. See Amnon Barzilai, "A Deep, Dark, Secret Love Affair," *Haaretz*, July 16, 2004 (www.haaretz.com).

51. In March 1967, for example, Singapore passed a National Service Act, patterned after Israel's system. See Er and Tan, *Lee's Lieutenants*, p. 58.

52. Singapore accredited an ambassador to Israel, based in Paris, only in 1996, and an honorary consul, based in Israel itself, in 1999. See Leifer, *Singapore's Foreign Policy*, p. 65.

53. Ibid.

54. Lee, *From Third World to First*, p. 26.

55. Ibid.

56. Adam Malik of Indonesia and Thanat Khoman of Thailand first broached the idea of ASEAN, and Rajaratnam came on soon thereafter. See ASEAN, "History: the Founding of ASEAN" (www.asean.org/asean/about-asean/history).

57. On the limited but real accomplishments of the Five Power Defense Arrangements, including formation of the Integrated Air Defense System, see Damon Bristow, "The Five Power Defense Arrangements: Southeast Asia's Unknown Regional Security Organization," *Contemporary Southeast Asia* 27, no. 1 (2005): 1–20.

58. Lee, *From Third World to First*, pp. 463–64.

59. See Allison and others, *Lee Kuan Yew*, pp. xxv, 41.

60. Ibid.

61. Ezra F. Vogel, *Deng Xiaoping and the Transformation of China* (Harvard University Press, 2011), pp. 287–91.

62. Daniel Bell, *The Coming of Post-Industrial Society: A Venture in Social Forecasting* (New York: Basic Books, 1973); and Daniel Bell, *The Cultural Contradictions of Capitalism* (New York: Basic Books, 1976).

63. Yap, Lim, and Kam, *Men in White*, p. 430.

64. Ibid., pp. 433–34.

65. Lee was apparently dissuaded in his attempt to hire Goh as his PPS by Minister of Finance Lim Kim San, following entreaties by Goh's boss at the EDB, J. Y. Pillay, who had originally sent Goh abroad to study. See ibid., p. 383.

66. On global e-government comparisons, see J. Ramon Gil-Garcia, *E-Government Success around the World: Cases, Empirical Studies, and Practical Recommendations* (Hershey, Pa.: IGI Global, 2013); Senior Minister Goh Chok Tong, "Integrating Public Services, Engaging Citizens," speech for the iGov Global Exchange, June 15, 2009 (www.ida.gov.sg).

67. On the history of e-government in Singapore, see Barney Tan and others, "The Evolution of Singapore's Government Infocomm Plans: Singapore's E-Government Journey from 1980 To 2007," Singapore eGovernment Leadership Centre and School of Computing, National University of Singapore, 2008 (http://unpan1.un.org/).

68. Infocomm Development Authority of Singapore, "Factsheet: Singapore's e-Government Journey" (www.ida.gov.sg/-/media/Files/Archive/News%20and%20Events/News_and_Events_Level2/20060530150726/eGovJourney.doc).

69. A full list of current e-government services in Singapore is available at www.ecitizen.gov.sg/eServices/Pages/default.aspx.

70. Infocomm Development Authority of Singapore, "Annual e-Government Perception Survey (Citizen) Conducted in 2015" (www.ida.gov.sg).

71. Singapore has held the top rank in the Waseda rankings at least five times since 2009. See Toshio Obi, ed., "2015 Waseda IAC International e-Government Ranking Survey," June 2015 (www.e-gov.waseda.ac.jp).

72. United Nations Department of Economic and Social Affairs, "United Nations e-Government Survey 2014" (https:publicadministration.un.org).

73. National Library Board, "TradeNet Is Officially Launched," October 17, 1989.

74. Marissa Lee, "The National IT Project That Went Global in a Big Way," *The Straits Times,* May 2, 2016.

75. On the latter two innovations, see Yap, Lim, and Kam, *Men in White*, p. 360.

76. Goh remarked in 1990 before parliament, "We wanted a law that could deal with the problem in a very fine way instead of having to resort to ISA or the Sedition Act or to use court prosecution under some other relevant laws to deal with those who cause disharmony through religion." Maintenance of Religious Harmony Bill, February 23, 1990, Parliament of Singapore—Official Report Parliamentary Debates (Hansard) (http://sprs. parl.gov.sg/).

77. Ibid., pp. 475–76.

78. Goh expressed these sentiments in his August 1999 National Day address. See C. M. Turnbull, *A History of Modern Singapore, 1819–2005* (Singapore: NUS Press, 2009), p. 359.

79. Ibid., p. 359; Yap, Lim, and Kam, *Men in* White, p. 492.

80. Yap, Lim, and Kam, *Men in* White, pp. 563–64.

81. Ibid., pp. 486–87. The U.S.-Singapore free trade agreement was the first ever concluded by the United States with an Asian nation.

82. Ibid., p. 478.

83. The inscription reportedly bears the words of Tang period Chancelllor Wei Zheng (580–643).

84. Lee's approach has included, in April 2012, establishing a Facebook page—a first for a Singaporean leader. See www.facebook.com/leehsienloong.

85. Yap, Lim, and Kam, *Men in White*, p. 512.

86. Ibid., pp. 510–11.

87. Ibid., pp. 490–91, 518–19. When Lee's first wife, Wong Ming Yang, died in 1982, for example, Lee asked a dialect-speaking staff sergeant, a primary-school dropout, to be one of the pall bearers at the funeral.

88. Ibid., p. 519.

89. Formed in 1999 through a merger of the National Computer Board and the Telecommunications Authority of Singapore, the Infocomm Development Authority of Singapore is a statutory board under the Ministry of Communications and Information, which manages the growing convergence of information technology and telephony through Singapore's 10-year infocomm master plan. See the IDA segment, "About Us: History" (www.ida.gov.sg/About-Us/What-We-Do/History).

90. See SPRING Singapore, "Sector Specific Accelerator (SSA) Programme" (www. spring.gov.sg/.../Pages/sector-specific-accelerator.aspx); and National Research Foundation, "Early Stage Venture Fund" (www.nrf.gov.sg/.../early-stage-venture-fund.aspx).

91. Yap, Lim, and Kam, *Men in White*, p. 513.

92. Garry Rodan, "Singapore in 2004: Long-Awaited Leadership Transition," *Asian Survey* 45, no. 1 (2005): 140–45.

93. The deal among Singapore's Tourism Board, Singapore GP, and Bernie Ecclestone was struck in 2007, but the first actual night race was run in 2008. See http://uniquelysingapore.org.

94. Yap, Lim, and Kam, *Men in White*, p. 453; "Singapore 21" was Prime Minister Goh Chok Tong's manifesto for the 1997 general elections. See Jasmine S. Chan, "Singapore: A Vision for the New Millennium," *Southeast Asian Affairs*, 2000, p. 260 (www. jstor.org/stable/279 12255).

95. Medisave was a compulsory savings program within the Central Provident Fund that generated funds to help cover medical costs on top of government subsidies; Medifund, generated from government fiscal surpluses, was to be a safety net for needy Singaporeans. On the details, see Yap, Lim, and Kam, *Men in White*, p. 454.

96. Goh took steps to support Singaporeans still in rental apartments in acquiring their own homes. See ibid., pp. 454–55.

97. Turnbull, *A History of Modern Singapore*, p. 362.

98. On Vogel's characterization of the Singaporean bureaucracy, see Quah, *Public Administration*, p. 6.

99. Singapore has a constitutional provision, introduced in September 1990, allowing for the appointment by the president of up to nine members of parliament (www.parliament.sov.sg/members-parliament).

Chapter 4

1. John Micklethwait and Adrian Wooldridge, *The Fourth Revolution: The Global Race to Reinvent the State* (New York: Penguin Press, 2014).

2. Thomas L. Friedman and Michael Mandelbaum, *That Used to Be Us: How America Fell Behind in the World It Invented and How We Can Come Back* (New York: Farrar, Straus and Giroux, 2011).

3. On the concept of a "plan-rational developmental state," see Chalmers Johnson, *MITI and the Japanese Miracle* (Stanford University Press, 1982), chap. 1.

4. Peter Evans, *Embedded Autonomy: States and Industrial Transformation* (Princeton University Press, 1995).

5. Peter Hall and David Soskice, eds., *Varieties of Capitalism: The Institutional Foundations of Comparative Advantage* (Oxford University Press, 2001); Theda Skocpol, *States and Social Revolutions: A Comparative Analysis of France, Russia, and China* (Cambridge University Press, 1979); and Stephan Haggard, *Pathways from the Periphery: The Roles of Growth in the Newly Industrializing Countries* (Cornell University Press, 1990); as well as Stephan Haggard and Matthew D. McCubbins, eds., *Presidents, Parliaments, and Policy* (Cambridge University Press, 2001).

6. Robert O. Keohane and Joseph S. Nye Jr., *Power and Interdependence,* 4th ed. (New York: Pearson, 2011); Hans J. Morgenthau, *Politics among Nations: The Struggle for Power and Peace* (New York: McGraw-Hill, 1993); and Robert Gilpin, *War and Change in World Politics* (Cambridge University Press, 1981).

7. George Liska, *Nations in Alliance: The Limits of Interdependence* (Johns Hopkins University Press, 1962); and George Liska, *Expanding Realism: The Historical Dimension of World Politics* (Lanham, Md.: Rowman and Littlefield, 1998).

8. On the concept of "minimalist government," see Kent E. Calder, "Japan's Minimalist Government," *Wall Street Journal*, February 13, 1981.

9. For a capsule summary, see "Widefare: Social Spending in Asia: Asia's Emerging Welfare States Spread Themselves Thinly," *The Economist*, July 16, 2013.

10. U.K. Department of Health, "The NHS Constitution for England," updated October 14, 2015.

11. On Japanese health care costs, see Ministry of Health, Labor, and Welfare (MHLW), "Overview of Medical Service Regime in Japan," Slide 3 (www.mhlw.go.jp). On Singaporean health care costs, see Ministry of Health Singapore, "Healthcare

Financing Sources," May 13, 2013. Patient co-payment share was calculated by the author based on table 1, where patient co-payment is equal to national health expenditure minus government expenditure and Medifund, Medisave, and MediShield expenditures.

12. Note that Medisave and MediShield are CPF accounts, which are actually individual saving accounts. The CPF and its role in health care are discussed later in the chapter.

13. MHLW, "Overview of Medical Service Regime in Japan," Slide 7.

14. See "Healthcare We All Can Afford," pamphlet prepared by Ministry of Health Singapore.

15. Figures for Japan and the United Kingdom are from the Organization for Economic Cooperation and Development (OECD), "Health at a Glance 2011," p. 157 (www.oecd.org/health/health-systems/49105858.pdf). Figure for Singapore calculated by the author with data provided in Ministry of Health Singapore, "Healthcare Financing Sources" (www.moh.gov.sg).

16. World Bank, "Health Expenditure, Public (% of Total Health Expenditure)," *World Development Indicators* (2014) (www-wds.worldbank.org/).

17. The Affordable Care Act (ACA) involves subsidies on health care premiums for individuals and families with incomes up to 400 percent of the poverty line, or US$94,200 for a family of four in 2013. See Tami Luhby, "What You'll Actually Pay for Obamacare," CNN, August 21, 2013 (money.cnn.com).

18. For details of the CPF program, see Central Provident Fund (CPF) Board, "CPF Overview" (http://cpf.gov.sg).

19. John Locke, of course, stressed the importance of property acquisition in his *Second Treatise*, published in 1690, and that concept—also valued by America's founding fathers—has become since the late 1960s a fundamental aspect of Singapore public policy. See C. B. McPherson, ed., *John Locke's Second Treatise of Government* (Indianapolis: Hackett, 1980).

20. CPF Board, "CPF Contribution and Allocation Rates from 1 January 2016" (www.cpf.gov.sg/Assets/Members/Documents/Jan2016_Con_Rate_Page.pdf).

21. As of December 31, 2014, the CPF had 1,951,000 active members. See CPF Board, "Annual Report 2015," p. 24. And Singapore recorded 2,185,200 resident labor force in 2014. See Department of Statistics–Singapore, *Yearbook of Statistics Singapore 2015,* table 5.1 (www.singstate.gov.sg/).

22. The CPF investment scheme provides an option for individual investment of CPF savings, within quite liberal guidelines, if the overall saving account has accumulated more than a government-specified minimum sum. See CPF Board, "CPF Investment Schemes" (www.cpf.gov.sg/).

23. The CPF full-retirement sum of required savings for members turning 55 on July 1, 2015, for example, was S$161,000. See CPF Board, "Retirement Sum Scheme" (www.cpf.gov.sg/).

24. Ministry of Finance Singapore, "Section IV. Is Our CPF Money Safe? Can the Government Pay All Its Debt Obligations?," *Our Nation's Reserves* (www.mof.gov.sg/Policies/Our-Nations-Reserves).

25. Up to 10 percent of investible savings may be invested in gold. Other investment products are also subject to the CPF Board's review. See CPF Board, "CPF Investment Schemes."

26. Housing and Development Board (HDB), Research & Planning Department, "Key Findings of Sample Household Survey 2008," *Statistics Singapore News Letter*, September 2010, p. 17.

27. Valerie Chew, "Public Housing in Singapore," *Singapore Infopedia*, 2009 (http://eresources.nlb.gov.sg).

28. Lee Kuan Yew, *From Third World to First: The Singapore Story, 1965–2000* (New York: Harper Collins, 2000), p. 96.

29. Valerie Chew, "Housing and Development Board," *Singapore Infopedia*, 2009.

30. See CPF Board, "Home Protection Scheme" (www.cpf.gov.sg/).

31. See HDB, "Public Housing in Singapore: Residents' Profile, Housing Satisfaction, and Preferences—HBD Sample Household Survey 2013" (www.hdb.gov.sg).

32. Samuel P. Huntington, *The Clash of Civilizations and the Remaking of World Order* (New York: Simon and Schuster, 2006).

33. In figure 4-7, Malay and Indian populations for Singapore are denoted as Ethnic Minority #1 and Ethnic Minority #2, respectively.

34. See, for example, Benedict R. Anderson, *Imagined Communities: Reflections on the Origin and Spread of Nationalism* (London: Verso, 1983).

35. Charles Tilly, ed., *The Formation of Nation States in Western Europe* (Princeton University Press, 1975); and Charles Tilly, *Coercion, Capital, and European States: AD 990–1990* (Oxford: Blackwell, 1990).

36. On this concept, see Eric Hobsbawm, *The Invention of Tradition* (Cambridge University Press, 1983).

37. The Housing Development Board is a statutory board under the jurisdiction of the Ministry of National Development, while the People's Association is a statutory board under the Ministry of Culture, Community, and Youth.

38. This policy change in 1989 affected 35 out of 125 neighborhoods in 25 HDB new towns. See National Library Board, "Ethnic Integration Policy Is Implemented," March 1, 1989 (http://eresources.nlb.gov.sg/).

39. Lee Kuan Yew has rather explicitly noted his high evaluation of communist mass-mobilization tactics and the importance of countering them. See Lee, *From Third World to First*, pp. 96–100, 123–24.

40. See www.pa.gov.sg.

41. See People's Association, "About Grassroots Organisations" (www.pa.gov.sg).

42. The National Heritage Board (NHB) is a statutory board under the Ministry of Culture, Community, and Youth.

43. See fiscal 2014 budget operating expenditure in Ministry of Finance, "Head X Ministry of Culture, Community and Youth," p. 189 (Singaporebudget.gov.sg).

44. "PM Lee Attends Opening Ceremony of New Singapore Chinese Cultural Centre," *AsiaOne*, September 29, 2014; and "Singapore's Unique Chinese Culture," *The Straits Times*, February 7, 2016.

45. On Japan, see, for example, Kent E. Calder, *Crisis and Compensation: Public Policy and Political Stability in Japan* (Princeton University Press, 1988).

46. Singapore government expenditures in general constituted 14.6 percent of GDP in fiscal 2014, of which 22 percent were devoted to defense, 21 percent to education, and 4 percent to government administration. See Singapore Ministry of Finance. *Budget Statement 2014*.

47. Comparative figures are for 2011, the latest available for all nations being compared at the time of writing.

48. See Ministry of Education Singapore, "Edusave" (www.moe.gov.sg/education/edusave).

49. Ibid.

50. Ministry of Education Singapore, "Eligibility: Who Is Eligible for a PSEA?" (www. moe.gov.sg/education/post-secondary/post-secondary-education-account/eligibility).

51. For children born after 2006, however, the age of eligibility for postsecondary education accounts has risen to 13 years of age.

52. Ministry of Manpower Singapore, "Committee of Supply," Speech to Parliament by Lee Yi Shyan, Minister of State for Trade & Industry and Manpower, March 9, 2011.

53. Singapore Workforce Development Agency, "What is WSQ?," updated July 15, 2015 (www.wda.gov.sg).

54. See OECD, *Economic Outlook for Southeast Asia, China and India 2014: Beyond The Middle-Income Trap,* p. 206.

55. OECD, "PISA 2012 Results in Focus" (www.oecd.org/pisa/keyfindings/).

56. Ibid.

57. PISA 2012 defined problem-solving competence as "an individual's capacity to engage in cognitive processing to understand and resolve problem situations where a method of solution is not obvious. It includes the willingness to engage with such situations in order to achieve one's potential as a constructive and reflective citizen." See OECD, "PISA 2012 Results: Creative Problem Solving" (ibid.).

58. See Ministry of Trade and Industry, "The Road Thus Far," chap. 1, p. 27 (www.mti.gov.sg/AboutMTI/Documents/app.mti.gov.sg/data/pages/507/doc/ ERC_Comm_MainReport_Part1_v2.pdf).

59. Speech by Indranee Rajah, senior minister of state, Ministry of Law and Ministry of Education, at the National Youth Business Conference 2014, "Dream Big. Do Big," October 4, at ITE College East.

60. Jacky Yap, "ACE and MOE announce S$15M 3-year plan to grow student entrepreneurs," *e27,* November 9, 2012.

61. For a list of start-up supports, see SPRING Singapore, "Nurturing Startups: Overview" (www.spring.gov.sg/).

62. Shea Driscoll, "Singapore Budget 2016: More Low-Wage Workers to Qualify for Workfare Income Supplement Scheme That Tops Up Their Income," *The Straits Times,* March 24, 2016; and Central Provident Fund Board, "More Frequent Workfare Income Supplement (WIS) Payouts: Frequently Asked Questions" (www.workfare.gov.sg/ Documents/FAQs.pdf).

63. Infocomm Development Authority of Singapore, "Bridging the Digital Divide," April 17, 2014.

64. Ministry of Social and Family Development, "Baby Bonus Scheme" (https:/app. msf.gov.sg/).

65. See Ministry of Health Singapore, "Medical Endowment Scheme: Annual Report 2014/2015."

66. Linda Low, "The Singapore Developmental State in the New Economy and Polity," *Pacific Review* 14, no. 3 (2001): 411–41.

67. Singapore's Department of Statistics defines government-linked companies as firms in which the government's effective ownership of voting shares is 20 percent or more. See Department of Statistics–Singapore, "Contribution of Government-Linked Companies to Gross National Product," Occasional Papers on Economic Statistics, 2001.

68. Carlos D. Ramirez and Ling Hui Tan, *Singapore, Inc. Versus the Private Sector: Are Government-Linked Companies Different?* International Monetary Fund Working Paper WP/03/156 (Washington: July 2003), p. 14.

69. On the privatization process and its implications, see Loizos Heracleous, "Privatisation: Global Trends and Implications of the Singapore Experience," *International Journal of Public Sector Management* 12, no. 5 (1999): 432–44.

70. For instance, the Project Jewel joint venture, involving the Changi Airport Group and Capital Mall Asia embarked in 2014 on construction of a S$1.47 billion retail and lifestyle complex at Changi Airport, scheduled to be completed in 2018. "Changi Airport's Project Jewel: 5 Things to Know about the New Lifestyle Complex," *The Straits Times*, December 4, 2014.

71. A new $220 million one-stop medical center near the Changi General Hospital is scheduled to be completed in 2017. "One-Stop Care at Upcoming Medical Centre at Changi General Hospital," *The Straits Times*, August 29, 2014.

72. Basic Element, Changi Airports International, and Sberbank, "Joint Press Release: Basic Element, Sberbank and Changi Airports International Form Airport Business Partnership," St. Petersburg, June 22, 2012 (www.changiairportgroup.com/export/sites/caas/assets/media_release_2012/22_Jun_2012_2.pdf).

73. Temasek, "Why Was Temasek Established?" (www.temasek.com.sg/Documents/).

74. Wilson Ng, "The Evolution of Sovereign Wealth Funds: Singapore's Temasek Holdings," *Journal of Financial Regulation and Compliance* 18 (December 2009): 2.

75. Temasek, "Portfolio Highlights: Geography," last updated March 31, 2016 (www.temasek.com.sg/porfolio).

76. Temasek, "Mr. Robert Zoellick Joins the Temasek Board," news release, August 1, 2013.

77. As of 2016, the Temasek portfolio is allocated most heavily to telecommunications (25 percent), financial services (23 percent), and transportation/industrials (18 percent). See Temasek, "Portfolio Highlights: Sector."

78. Ramirez and Tan, *Singapore, Inc.*, p. 14.

79. Temasek, "Portfolio Highlights: Major Investments."

80. See Johnson, *MITI and the Japanese Miracle*, and Steven Vogel, *Freer Markets, More Rules: Regulatory Reform in Advanced Industrial Countries* (Cornell University Press, 1998).

81. Singapore has 16 ministries, including the Ministry of National Development, which supervises the Housing and Development Board; and the Ministry of Commerce and Industry, which supervises the Economic Development Board. For details on ministerial configurations, see Singapore Government Directory (www.sgdi.gov.sg).

82. See Economic Development Board, "About EDB" (www.edb.gov.sg/content/edb/en/about-edb.html).

83. See EDB, "Contact Us-Global Offices."

84. Lim Swee Say, minister for the prime minister's office; S. Dhalabalan, chair of Temasek Holdings; Manohar Khiatani, CEO of Jurong Town Corporation; Liew Heng San, CEO of the Central Provident Fund; and Philip Yeo, chair of SPRING Singapore, are also alumni of the EDB.

85. On the concept of embedded autonomy, often associated with technocratic flexibility, see Peter Evans, *Embedded Autonomy: States and Industrial Transformation* (Princeton University Press, 1995).

86. See the biography of Beh Swan Gin, chair of the EDB since 2014, Economic Development Board, "Dr Beh Swan Gin," last updated April 26, 2016 (www.edb.gov.sg/... top-of/the-board/).

87. See EDB, "Our Board Members," last updated March 9, 2016 (www.edb.gov.sg).

88. See EDB, "International Advisory Council," last updated June 27, 2016 (www. edb.gov.sg).

89. See "EDB International Advisory Council (IAC) Makes Recommendations for Singapore's Economic Future," September 20, 2013 (www.edb.gov.sg).

90. Deputy Prime Minister Shanmugaratnam pointed out the role of EDB facing a new phase of national economic development transitioning from value adding to value creation. See Ministry of Finance, Speech by Mr.Tharman Shanmugaratnam, deputy prime minister and minister for finance, at EDB Society's 25th Anniversary Gala Dinner, July 23, 2015 (www.mof.gov.sg).

91. In this respect, the background of EDB chair Beh Swan Gin, a medical doctor and biomedical sciences specialist who most recently served as permanent secretary of the Ministry of Law, is of particular interest.

92. Monetary Authority of Singapore, "New FinTech Office: A One-Stop Platform to Promote Singapore as a FinTech Hub," media release, April 1, 2016.

93. See Agency for Science, Technology and Research, "About A*STAR" (www. a-star.edu.sg).

94. Urban Redevelopment Authority (URA), statutory board under the Ministry of National Development, has commercial projects at science park Fusionopolis that host A*Star's research and development activities. See URA, "Commercial Projects in Pipeline at End of 2nd Quarter 2014," p. 1 (www.ura.gov.sg/uol/media-room/news/).

95. Jurong Town Corporation (JTC), statutory board under the Ministry of Trade and Industry, developed science research parks Biopolis and Fusionopolis, which house A*STAR's research and development activities. See A*STAR, "A Vision for Convergence" (www.a-star.edu.sg...A-Vision-for-Convergence.aspx) and JTC, "One North" (www.jtc. gov.sg/RealEstateSolutions/one-north/).

96. For an insightful review of these challenges, see the 2015 Rajaratnam Lecture of Prime Minister Lee Hsien Loong (www.mfa.gov.sg/...media_centre/).

97. Kent E. Calder, *Embattled Garrisons: Comparative Base Politics and American Globalism* (Princeton University Press, 2007), pp. 60–62, 236–37.

98. Singapore, at just over 700 square kilometers, is roughly one-eighth as large as the next smallest member of ASEAN, Brunei. See World Bank, "Land Area," *World Development Indicators* (2015).

99. In 2013 Singapore's defense budget was US$9.86 billion, compared to Vietnam's defense spending of $3.8 billion, Malaysia's $5 billion, and Indonesia's $8.4 billion. See International Institute of Strategic Studies, *The Military Balance 2014* (London: International Institute for Strategic Studies, 2014).

100. The United States in April 2014 also concluded a separate Enhanced Defense Cooperation Agreement providing for access by U.S. forces to designated Philippine bases, although the provision of permanent facilities, or the entry of nuclear weapons onto the prospective temporary facilities, were specifically excluded. On the details of the agreement, see www.gov.ph/downloads/2014/04apr/20140428-EDCA.pdf.

101. Calder, *Embattled Garrisons*, p. 61. The headquarters of the U.S. Navy Western Pacific Logistics Group has been located in Singapore since July 1992, following the U.S. military withdrawal from the Philippines.

102. Ibid.

103. "Agreement Calls for 4 U.S. Littoral Combat Ships to Rotate through Singapore," *Defense News*, June 2, 2012 (www.defensenews.com); and "Four U.S. Warships to Operate out of Singapore by 2018," *The Straits Times*, November 5, 2015.

104. Exercise Tiger Balm is the oldest bilateral training exercise in Singapore armed forces history and now involves National Guard as well as regular U.S. Army troops. It has been supplemented since 2007 by Lightning Strike, sponsored by U.S. Army Pacific. On details of these exercises, see www.army.mil.

105. Exercise CARAT, which began in 1995, focused in 2014 on surface gunnery, air defense, search and rescue, shipboard helicopter operations, and marine interdiction, involving 1,400 from the two countries, with broader multilateral aspects as well as the bilateral dimension. See Loke Kok Fai, "Singapore, U.S. Kick Off Joint Military Exercise in South China Sea," *Channel NewsAsia*, July 29, 2014.

106. On Peace Carvin II, see www.pacaf.af.mil. The Singapore Air Force also exercises jointly with combined U.S. forces of different branches of service through Exercise Forging Sabre, initiated in 2005, the location of which changes annually. On the 2009 event, held at Fort Sill, Oklahoma, see www.globalsecurity.org/military/library/news/2009/11/mil-091125-arnews05.htm.

107. Exercise Red Flag, a multilateral air exercise involving the Philippines, Canada, the United Kingdom, Japan, New Zealand, and Australia, as well as the United States and Singapore, was originally known as Exercise Cope Thunder, but redesignated as Red Flag in 2006 (www.globalsecurity.org/military/ops/cope-thunder.htm).

108. On the details of this agreement, see www.state.gov/documents/organiztion/95360.pdf.

109. On such difficulties, see, for example, Calder, *Embattled Garrisons*, pp. 130–36, 147–48, and 151–52; as well as William L. Brooks, *The Politics of the Futenma Base Issue in Okinawa: Relocation Negotiations in 1995–1997 and 2005–2006*, Asia-Pacific Policy Papers 9 (Washington: Reischauer Center for East Asian Studies, 2000); and William L. Brooks, *Cracks in the Alliance? Futenma Log: Base Relocation Negotiations, 2009–2013*, Asia-Pacific Policy Papers 12 (Washington: Reischauer Center for East Asian Studies, 2011).

110. "Singapore Troops to Join Taiwan Drills," *Taipei Times*, March 5, 2013.

111. Lee Min Kok, "China and Taiwan to Hold Historic Talks in Singapore: Six Things about Cross-Strait Relations," *The Straits Times*, November 5, 2015.

112. This observation is from the International Institute for Democracy and Electoral Assistance (www.idea.int/asia-pacific/burma/upload/chap1.pdf).

113. Michael Leifer, *Singapore's Foreign Policy: Coping with Vulnerability* (London: Routledge, 2000), p. 84.

114. The World Water Council was founded in 1996 at the initiative of renowned water specialists and international organizations, in response to the global community's increasing concern about world water issues. On the World Water Council and Singapore International Water Week, see www.worldwatercouncil.org/about-us/vision-mission-strategy.

115. On the penumbra of power concept, see Kent E. Calder, *Asia in Washington: Exploring the Penumbra of Transnational Power* (Brookings, 2014).

116. For additional details on how Singapore uses its ambassadors in Washington to further its diplomatic interests, see Calder, *Asia in Washington*.

117. For more details, see www.mfa.sg.washington.

Chapter 5

1. McKinsey and Company, "How to Make a City Great," September 2013 (http://mckinsey.com).

2. The United Nations Development Program forecasts an urban population in 2050 of over 6,339,000,000 (see http://esa.un.org/undp/wup/Highlights/

WUP2014-Highlights.pdf). See also United Nations Department of Economic and Social Affairs (UNDESA), *World Urbanization Prospects: The 2014 Revision* (June 2014), p. 1.

3. Karl Wilson, "Urban Future," *China Daily: Asia Weekly*, June 20–26, 2014, p. 1.

4. UNDESA, *World Urbanization Prospects: The 2014 Revision.*

5. According to *The New Statesman,* in 2014 Jakarta and Manila were the 21st and the 22nd most polluted cities in the world, in terms of air quality (www.newstatesman.com).

6. Three more of the top 20 are in Pakistan, and 3 others in Bangladesh, making 16 of the top 20 in South Asia. Figures are for PM 2.5 levels, as determined by the World Health Organization, out of 1,600 major cities worldwide. See Madison Park, "Top 20 Most Polluted Cities in the World," CNN, May 8, 2014 (www.cnn.com).

7. Charles Goldblum, "Singapore's Holistic Approach to Urban Planning: Centrality, Singularity, Innovation, and Reinvention," in *Singapore from Temasek to the 21st Century: Reinventing the Global City,* edited by Karl Hack and Jean-Louis Margolin, with Karine Delaye (Singapore: NUS Press, 2010), pp. 384–408.

8. Chalmers Johnson, *MITI and the Japanese Miracle* (Stanford University Press, 1982); and Meredith Woo-Cumings, ed., *The Developmental State* (Cornell University Press, 1999).

9. The categories featured in the Asian Green City Index include energy conservation, land and building use, transport, waste management, water, sanitation, air quality, and environmental governance. In all these categories, Singapore is above average. See Karl Wilson, "Singapore Model Sets Global Standard," *China Daily: Asia Weekly*, June 20–26, 2014, p. 7.

10. See Mahizhan Arun, "Smart Cities: The Singapore Case," *Cities* 6, no. 1 (1999): 13–18; and iN2015 Steering Committee, *Innovation, Integration, and Internationalisation* (www.ida.gov.sg/media/Files/Infocomm%20Landscape/iN2015/Reports/01_iN2015_Main_Report.pdf).

11. On the progression of the Singapore government's computerization efforts, including Tradenet, Medinet, and Lawnet, see www.ida.gov.sg/-/media/Files/Infocomm%20Landscape/iN2015/Reports/01-iN2015_M_Report.pdf.

12. National Computer Board, *A Vision of an Intelligent Island: The IT 2000 Report* (Singapore: National Computer Board, 1992).

13. For the details, see the Infocomm Development Authority of Singapore, "iN 2015 Masterplan" (www.ida.gov.sg/Infocomm-Landscape/iN2015-Masterplan).

14. Ibid. In this effort, iN2015 proposed to double the value added of Singapore's infocomm industry to S$26 billion, triple infocomm export revenue to S$60 billion, and create 80,000 jobs.

15. The Intelligent Energy System pilot project was implemented in 2009 by the Energy Market Authority, a statutory board administered by the Ministry of Trade and Industry. See "Smart Grid Technology Primer: A Summary," National Climate Change Secretariat and National Research Foundation, 2011 (http://app.nccs.gov.sg.)

16. In 2013, according to UN statistics, 57 percent of Singapore's waste was recycled—an extremely high proportion in comparison with Germany's 46.6 percent, Sweden's 35.4 percent, the United Kingdom's 26.9 percent, the United States' 23.8 percent, France's 18.2 percent, and Japan's 16.8 percent. United Nations Statistics Division, "Municipal Waste Treatment," *Environmental Indicators* (http://unstats.un.org/unsd/environment/wastetreatment.html); and Wilson, "Singapore Model Sets Global Standard."

17. See 2014 data from Infocomm Development Authority of Singapore, "Infocomm Usage—Households and Individuals" (www.ida.gov.sg/Tech-Scene-News/Facts-and-Figures/Infocomm-Usage-Households-and-Individuals).

18. Infocomm Development Authority of Singapore, "Bridging the Digital Divide," April 17, 2014 (www.ida.gov.sg).

19. Singapore has a population density of 7,736.5 people per square kilometer, versus 348.7 per square kilometer in Japan, 505 in South Korea, and only 34.6 in the United States. See World Bank, "Population Density," *World Development Indicators* (2014).

20. In some parts of Singapore, land prices during 2011–13 were reportedly rising 30 percent a year, or three times the pace of apartment costs. Average land costs as a share of total development costs for non-landed housing sites rose from 42 percent in 2008 to 62 percent in 2013. See Pooja Thakur, "Singapore's Soaring Land Prices 'Suicidal' for Developers," *Bloomberg News*, February 20, 2014; and Nikki De Guzman, "Land Cost Takes Over Property Prices and Income Growth," *Yahoo News*, September 10, 2013.

21. Joan C. Henderson, "Planning for Success: Singapore, the Model City-State?," *Journal of International Affairs* 65 (Spring/Summer 2012): 69–83.

22. Center for Livable Cities and Urban Land Institute, *Principles for Livable High-Density Cities: Lessons from Singapore*, 2013 (www.uli.org).

23. Urban Redevelopment Authority (URA), "Introduction to Concept Plan."

24. Henderson, "Planning for Success: Singapore, The Model City-State?"

25. "Singapore Holds Heritage Town Award Presentation Ceremony," *Gov Monitor*, February 21, 2011; and Belinda Yuen, "Searching for Place Identity in Singapore," *Habitat International* 29, no. 2 (2005): 197–214.

26. Goldblum, "Singapore's Holistic Approach to Urban Planning," p. 388.

27. URA, "The Planning Act Master Plan Written Statement 2014," revised January 15, 2016.

28. URA, "Introduction to Master Plan."

29. For more information about development control, browse URA, "Development Control" (www.ura.gov.sg/uol/DC.aspx#).

30. Ministry of National Development, "How We Will Live, Work, and Play in Singapore 2030" (www.mnd.gov.sg/landuseplan/environment_live_work_play.htm); and Infocomm Development Authority of Singapore, "Smart Work Centres" (www.ida.gov.sg/.../New-Ways-of-Work/).

31. Marsita Omar and Nor-Afidah Abd Rahman, "Certificates of Entitlement (COEs)," *Singapore Infopedia* (National Library Board Singapore, 2006) (http://eresources.nlb.gov.sg/infopedia/articles/).

32. Singapore's "compact city" initiative favors density, making walking more feasible, while an extensive infrastructure of cycling paths, including the 150-kilometer Round Island Route, encourages cycling. See Centre for Liveable Cities and Urban Land Institute, "10 Principles for Liveable High-Density Cities: Lessons from Singapore," press release, 2013 (www.ULI_Density_10Princ%20(3)pdf).

33. On the Singapore approach, see Carlos Felipe Pardo, "Sustainable Urban Transport," *Shanghai Manual—A Guide for Sustainable Urban Development in the 21st Century* (Beijing: China International, 2011), pp. 29–38.

34. Land Transport Authority, "Household Interview Travel Survey 2012: Public Transport Mode Share Rises to 63%," October 7, 2013 (www.lta.gov.sg/apps/news/).

35. KPMG International, "Infrastructure 100: World Market Report 2014," p. 52 (www.kpmg-institutes.com/institutes/government-institutes/articles/).

36. Singapore's commuting costs in relation to GDP per capita were also lower than those for Hong Kong (9.2 percent). The only major cities lower than Singapore were Copenhagen and Madrid. See Credo Business Consulting LLP, "The Mobility Opportunity: Improving Public Transport to Drive Economic Growth," report commissioned by Siemens AG, p. 9 (www.credo-group.com/download/MobilityOpportunityStudy.pdf).

37. Since 2008 the Singapore government has committed S$60 billion to double Singapore's light-rail network to 280 kilometers, and to add 800 buses (www.public transport.sg).

38. Lew Yii Der and Leong Wai Yan, "Managing Congestion in Singapore—A Behavioral Economics Perspective," *Journeys,* May 2009.

39. Say Tay Tan, F. L. Leong, and B.C.A Leong, *Economics in Public Policies: The Singapore Story* (Singapore: Marshall Cavendish Education, 2009).

40. Johnathan E. D. Richmond, "Transporting Singapore—The Air-Conditioned Nation," *Transport Review* 28 (May 2008): 357–90 (http://the-tech.mit.edu/-richmond/professional/aircon.pdf).

41. Land Transport Authority, "Transition to a Government Contracting Model for the Public Bus Industry," May 21, 2014.

42. Stephanie Ho, "Mass Rapid Transit (MRT) System," *Singapore Infopedia*, November 5, 2013.

43. Public Transport Council, a statutory board under the Ministry of Transport, regulates public transport fares to create an affordable public transport system. See Public Transport Council, "About Us" (www.ptc.gov.sg/index/aspx.)

44. See Credo Business Consulting LLP, "The Mobility Opportunity," p. 9.

45. The World Bank and the so-called Harvard Team recommended partial or all-bus rapid transit systems, while Singapore ultimately decided on all-rail. See www.smrt.com.sg.

46. SMRT was, for example, awarded "Best Passenger Experience" at the fourth annual MetroRail conference in Copenhagen (April 2008). See ibid.

47. See, for example, Harvey Dzodin, "Singapore Is the Future of China in Urban Order," Xinhuanet.com, August 30, 2014.

48. Land Transport Authority, "Certificate of Entitlement (COE)."

49. Land Transport Authority, "Vehicle Quota System," "Certificate of Entitlement (COE)," and "Tax Structure for Cars."

50. Neel Chowdhury, "Strategic Singapore," *Time*, March 3, 2011.

51. Lim Tin Seng, "Area Licensing Scheme," *Singapore Infopedia*, August 15, 2014.

52. G. Santos, W. W. Li, and W. T. Koh, "Transport Policies in Singapore," *Research in Transport Economics* 9, no. 1 (2004): 209–35.

53. Ministry of the Environment and Water Resources, "A Lively and Livable Singapore," p. 57 (https://app.mewr.gov.sg/data/ImgCont/1299/Chapter05_Commute.pdf).

54. Land Transport Authority, "In-Vehicle Unit."

55. Christopher Tan, "ERP Rates at Four Locations in Singapore Will Be Raised from Monday, May 4," *The Straits Times*, April 27, 2015.

56. Ministry of the Environment and Water Resources, *The Singapore Green Plan: Toward a Model Green City* (Singapore: Ministry of the Environment and Water Resources, 1992); and Chua Lee Hoong, *The Singapore Green Plan 2012* (Singapore: Ministry of the Environment and Water Resources, 2012).

57. See Prime Minister's Office Singapore, "Speech by Prime Minister Lee Hsien Loong at the Launch of Clean and Green Singapore 2014."

58. When Lee Kuan Yew proposed in 1967 his vision for Singapore as the Garden City, he indicated that the first stage should be cleaning away rubbish and litter in the street, since litter often results from lack of civic consciousness. See "S'pore to Become Beautiful, Clean City within Three Years," *The Straits Times*, May 12, 1967, p. 4; and National Library Board, "'Garden City' Vision Is Introduced," May 11, 1967 (http://eresources.nlb.gov.sg/).

59. Singapore Green Plan 2012 (released in 2002) aims to make new parks and park connectors major tools for conserving nature. See Chua, *The Singapore Green Plan 2012*, p. x.

60. Park connectors are green pedestrian roads and cyclist routes that have played a major role in making walking and cycling popular in Singapore. The 2008 Leisure Plan aims to triple park connector routes from 100 to 360 kilometers. See Urban Redevelopment Authority, "URA Launches New Island-wide Leisure Plan," May 21, 2008. On the Singapore Park Connector Network, see a descriptive online map provided by the National Parks Board (www.nparks.gov.sg). See also Chua, *The Singapore Green Plan 2012*, p. 22.

61. Valerie Chew, "Singapore Green Plan," *Singapore Infopedia*, 2010.

62. National Parks Board, "Community in Bloom Initiatives," March 8, 2016 (www.nparks.gov.sg/gardening/).

63. For a list of campaigns, see National Environment Agency, "All Campaigns," last updated November 2015 (www.nea.gov.sg/events-programmes/).

64. "Edutainment" is a Singaporean term denoting a fusion of education and entertainment. Among the many edutainment projects in Singapore, apart from those described here, are the Experience Center (depicting high-tech, next-generation services), and Science Center Singapore. See www.singapore-attractions.com/members/edutainment.php.

65. Chua, *The Singapore Green Plan 2012*, p. 25.

66. URA, "Master Plan: Civic and Cultural District by the Bay."

67. National Library Board, "Esplanade—Theatres on the Bay Opens," October 12, 2012 (http://eresources.nlb.gov.sg/infopedia/articles/)

68. See Gardens by the Bay (www.gardensbythebay.com.sg/en.html).

69. See www.formula1.com.

70. Derek da Cunha, *Singapore Places Its Bets: Casinos, Foreign Talent, and Remaking a City-state* (Singapore: Straits Times Press, 2010).

71. Dan Smith, *The Penguin State of the World Atlas,* 9th ed. (New York: Penguin Books, 2012), p. 91.

72. Ibid.

73. Agriculture and Agri-Food Canada, "Market Overview—Singapore," *Market Access Secretariat-Global Analysis Report* (Ottawa, June 2014), p. 3.

74. United Nations Department of Economic and Social Affairs Population Division, "File 3: Urban Population at Mid-Year by Major Area, Region and Country, 1950–2050 (Thousands)," *World Urbanization Prospects: The 2014 Revision* (June 2014).

75. Nikos Alexandratos and Jelle Bruinsma, *World Agriculture towards 2030/2050: The 2012 Revision* (Rome: Food and Agricultural Organization, 2012) (www.fao.org).

76. Kalinga Seneviratne, "Farming in the Sky in Singapore," *Our World*, December 12, 2012 (http://ourworld.unu.edu).

77. See Alexandra Kain, "Singapore's Ecological EDITT Tower," *Inhabitat*, October 15, 2008 (http://inhabitat.com/editt-tower-by-trhamzah-and-yeang/).

78. Sky Greens, "About Sky Greens: How We Started" (www.skygreens.com/about-skygreen).

79. Seneviratne, "Farming in the Sky in Singapore."

80. Ibid.

81. "Lettuce Sees the Future: Japanese Farmer Builds High-Tech Indoor Veggie Factory," *GE Reports*, July 9, 2014 (www.gereports.com).

82. The vegetable factory is operated by Panasonic's in-house subsidiary, Automotive and Industrial Systems Company, which in Japan has already developed a greenhouse for growing spinach, at which it can automatically adjust temperatures and humidity. For details, see Kyodo News International, "Panasonic Starts Trial Operation of Vegetable Factory in Singapore," July 17, 2014 (www.globalpost.com).

83. For more country-specific details, see Smith, *The Penguin State of the World Atlas*, p. 111.

84. Emily Corcoran and others, eds., "Sick Water? The Central Role of Wastewater Management in Sustainable Development," A Rapid Response Assessment, United Nations Environment Programme, UN-HABITAT.

85. Smith. *The Penguin State of the World Atlas*, p. 111; Food and Agriculture Organization of the United Nations, "Water Uses–Thematic Discussion" (www.fao.org/nr/water/aquastat/water_use/index.stm).

86. United Nations Environment Program Division of Technology, Industry and Economics, "An Environmentally Sound Approach for Sustainable Urban Water Management: An Introductory Guide for Decision-Makers" (www.unep.or.jp/ietc/publications/urban/urbanenv-2/9.asp).

87. James Low, "Sustaining the Value of Water," in *Case Studies in Public Governance: Building Institutions in Singapore*, edited by June Gwee (New York: Routledge, 2012), p. 108.

88. Public Utilities Board, "Water Tariff" (www.pub.gov.sg).

89. This program works to transform simple drains, canals, and reservoirs into beautiful streams, well-integrated into surrounding parks and other environments, with plans for transforming 100 sites by 2030. Singapore International Waterweek, "PUB's Active, Beautiful, Clean Waters (ABC Waters) Programme Wins at Global Water Awards 2013."

90. Jean Lim,"NEWater," *SingaporeInfopedia,* 2010, National Library Board (http://eresources.nlb.gov.sg/infopedia/articles/).

91. Research Office Legislative Council Secretariat, "NEWater in Singapore," February 26, 2016 (www.legco.gov.hk/...1516fsc22-newater-in-singapore-20160226-e.pdf).

92. Among the awards NEWater received are the Stockholm Industry Water Award (2007) and the UN-Water Best Practice Award.

93. Lux Research, "Singapore Universities Top Ranking of Water Research Institutes," April 30, 2013.

94. Hyflux, "Tuaspring Wins Distinction in Desalination Plant of the Year Category at Global Water Awards 2014," *Featured Stories,* April 7, 2014.

95. Mayuko Tani, "Singapore's Hyflux Enters Latin American Water," *Nikkei Asian Review*, June 26, 2014.

96. International Enterprise Singapore (IES), "Singapore–South African Report Economic Relations Grow with IE Singapore's First Office in Africa," January 25, 2013.

97. Smith, *The Penguin State of the World*, p. 115.

98. Figures for final energy consumption are from the International Energy Agency (www.iea.org). For the 2004–12 period, China's share of the global energy consumption increase was 56 percent, and India's was an additional 12 percent.

99. World Bank, "CO2 Emissions," *World Development Indicators* (2011).

100. Central Intelligence Agency, *World Factbook 2016–17*. Figures are country comparisons for crude oil imports.

101. Singapore Energy Market Authority (EMA), "Natural Gas Consumption by Sub-Sector," *Singapore Energy Statistics 2015*, table 3.7, p. 59 (www.ema.gov.sg).

102. EMA, "Fuel Mix for Electricity Generation."

103. Neil McGregor, "Milestones in Singapore's Energy Strategy," *The Business Times*, June 20, 2012.

104. See Alpana Roy, "Singapore as Asia's Liquid Natural Gas Hub: Challenges and Prospects," unpublished paper, SAIS/Johns Hopkins University, December 12, 2012.

105. Chou Hui Hong and Ramsey Al-Rikabi, "Singapore Bids for Role as LNG Hub with Second Terminal," *Bloomberg News,* February 25, 2014.

106. U.S. Energy Information Administration (EIA), *International Energy Outlook 2016*, pp. 41–42. EIA forecasts China will account for 63 percent of the natural gas consumption growth in non-OECD Asia from 2012 to 2040, and India will account for 8 percent.

107. Ibid., pp. 49–50.

108. "IEA Chief Backs Natural Gas Spot Market in Asia," *China Post*, October 12, 2012. On the exchange, which was established in the Shanghai FTZ with Petrochina, Sinopec, and CNOOC as partners, see "China Launches New Oil and Gas Trading Platform—Xinhua," Reuters, July 1, 2015.

109. Francis Kim, "LNG Traders Flock to Singapore to Tap China, India Demand," Reuters, March 1, 2011.

110. On the Singapore Intelligent Energy System, see www.ema.gov.sg/cmsmedia/Newsletter/2012/04/eyeon-emaIES.html.

111. Dennis Gross, "Singapore: Smart Grid City," *Cleantech*, August 1, 2010.

Chapter 6

1. In the words of the Economic Development Board (EDB), "Singapore will become an Intelligent Island, a global centre of excellence for science and technology, a high value-added location for production, and a critical strategic node in global networks of commerce, communications, and information." EDB, presentation at the Singapore Economic Forum, July 10, 1995 (http://web.usm.my.aamj.1.2.1996/1-2-7.pdf).

2. Shanghai port ranked first, and handled 35.29 million TEU (twenty-foot equivalent unit) in 2014, while Singapore ranked second, and handled 33.87 million TEU. See World Shipping Council, "Top 50 World Container Ports" (www.worldshipping.org/.../global-trade/). Singapore's port has been frequently recognized as the "Best Seaport in Asia" by the Asian Freight, Logistics and Supply Chain Awards (AFSCA). See "Singapore Named Best Seaport in Asia for 28th Time," *Channel NewsAsia*, June 15, 2016.

3. Maritime and Port Authority Singapore, "Global Hub Port" (www.mpa.gov.sg).

4. Changi was ranked as the world's best airport in 2010 and 2013–16 by Skytrax World Airport Awards. Hong Kong was ranked no. 1 in 2011 and Incheon was no. 1 in 2012. See www.worldairportawards.com.

5. EDB, "Logistics and Supply Chain Management" (www.edb.gov.sg).

6. Singapore was ranked 5th place globally, but no. 1 in Asia, ahead of Hong Kong (no. 9) and Japan (no. 12). See World Bank, "Global Ranking 2016," *International Logistics Performance Index (LPI) Global Ranking*.

7. EDB, "Logistics and Supply Chain Management."

8. See www.rvo.nl/sites/default/files/Logistics%20industry%20Singapore%20-%20 Sep'12.pdf.

9. EDB, "Logistics and Supply Chain Management."

10. Daniel Tay, "This Building Could Be the Future of e-Commerce Logistics in Southeast Asia," *Tech in Asia*, October 14, 2014; and "Topping Out Ceremony Marks Milestone for SingPost Regional e-Commerce Logistics Hub," *Singapore Post*, March 1, 2016.

11. Newley Purnell, "Singapore Post to Build Logistics Hub in E-Commerce Bet," *Wall Street Journal*, October 15, 2014.

12. On the central role of infocom technology in facilitating information flow and accessibility, see Infocomm Development Authority (IDA) of Singapore, "iN2015 Masterplan" (www.ida.gov.sg/Tech-Scene-News/iN2015-Masterplan).

13. Jonathan Koh, "Towards a Single Window Trading Environment: Singapore's TradeNet," CrimsonLogic Report, p. 13 (www.crimsonlogic.com/Documents/).

14. IDA, "Innovation, Integration, Internationalisation," Report by the iN2015 Steering Committee, p. 37.

15. In 2014, 75.6 percent of the Middle East's exports, or approximately 14.9 million barrels per day out of 19.7 total went to Asia (China, India, Japan, Singapore, and other Asia-Pacific). See British Petroleum, *Statistical Review of World Energy 2015*.

16. The International Energy Agency (IEA) expects Persian Gulf exports to Northeast Asia to rise from 12 million in 2013 to around 22 million barrels a day by 2040. See IEA, *World Energy Outlook 2014*.

17. Singapore's first liquefied natural gas terminal was opened in May 2013, with a second one announced in February 2014. On prospects for a Singapore gas hub, see Rudolf ten Hoedt, "Singapore's Push to Be Asia's First LNG Trading Hub, and the Uncertain Future of the Asian Gas Market," *Energy Post*, October 28, 2014.

18. Woo Shea Lee, Yip Yoke Har, and Ang Sock Sun, "Easing Taxes to Create Global Insurance Hub," *The Business Times*, March 24, 2016.

19. China (31 percent), Japan (11 percent), Korea, Hong Kong, and India together held 51 percent of world reserves in 2015. World Bank, "Total reserves minus gold (current US$)," *World Development Indicators* (2015).

20. Ibid.

21. For example, Saudi Arabia held 6 percent of world total reserves in 2015.

22. See "Singapore to Emerge as Top Finance Hub by 2014: Study," Reuters, July 4, 2013.

23. On Singapore financial innovations, see Robert F. Emery, *The Asian Dollar Market*, Federal Reserve System Discussion Paper (1975) (www.federalreserve.gov).

24. Lee Kuan Yew, *From Third World to First: the Singapore Story 1965–2000* (New York: HarperCollins, 2000), p. 77.

25. Laurie Cohen, "Singaporeans Learn Tricks of Trade at Merc," *Chicago Tribute,* June 10, 1984.

26. Including US$291 billion (spot, outright forward, FX swap) and US$79 billion (FX options). See Singapore Foreign Exchange Market Committee, "Survey of Singapore Foreign Exchange Volume in April 2014," July 25, 2014.

27. Including spot, outright forward, FX swap, and option. See New York Federal Reserve, "Foreign Exchange Committee Releases FX Volume Survey Results," Foreign Exchange Committee Announcement, July 28, 2014.

28. Including spot, FX swap, outright forward, and option. See Tokyo Foreign Exchange Market Committee, "Results of Turnover Survey of Tokyo Foreign Exchange Market," July 28, 2014, table 1 (http://www.fxcomtky.com/survey/pdf_file/survey_2014_02_e.pdf).

29. World Bank, "Net Inflows of Foreign Direct Investment, % of GDP," *World Development Indicators* (2014).

30. International Enterprise Singapore, "The Singapore Advantage," July 2014, p. 2.

31. "GM to Move International Headquarters to Singapore from China," Reuters, November 13, 2013.

32. Jack Neff, "From Cincy to Singapore: Why P and G, Others Are Moving Key HQs," *Advertising Age*, June 11, 2012.

33. Economic Development Board, "P&G Opens $250 million Innovation Centre," March 28, 2014. Areas of research include biochemical, molecular, and genomics for P&G's brands.

34. Amit Banati, "Kellogg Moves Asia-Pacific Headquarters to Singapore, Looks to Create Breakfast Category," September 19, 2013 (www.lpk.com).

35. Singapore's corporate income taxes have decreased from 26 percent in 2000 to 17 percent in 2016. Since 2003 Singapore has also adopted a single-tier income tax system, so stakeholders are not subject to double taxations. See Economic Development Board, "Taxation," last updated March 11, 2016; and Hawksford Singapore, "Singapore Corporate Tax Guide" (www.guidemesingapore.com/taxation/corporate-tax/singapore-corporate-tax-guide).

36. Ministry of Trade and Industry Singapore, "Mr Lee Yi Shyan at the Asia-Pacific Trade Forum 2014," November 24, 2014.

37. See Chia Siow Yue, "The Singapore Model of Industrial Policy: Past Evolution and Current Thinking," Second LAEBA Annual Meeting, Buenos Aires, Argentina, November 28–29, 2005.

38. National Library Board, "Formation of SIJORI Growth Triangle Is Announced," December 20, 1989.

39. On the concept of the "knowledge economy," see Peter Drucker, *The Age of Discontinuity: Guidelines to Our Changing Society* (New York: Harper and Row, 1969); as well as Fritz Machlup, *The Production and Distribution of Knowledge in the United States* (Princeton University Press, 1962).

40. National Research Foundation–Research, Innovation, Technology Administration (RITA) System, "R&D Development," last updated May 13, 2016 (www.nrf.gov.sg/research/overview); and A*STAR, "STEP 2015 Science, Technology & Enterprise Plan 2015: Asia's Innovation Capital," May 2011.

41. For examples of the living laboratory concept in operation in the area of clean energy, such as the CleanTech Park, see Energy Efficient Singapore, "Test-Bedding & R&D: CleanTech Park Living Lab Program" (www.e2singapore.gov.sg).

42. According to A*STAR, Phase 1 of Biopolis was completed in 2003 at a cost of S$500 million and Phase 1 of Fusionopolis opened in October 2008 at a cost of S$600 million. No further official figures have been published.

43. Economic Development Board (EDB), "Biopolis, Fusionopolis, Mediapolis" (www.edb.gov.sg).

44. Chia Yan Min, "A Home for World's Best Scientists," *The Straits Times*, January 3, 2014.

45. "Roche Establishes New Medical Research Hub in Singapore," *Asia-Pacific Biotech News* 14, no. 2 (2010): 34 (www.asiabiotech.com).

46. "Singapore Aims to Become 'Investment Hub for Global Diagnostics Industry,'" December 2, 2014 (www.out-law.com).

47. EDB, "Biopolis, Fusionopolis, Mediapolis."

48. See Campus for Research Excellence and Technological Enterprise, "CREATE Milestones."

49. On the SMART program, see https://smart.mit.edu/about-smart/about-smart.html.

50. National Research Foundation, "CREATE."

51. National Research Foundation, "R&D Development," last updated May 13, 2016.

52. FIA (Food Industry Asia), "Singapore an Emerging Global Hub for Food Science and Nutrition" (http://foodindustry.asia/singapore-an-emerging-global-hub-for-food-science-and-nutrition).

53. National Research Foundation, "R&D Development," last updated May 13, 2016.

54. Following National University of Singapore, Peking University and University of Tokyo place 42nd and 43th, respectively, in 2015–16.

55. Times Higher Education, "150 under 50 Rankings 2016" (www.timeshigher education.com).

56. ICEF Monitor, "Singapore Solidifies Its Reputation as a Regional Education Hub," June 6, 2014.

57. Ministry of National Development, "Urban Sustainability R&D Congress 2015."

58. Ministry of National Development, "Urban Sustainability R&D Congress 2011."

59. The SIWW recorded over S$36.3 billion in business announcements by 2014. See Singapore International Water Week, "Singapore International Water Week 2016" (www.siww.com.sg/sites/default/files/siww_2016_event_highlights_en_updated_jan_2016.pdf).

60. See World Cities Summit Corporate Sponsorship Brochure.

61. World Cities Summit, "Lee Kuan Yew World City Prize: About the Prize."

62. Lee Kuan Yew World City Prize, "2012 Prize Laureate: City of New York."

63. Lee Kuan Yew World City Prize, "2014 Prize Laureate: City of Suzhou, Jiangsu Province."

64. Singapore International Energy Week (SIEW), "FAQs" (www.siew.sg/about-siew/faqs).

65. SIEW, "Past Events: SIEW 2014."

66. "A Report on the Singapore Mission," GRIPS Development Forum, Tokyo, September 13, 2010 (www.grips.ac.jp/teacher/oono/hp/docu02/singapore_BTOR.pdf).

67. Ibid.

68. Ibid.

69. See Singapore Cooperation Program, "Bilateral Technical Assistance Programs."

70. SCE has become a subsidiary of International Enterprise Singapore (IES), a statutory board that promotes Singapore's external economy under the Ministry of Trade and Industry. IES, *Thirty Years of Globalising Singapore: International Enterprise Singapore Annual Report 2012–2013* (Singapore, 2012), p. 50.

71. Data as of November 2015; Singapore Cooperation Enterprise (SCE), "Our Reach," 2016.

72. On these International Partnership Teams, see SCE, "International Partnerships" (www.sce.gov.sg/international-partnerships.aspx).

73. Singapore Cooperation Programme, "Third Country Training Programmes."

74. See Singapore Business Federation, *Singapore: Your Global-Asia Hub Business Services Resource Guide 2012–2013* (http://knowledge.insead.edu/entrepreneurship-innovation/insead-at-50-the-defining-years-1356).

75. In 2014 Singapore's merchandise exports totaled US$409.8 billion, and commercial services exports totaled US$140.1 billion. See World Trade Organization, "Singapore," *Country Profiles*, September 2015.

76. EDB, "Industry Background: Energy" (www.edb.gov.sg/content/edb/en/industries/industries/energy.html); C. M Turnbull, *A History of Modern Singapore, 1819–2005* (Singapore: National University of Singapore, 2009), 311.

77. Trading Economics, "Singapore Exports" (www.tradingeconomics.com/singapore/exports).

78. In 2014 Singapore's non-oil merchandise exports totaled S$390.4 billion, of which S$239.1 billion was re-exports. See Department of Statistics–Singapore, "16.1 Merchandise Trade by Type," *Yearbook of Statistics Singapore 2016*.

79. Marsita Omar, "Jurong Reclamation," *Singapore Infopedia* (Singapore: National Library Board, 2010).

80. Data for 2015. See Wilson Wong and Lim Yi Ding, "Trends in Singapore's International Trade in Services," *Statistics Singapore Newsletter*, March 2016, p. 2.

81. Changi Airport International, for example, played a key role in helping 600,000 passengers transit Sochi during the 2014 Winter Olympics. See "Opportunities for Singapore Companies in Russia, from Airports to Property and Planning," *The Straits Times*, May 21, 2016.

82. PSA International's Gwadar port management role ended in 2013 and was assumed by China Overseas Port Holding Company. See Syed Irfan Raza, "China Given Contract to Operate Gwadar Port," *Dawn*, February 18, 2013.

83. Hotel management, as in the Gulf, is a key Singapore service export.

84. See Singapore Personal Access (SingPass), "About Us."

85. Singapore ranked 3rd in the UN E-Government Development Index 2014 (https://publicadministration.un.org/egovkb/en-us/Reports/UN-E-Government-Survey-2014), while Japan's Waseda University ranked the country 1st in its 2015 Waseda-IAC International e-Government Rankings (www.waseda.jp/top/en-news/28775).

86. Marissa Lee, "The National IT Project That Went Global in a Big Way," *The Straits Times*, May 2, 2016.

87. For details on these innovative e-government programs, see www.crimsonlogic.com.

88. Karl Polanyi, *The Great Transformation: The Political and Economic Origins of Our Time* (Boston: Beacon Press, 1944); Barrington Moore Jr., *Social Origins of Dictatorship and Democracy: Lord and Peasant in the Making of the Modern World* (Boston: Beacon Press, 1966); and Joseph A. Schumpeter, *Capitalism, Socialism, and Democracy* (London: George and Allen Unwin, 1976).

89. United Nations Department of Economic and Social Affairs (UNDESA) Population Division, "File 1: Population of Urban and Rural Areas at Mid-Year . . . and Percentage Urban, 2014," *World Urbanization Prospects: The 2014 Revision* (June 2014).

90. UNDESA Population Division, "File 3: Urban Population at Mid-Year by Major Area, Region and Country, 1950–2050," *World Urbanization Prospects: The 2014 Revision* (June 2014).

91. Cheryl Sim, "China-Singapore Suzhou Industrial Park" *Singapore Infopedia*. (Singapore: National Library Board, 2015).

92. United Nations, *World Urbanization Prospects: The 2014 Revision*, p. 13.

93. See, for example, Prime Minister's Office Singapore, transcript of Prime Minister Lee Hsien Loong's speech at Smart Nation Launch, November 24, 2014.

94. Charles Goldblum, "Singapore's Holistic Approach to Urban Planning: Centrality, Singularity, Innovation, and Re-invention," in *Singapore from Temasek to the 21st Century: Reinventing the Global City,* edited by Karl Hack and Jean-Louis Margolin, with Karine Delaye (Singapore: NUS Press, 2010), pp. 390–91.

95. One recent example of this continuous innovation is Clean Tech Park, the first co-themed business park in Asia. See Elga Reyes, "Clean Tech One Officially Opens in Singapore's First Eco-Business Park," *Eco-Business*, August 16, 2013 (www.eco-business.com).

96. Singapore-MIT Alliance for Research and Technology (SMART), "Future Urban Mobility (FM) IRG."

97. On Deng's fateful 1978 Singapore visit, the rapport established, and the implications for bilateral China-Singapore relations, see Ezra F. Vogel, *Deng Xiaoping and the Transformation of China* (Harvard University Press, 2011), pp. 290–91.

98. On details of SCE operations in China, see SCE, "Our Reach: China."

99. On Fullerton Financial's microcredit activities in China, see Temasek, "Temasek Review 2014," p. 74.

100. Fullerton Financial has 400 rural branches in India and services 1.2 million self-employed entrepreneurs and working families in Indonesia. See ibid.

101. "Suzhou Industrial Park: 10 Things to Know about the China-Singapore Project," *The Straits Times*, October 25, 2014.

102. See "The Sino-Singapore Tianjin Eco-City: A Practical Model for Sustainable Development," UNEP South-South Cooperation Case Study, March 2013.

103. Sino-Singapore Guangzhou Knowledge City, "About Us: Milestones."

104. Sino-Singapore Guangzhou Knowledge City, "Industry Development: Industry Plan."

105. Sino-Singapore Guangzhou Knowledge City, "About SSGKC: Overview."

106. Sino-Singapore Guangzhou Knowledge City, "About Us: Company Profile."

107. On this agreement, see "Chongqing and China Mobile to Build IoT Industrial Highland," *Chongqing News*, October 8, 2012 (www.english.cqnews.net).

108. "Chongqing's Industrial Clusters, Forward Thinking Offer Useful Example amid Tricky Environment," *Global Times*, March 8, 2016.

109. On this phenomenon, see Kent E. Calder, *The New Continentalism: Energy and Twenty-First-Century Eurasian Geopolitics* (Yale University Press, 2012), especially pp. 167–69.

110. Kor Kian Beng, "Lower Logistics Costs with Euro-Sino-S'pore Route," *The Straits Times*, April 17, 2016.

111. Kor Kian Beng, "Singapore-China Chongqing Project 'Making Good Progress,'" *The Straits Times*, April 16, 2016.

112. Kor Kian Beng, "Lower Logistics Costs with Euro-Sino-Singapore Route."

113. Monetary Authority of Singapore, "Cross-Border RMB Flows and Capital Market Connectivity between China and Singapore to Strengthen," November 9, 2015.

114. Professor Jae-ho Chung of Seoul National University, one of Korea's foremost China specialists, recently noted with approval Singapore's ability to keep both the United States and China happy. See Jae-ho Chung, "Korean Diplomacy Needs to Learn from Singapore on How to Hide the True Intention," *Chosun Ilbo*, November 17, 2012.

115. "BPA Leads Advanced Singapore Research," Busan Port Authority press release, July 7, 2014 (www.busanpa.com).

116. Yeonwoo Joong and others, *A Possible Director for Sino-Korea Business Cooperation in Prospective Cities in China, and Development of Business Model* (Seoul: Korea Land and Housing Corporation Land and Housing Research Institute, 2012).

117. In 2014 the foundation was sponsoring 118 programs in Southeast Asia, with S$64.7 million committed; 39 programs in Northeast Asia, with S$28.7 million committed, and 33 in South Asia, with S$16.1 million committed. See Temasek Foundation, "Temasek Foundation Summary Report 2014/2015," p. 2.

118. This park was conceptualized in 1992 by then–prime ministers Goh Chok Tong and Narasimha Rao. International Tech Park Bangalore (ITPB), "History." International Tech Park Bangalore (ITPB), "Ascendas Acquires Tata Stake in International Tech Park, Bangalore," April 12 2005 (www.itpbangalore.com/press/05_taka.html).

119. SCE, "Our Reach: International Partnerships."

120. Radheshyam Jadhav, "Government Mulls Singapore Model of Development for Cities," *The Times of India*, September 9, 2013.

121. Chan Yi Wen, "Singapore Signs Deal to Master-Plan Indian State's New Capital," *The Business Times*, December 9, 2014.

122. "Amaravathi Master Plan to Guide Development up to 2050," *MasterPlans India*, May 27, 2015; Lee U-Wen, "Surbana, Jurong Int'l to Master-Plan New Indian City," *The Business Times*, January 13, 2015.

123. International Enterprise Singapore, "Smart Cities Discussion: A Smarter India, One City at a Time," India Singapore Economic Convention 2015, December 9, 2015.

124. "Singapore to Help India in Smart Cities Project," *The Times of India*, August 16, 2014.

125. Singapore Ministry of Foreign Affairs, "Deputy Prime Minister and Minister for Finance Tharman Shanmugaratnam and Russian First Deputy Prime Minister Igor Shuvalov Co-Chair The Fourth Session of The High-Level Russia-Singapore Inter-Governmental Commission 19 June 2013," MFA press release, June 20, 2013.

126. Kaznex Invest, "Singapore Model to Be Applied for Kazakhstan's SEZ Development," July 16, 2013.

127. Encyclopædia Britannica Online, s.v. "Paul Kagame," accessed July 16, 2016.

128. "List of African Countries by Population (2015)," *Statistics Times*, updated March 27, 2015.

129. World Bank, "GDP per capita (constant 2010 US$)," *World Development Indicators* (2015).

130. Patricia Crisafulli and Andrea Redmond, *Rwanda, Inc.: How a Devastated Nation Became an Economic Model for the Developing World* (New York: Palgrave Macmillan, 2012), pp. 13–14, 133.

131. On how Kagame found and embraced the Singapore paradigm, see "Africa's Singapore?," *The Economist*, February 25, 2012; and "Rwanda: the Singapore of Africa?," *The Southern Times*, May 23, 2011.

132. Edwin Musoni, "President Kagame Calls for Increased Efforts to Development," *The New Times*, January 14, 2013.

133. On the details, see Jeff Chu, "Rwanda Rising: A New Model of Economic Development," *Fast Company*, April 1, 2009.

134. Bill Clinton, Tony Blair, Howard Schultz (CEO of Starbucks), and Eric Schmidt (chair of Google) are among Kagame's core international contacts.

135. For a list of council members as of 2009, see "Rwanda: Presidential Advisory Council members meet on Sunday 22/09/13 in New York," *Rising Continent*, September 25, 2013.

136. "Rwanda Completes $95 Million Fiber Optic Network," Reuters, March 16, 2011.

137. Lena Ulrich and Ronald S. Thomas, "Building National Competitive Advantage: Rwanda's Lessons from Singapore," *Thunderbird International Business Review* 56, no. 3, (2014): 238.

138. For more information, see Carnegie Mellon University, "Carnegie Mellon University in Rwanda" (www.cmu.edu/rwanda/index.html).

139. See, for example, Felly Kimenyi, "Kagame Reiterates Need to Use English as Education Medium," *The New Times*, October 15, 2008.

140. On Rwanda's emulation of Singapore's approach to corruption, see Crisafulli and Redmond, *Rwanda, Inc.*, p. 233.

141. World Bank, "GDP Growth (Annual %)," *World Development Indicators*, 2004, 2010.

Chapter 7

1. Benjamin Barber, *If Mayors Rule the World: Dysfunctional Nations, Rising Cities* (Yale University Press, 2013).

2. Tanaka Akihiko, *The New Middle Ages: The World System in the 21st Century* (Tokyo: International House of Japan, 2002).

3. On Singapore cases by Harvard Business School faculty and staff, see www.hbs.edu/faculty/Pages/search.aspx?qt=Singapore&mclickorder=qt-1:&page1.

4. See "Modernizing the Mandarins," *The Economist*, August 9, 2014.

Bibliography

Allison, Graham, and Robert D. Blackwill, with Ali Wyne. 2013. *Lee Kuan Yew: The Grand Master's Insights on China, the United States, and the World*. MIT Press.

Arun, Mahizhan. 1999. "Smart Cities: The Singapore Case." *Cities* 6, no. 1: 13–18.

Barber, Benjamin R. 2013. *If Mayors Ruled the World: Dysfunctioning Nations, Rising Cities*. Yale University Press.

Barr, Michael D. 2000. "Lee Kuan Yew's Fabian Phase." *Australian Journal of Politics and History* 46 (March): 110–26.

———. 2000. *Lee Kuan Yew: The Beliefs Behind the Man*. Richmond, Surrey: Curzon Press.

Barr, Michael D., and Zlatko Skrbis. 2008. *Constructing Singapore: Elitism, Ethnicity, and the Nation-Building Project*. Copenhagen: NIAS Press.

Bhaskaran, Manu. 2003. *Reinventing the Asian Model: The Case of Singapore*. Singapore: Asian Universities Press.

Bloodworth, Dennis. 1986. *The Tiger and the Trojan Horse*. Singapore: Times Books International.

Calder, Kent E. 1988. *Crisis and Compensation: Public Policy and Political Stability in Japan*. Princeton University Press.

———. 2007. *Embattled Garrisons: Comparative Base Politics and American Globalism*. Princeton University Press.

———. 2014. *Asia in Washington: Exploring the Penumbra of Transnational Power*. Brookings.

Calder, Kent E., and Roy Hofheinz Jr. 1982. *The Eastasia Edge*. New York: Basic Books.

Chew, Emrys, and Chong Guan Kwa, eds. 2012. *Goh Keng Swee: A Legacy of Public Service*. Singapore: World Scientific.

Ching, Leong, ed. 2015. *Great Singapore Stories: Founding Fathers*. Singapore: Straits Times Press.

Choi, C. C., and Raymond Toh. 2010. "Household Interview Surveys from 1997 to 2008: A Decade of Changing Travel Behavior." *Journeys* (May): 52–61.

Chua, Lee Hoong. 2012. *The Singapore Green Plan 2012*. Singapore: Ministry of the Environment.

Crisafulli, Patricia, and Andrew Redmond. 2012. *Rwanda, Inc.: How a Devastated Nation Became an Economic Model for the Developing World*. New York: Palgrave Macmillan.

Davis, Lindsay, ed. 2013. *The Wit and Wisdom of Lee Kuan Yew*. Singapore: Editions Didier Millet.

Desker, Barry, and Ang Cheng Guan, eds. 2016. *Perspectives on the Security of Singapore: The First Fifty Years.* Singapore: World Scientific.

Drysdale, John. 1984. *Singapore: Struggle for Success.* Singapore: Times Books International.

Er, Lam Peng, and Kevin Y. L. Tan, eds. 1999. *Lee's Lieutenants: Singapore's Old Guard.* Sydney: Allen and Unwin.

Frost, Mark Ravinder, and Yu-mei Balasingamchow. 2009. *Singapore: A Biography.* Hong Kong University Press.

Gliesquiere, Henri. 2007. *Singapore's Success: Engineering Economic Growth.* Singapore: Thomson Asia.

Grew, Raymond, ed. 1978. *Crises of Political Development in Europe and the United States.* Princeton University Press.

Hack, Karl, and Jean-Louis Margolin, eds., with Karine Delaye. 2010. *Singapore from Temasek to the 21st Century: Reinventing the Global City.* Singapore: NUS Press.

Hague, M. Shamsul. 2004. "Governance and Bureaucracy in Singapore: Contemporary Reforms and Implications." *International Political Science Review* 25, no. 2: 227–40.

Henderson, Joan C. 2012. "Planning for Success: Singapore, the Model City-State?," *Journal of International Affairs* 65 (Spring/Summer): 69–83.

Johnson, Chalmers. 1982. *MITI and the Japanese Miracle.* Stanford University Press.

Josey, Alex. 1980. *Lee Kuan Yew: The Critical Years, 1971–1978.* Singapore: Times Books International.

———. 1980. *Lee Kuan Yew: The Crucial Years.* Singapore: Times Books International.

Kingdon, John W. 1984. *Agendas, Alternatives, and Public Policies.* Boston: Little Brown.

Koh, Tommy, and Li Lin Chang, eds. 2004. *The United States–Singapore Free Trade Agreement: Highlights and Insights.* Singapore: Institute of Policy Studies.

Kumar, Sree, and Sharon Siddique. 2010. "The Singapore Success Story: Public-Private Alliance for Investment Attraction, Innovation, and Export Development." UN ECLAC, CEPAL-Serie Comercio International 99 (March).

Kwang, Han Fook, Warren Fernandez, and Sumika Tan. 1998. *Lee Kuan Yew: The Man and His Ideas.* Singapore: Straits Times Press.

Lai, Ah Eng, ed. 2004. *Beyond Rituals and Riots: Ethnic Pluralism and Social Cohesion in Singapore.* Singapore: Eastern Universities Press.

Lee, Kuan Yew. 1998. *The Singapore Story: Memoirs of Lee Kuan Yew.* Singapore: The Straits Times Press.

———. 2000. *From Third World to First: The Singapore Story, 1965–2000.* New York: Harper Collins.

———. 2011. *Hard Truths to Keep Singapore Going.* Singapore: The Straits Times Press.

Leifer, Michael. 2000. *Singapore's Foreign Policy: Coping with Vulnerability.* London: Routledge.

Li, M. Z. F., D. C. B. Lau, and D. W. M. Seah. 2011. "Car Ownership and Urban Transport Demand in Singapore." *International Journal of Transport Economics* 38, no. 1: 47–70.

Mahbubani, Kishore. 2015. *Can Singapore Survive?* Singapore: Straits Times Press.

Mahbubani, Kishore, and others. 2013. *Lee Kuan Yew School of Public Policy: Building a Global Policy School in Asia.* Singapore: World Scientific.

Micklethwait, John, and Adrian Wooldridge. 2014. *The Fourth Revolution: The Global Race to Reinvent the State.* New York: Penguin Press.

Minchin, James. 1986. *No Man Is an Island: A Study of Singapore's Lee Kuan Yew*. Sydney: Allen and Unwin.

Ministry of the Environment and Water Resources. 1992. *The Singapore Green Plan: Toward a Model Green City*. Singapore.

Plate, Tom. 2010. *Conversations with Lee Kuan Yew*. Singapore: Marshall Cavendish International.

Porter, Michael E., Boon Siong Neo, and Christian Ketels. 2009. *Remaking Singapore*. Harvard University Business School.

Quah, Euston, ed. 2016. *Singapore 2065: Leading Insights on Economy and Environment from 50 Singapore Icons and Beyond*. Singapore: World Scientific.

Quah, Jon S. T. 2010. *Public Administration Singapore-Style*. Bingley, United Kingdom: Emerald Group.

Ramakrishna, Kumar. 2015. *"Original Sin"? Revising the Revisionist Critique of the 1963 Operation Coldstore in Singapore*. Singapore: Institute of Southeast Asian Studies.

Richmond, Johnathan E. D. 2008. "Transporting Singapore—The Air-Conditioned Nation." *Transport Reviews* 28 (May): 357–90.

Rosecrance, Richard. 1999. *The Rise of the Virtual State: Wealth and Power in the Coming Century*. New York: Basic Books.

Santos, G., W. W. Li, and W. T. Koh. 2004. "Transport Policies in Singapore." *Research in Transport Economics* 9, no. 1: 209–35.

Soon, Carol, and Hoe Su Fern, eds. 2016. *Singapore Perspectives 2015: Choices*. Singapore: World Scientific.

Tan, S. T., F. L. Leong, and B. C. A. Leong. 2009. *Economics in Public Policies: The Singapore Story*. Singapore: Marshall Cavendish Education.

Tortajada, Cecilia, Yugal Kishre Joshi, and Asit K. Biswas. 2013. *The Singapore Water Story: Sustainable Development in an Urban City State*. London: Routledge.

Townsend, Anthony M. 2013. *Smart Cities: Big Data, Civic Hackers, and the Quest for a New Utopia*. New York: W. W. Norton.

Trocki, Carl A. 2006. *Singapore: Wealth, Power, and the Culture of Control*. New York: Routledge.

Turnbull, C. M. 2009. *A History of Singapore: 1819–2005*. Singapore: NUS Press.

Vogel, Ezra F. 1979. *Japan as Number One: Lessons for America*. Harvard University Press.

———. 2011. *Deng Xiaoping and the Transformation of China*. Harvard University Press.

Weiner, Myron. 1971. *Crises and Sequences in Political Development*. Princeton University Press.

Welsh, Bridget, and others, eds. 2009. *Impressions of the Goh Chok Tong Years in Singapore*. Singapore: NUS Press.

Woo-Cumings, Meredith, ed. 1999. *The Developmental State*. Cornell University Press.

World Economic Forum. 2013. *Global Competitiveness Report* (2013–14). Geneva: SRO-Kundig.

Yuen, Belinda. 2005. "Searching for Place Identity in Singapore." *Habitat International* 29, no. 2: 197–214.

Index

Figures and tables are indicated by "f" and "t" following page numbers.

Vogel, Ezra, 4, 39
Wang Yang, 154
Water: desalination of, 128, 161; imports, 18, 127; international conference on, 104, 128, 143; management strategies for, 122, 125–28, 127*f*, 166–67; quality of, 10, 126
Wealth management, 136–37
Weber, Max, 30–31
Welfare. *See* Social welfare
Wen Jiabao, 151, 153
Wilson, Harold, 24–25, 35–36, 49
Wooldridge, Adrian, 61
World Bank: advisory support by, 160; outreach endeavors by, 144, 146;

performance rankings by, 4, 6, 134, 156; policy concerns for, 173; transportation-policy development by, 118
World Cities Summit, 143
World Economic Forum, 4, 9, 11, 156
World Health Organization (WHO), 7
World Wide Web. *See* Internet

Xi Jinping, 14, 49, 151, 155

Yip, Leo, 46

Zoellick, Robert, 91